Acclaim for *With Grit and By Grace*

"This is a must-read memoir of the years when women believed everything was possible—and made it so. Having served with Betty Roberts in the Oregon Legislature during the 1970s, I witnessed the great strides she made in enacting legislation that helped pull women out of the shadows of discrimination. Her commitment, perseverance, and common sense gave me a deep appreciation of women's capabilities and their struggles. The growing number of capable and dedicated women who now serve in public office are a fitting tribute to her efforts."

—Congressman Earl Blumenauer

"*With Grit and By Grace* tells the story of the women's movement from a political insider's perspective. Betty Roberts had already served six years in the Oregon Legislature when a cadre of young, impatient, college-educated, female activists showed up in the early 1970s. With Roberts as the chair of a bipartisan women's caucus, we women legislators and organizers moved political mountains to ratify the ERA and pass dozens of bills to end gender discrimination. *With Grit and By Grace* tells this monumental story. It's a history that every woman should know—it explains how far we have come and illuminates a path for the millennial generation to continue the fight."

—Norma Paulus, former Oregon Secretary of State (the first woman to hold a statewide elected office in Oregon) and Oregon Superintendent of Public Instruction

"*With Grit and By Grace* is a fascinating look into the campaigns of a pioneering woman in American politics. Betty Roberts tells the story of what goes into the decision to run for office and the many challenges faced on the campaign trail. For those of us who study and analyze women's progress in elective office, this book provides unique insights into what it means for a woman to take on the political power structure. Betty's efforts in the early years of the women's political movement made it possible for many other women to follow in her footsteps."

—Debbie Walsh, Director, Center for American Women and Politics, Rutgers University

"Long overdue and profoundly welcome, *With Grit and By Grace* tells the story of how one woman cracked—and broke through—glass ceilings, ultimately becoming the first woman on the Oregon Supreme Court. Once there, Betty Roberts helped her colleagues on the bench to understand the pervasive gender stereotypes that influenced their legal thinking. My own life's work has been educating judges about gender bias, and Justice Roberts was an early example of how female judges all over the country have helped the courts recognize the true meaning of impartiality, fairness, and justice. *With Grit and By Grace* will fascinate and encourage every woman who is blazing her own trail today."

—Lynn Hecht Schafran, Director, National Judicial Education Program, and recipient of the Margaret Brent Women Lawyers of Achievement Award

"*With Grit and By Grace* will captivate women of all ages—those who experienced discrimination in the past and younger readers who encounter today's glass ceilings. I first knew Betty Roberts when I argued cases before her court as one of few women in Oregon appellate work. Her presence alone gave women lawyers hope and encouragement. I could not then imagine the roadblocks she had overcome to be in that position, but as I learned her story I knew it had to be told. We can all relate to the 'grit' and 'grace' she describes as giving voice to our own stories."

—Katherine O'Neil, Member of the Board of Governors of the American Bar Association, and Founding President of Oregon Women Lawyers

With Grit and By Grace

After her retirement from the Oregon Supreme Court in 1986, **BETTY ROBERTS** began a new career in mediation and arbitration, and made international headlines in March 2004 when she performed the state's first same-sex marriage ceremonies in Multnomah County. She lives in Portland, Oregon.

GAIL WELLS is the author of several books, including *The Little Lucky: A Family Geography* and *The Tillamook: A Created Forest Comes of Age* (both OSU Press). She is an independent writer and editor specializing in natural-resource and historical topics. She lives in Corvallis, Oregon.

With Grit and By Grace

Breaking Trails in Politics and Law, A Memoir

Betty Roberts

with

Gail Wells

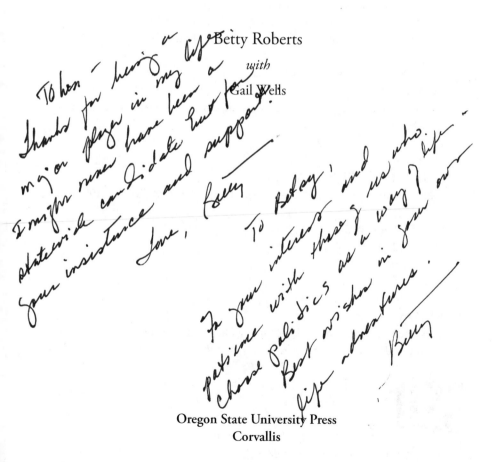

To Lou — a
Thanks for being a
major player in my life
I might never have been a
statewide candidate but for
your insistence and support.
Love, Betty

To Betsy, and who
To your interest and who
pastime with those of us who
choose politics as a way of life —
Best wishes in your own
life adventures.
Betty

Oregon State University Press
Corvallis

The paper in this book meets the guidelines for permanence and durability of the Committee on Production Guidelines for Book Longevity of the Council on Library Resources and the minimum requirements of the American National Standard for Permanence of Paper for Printed Library Materials Z39.48-1984.

Library of Congress Cataloging-in-Publication Data
Roberts, Betty, 1923-
  With grit and by grace : breaking trails in politics and law, a memoir / Betty Roberts with Gail Wells.
     p. cm.
  Includes index.
  ISBN-13: 978-0-87071-199-2 (alk. paper)
  1. Roberts, Betty, 1923- 2. Judges--Oregon--Biography. I. Wells, Gail, 1952- II. Title.
  KF8745.R595A3 2008
  340.092--dc22

                                                        2007040551

Oregon State University Press
121 The Valley Library
Corvallis OR 97331-4501
541-737-3166 • fax 541-737-3170
http://oregonstate.edu/dept/press

For Dian, John, Jo, and Randy
Without whom this life would not have been lived;
this story would not have been told.

The Glass Ceiling at the Oregon Supreme Court (Photograph by Justice
Virginia Linder)

Democracy relies on the telling of stories. If a people are to govern themselves, they must know as much of the truth as they can. But something more is gained in the process. The constant exchange of stories that democracy requires is itself a profound experience. Unexamined memories, forgotten regions of the psyche and the soul must be continually explored for the form to remain alive. In my lifetime I have seen democracy begin to expand, not only to include those who have been excluded, but to provide a listening arena, a vocabulary, an intelligent reception for stories that have been buried. Not just stories of the disenfranchised and the marginalized, but marginalized and disenfranchised histories even in the lives of the accepted and the privileged.

Susan Griffin, *What Her Body Thought*

Contents

Preface

On Monday morning, February 8, 1982, three days after my fifty-ninth birthday, I raised my right hand and said, "I, Betty Roberts, do solemnly swear ..."

The formal ritual of repeating the words after Arno Denecke, the Chief Justice of the Oregon Supreme Court, would dramatically change the 124-year history of the all-male court to include its first woman justice.

After the final words "... so help me God," the applause went on and on, thundering the audience's enthusiasm for the breakthrough my appointment represented for women. I swallowed once, twice, as I prepared to make my remarks.

Today, one woman. Tomorrow, many more.

❧ ❧

It had been a long and circuitous journey from my childhood in Wichita Falls, Texas, where I grew up in a poor family from the wrong side of the tracks. Looking back, it was a journey I could never have imagined for myself. In the early years there were no role models in my life to emulate—no teacher, no politician, no lawyer or judge. In any case, the role of politician, lawyer, or judge was not considered fitting for a woman. Becoming a wife and mother was the conventional and accepted path, but after I moved to Oregon, my life took a sudden turn when I broke with convention and returned to college.

Without signposts I had to find my own way. The trail I took often presented obstacles and roadblocks that seemed insurmountable, but with determination and support from others I met along the way, I overcame them. Ultimately I was able to see ahead to where I could make a difference—first becoming a teacher, then a state legislator and lawyer, and finally a judge and justice.

During my long career in Oregon politics I played an important role in many of the state's historical events. As a legislator I was able to participate in and influence the passage of our first comprehensive land use legislation, extensive environmental protection issues, consumer protection legislation, and the opening of government workings to ordinary citizens. I took the lead on decriminalizing abortions, on allowing women to retain their names upon marriage or divorce, and ratification of the Equal Rights Amendment.

These issues were played out against the backdrop of one of the most tumultuous periods of our nation's history. The late 1950s, '60s and early '70s were a societal earthquake as the civil rights movement, the anti-Vietnam peace movement, and the women's movement coexisted and combined to change this nation's history. During that time many of us were jolted into rethinking and reshaping our own lives, our government, and our society.

In telling my story, I hope to illuminate the events of that turbulent time, with emphasis on the women's movement through my experiences as a woman who was intimately engaged in the politics of changing our society in ways that are still evolving. I hope the history related here will encourage a better understanding of how the twentieth century unfolded, often with great sacrifices and always with promise.

The revelations in this book of both the disappointments and the victories of the women who created the so-called "second wave" of feminism will help today's women become acutely aware of their own possibilities, learn to create their own opportunities and to take advantage of them. In today's world, every woman should be able to explore her own life, discover her own uniqueness, break her own trails, and pioneer her own destiny.

Chapter 1

Bloodlines and Clotheslines

The Johnson Memorial Cemetery in Munday, Texas, like most rural cemeteries on the northwest plains of Texas, doesn't get much maintenance. I stood surveying patches of grass stubble and malnourished weeds, a ragged carpet for the headstones I passed in search of the one I had come to see. It must be here somewhere; my sister said so. Excitement and anxiety grew as the four of us, my brother, husband, daughter, and I fanned out in different directions. Then my husband called out. There it was.

Mary Elizabeth Stone
November 10, 1849 – July 27, 1927

My great-grandmother, my link to the past, and the oldest ancestor I could remember who'd influenced my life.

The wind that October day in 1995 was surprisingly calm for northwest Texas. It was strong enough, however, to kick up a small dust devil that twisted and twirled as it danced across the road. It reminded me of the ominous cone-shaped giants I used to see as a child, sweeping from the sky, touching down at one unlucky spot to blow down houses and trees and suck people and animals away, and then moving on.

"When my time comes," I said to my daughter and husband, "I don't want my ashes scattered in Texas. They'd just blow back to Oregon anyway."

Here the wide, unobstructed horizon of the dark land meets the bluest sky. The vastness of the space allows a person's spirit to stretch, seeking the horizon only to find another horizon waiting to be explored, and then another and another. Just the way life unfolds, I thought.

Great-grandmother Stone had raised six children of her own. When she lost an adult daughter because of childbirth complications, she took in a seventh, a baby girl, my mother, and raised her, too.

My mother's family had migrated to Texas from Georgia after the Civil War. They settled near Graham, where the rock-strewn land made farming impossible. Turning to cattle ranching and raising horses for sale to the Army, a couple of my enterprising distant cousins had the brilliant idea of corralling buffalos for the meat and hides. According to family folklore, they built a corral and went out to round up a herd and successfully started them stampeding toward the corral. Amazingly, the buffalos went into the corral. And right on out the other side.

Others in the family considered farming a more reliable enterprise. They moved on, my great-grandmother and my mother with them, some one hundred miles northwest to a place called Goree, Texas. Mary Stone and her little granddaughter lived together in a tiny house on the edge of a large tract of land owned by Great-grandmother Stone's daughter, Tessie, and Tessie's husband, Bill Coffman. My mother grew up among a loving, prosperous family and looked upon her cousins as brothers and sisters. Goree and the Coffman family would provide a haven for me, too, in my growing-up years.

My father's family had a more mysterious beginning in Texas. Two young men, my father's father and his brother, perhaps still in their teens, left Alabama on one horse sometime after the Civil War, so the story goes. My father, the youngest of four boys, was born somewhere in central west Texas, probably in the area of Copperas Cove, where as a young man he played on a traveling baseball team. He met my mother when the team came to Goree. An elderly aunt told me he worked in a hardware store in Goree and that his parents lived there for a while, but they were "bush" people, meaning they didn't clear the land for farming, and soon moved on.

Whatever the truth of that, my mother, Mary Pearl Higgins, and my father, David Murray Cantrell, were married in Goree, Texas, in December 1915. Murray, as he was known, came from Cushing, Oklahoma, where he was working for an oil company, to claim Pearl as his bride. He later worked for the Atcheson, Topeka and Santa Fe Railroad, where his job was to go to refineries and oil companies to "gauge the oil," to determine its quality for use in the railroad business.

Because my father's work sent the family to different locations in that oil-rich part of the country, my older sister Mary Adella was born in Kansas, my older brother Bobbie Joe in Texas. By the time I, Betty Lucille, came along in 1923, the family was back in Kansas, and it was there that I locate my first childhood memories of a near-idyllic life.

My father had a good job. He took us to circuses and he always had gum for us when he came from work. I'd meet him at the road and ride to the house on the running board of his black Ford coupe, he holding his arm tight around me so I wouldn't fall off. We had a nice house with nice furnishings, and my mother kept it neat and tidy. Mother was a resolute believer in cleanliness and education. She had finished the tenth grade, which was as far as a Texas public-school education went in those days, and had received her diploma when she was twenty. She was proud of that. She started each of us in first grade at age five instead of six. She told us, "You children were all so advanced and exceptional that I thought it was the best thing to do."

We dressed in fine clothes when we went to the silent movies to see Clara Bow or Charlie Chaplin. Mother sang when she cleaned the house. She'd put a record on the wind-up Victrola and sing "Tiptoe Through the Tulips," her favorite, with the sun shining through the lace curtains as she push-vacuumed the living-room rug. She bought books for us and saw to it that we had music and dance lessons.

Then, abruptly and without warning, our family's world fell apart. We would have to move to Texas without Daddy. There would be no more tap-dancing lessons or nice clothes for us children, and Mother wouldn't sing any more. Sometimes we wouldn't have enough to eat.

❧ ❧

When the doctor came to our house, I knew something was terribly wrong. We stood around the bed and watched the doctor take blood from Dad's arm. I could tell from the muted tone of the doctor's conversation with Mother, and from the desperate looks on the faces of Mother and my sister, that my daddy was very ill. The doctor made arrangements to have him admitted to a sanatorium in Claremore, Oklahoma, more than a hundred miles away.

The Cantrell family in Kansas, 1927: back row, left to right, Mary Adella, Pearl (mother), Betty Lucille; front row, Bobbie Joe, Murray (father)

Many years later I learned that his strange affliction was common during Prohibition in our part of the country. It had a name, "Jake leg," or "Jake foot," and was easily identifiable by the way a person walked, if he could walk at all. The sound of the walk was a thump of the crutches or canes, the toes tap-tapping, and the slap of the heel—*thump-tap-tap-slap, thump-tap-tap-slap,* a sound so familiar in my childhood that I can still hear it in my mind.

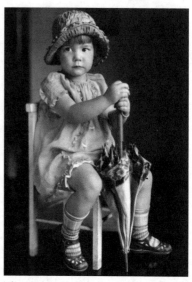

The author in Kansas in the 1920s

The cause of this paralysis of the muscles was a bootlegged patent medicine called "Jamaican Ginger," known by its slang name Jake, which drinkers in those days often substituted for more expensive bootleg whiskey. The real Jamaican Ginger had enough ginger to make it bitter and unpalatable, so bootleggers substituted tri-ortho-cresyl phosphate, a chemical that damaged the nerves but fooled the Prohibition Bureau. The outlawed mixture cost less than 50 cents for a two-ounce bottle. It was illegally sold by many drugstores and even dispensed at the soda fountain, where a milkshake could be served as a chaser. It's possible that was how my father drank the poison.

Dad liked the conviviality of sharing a drink with friends, usually on Saturdays. Looking back on it, I think it's quite likely that, while Dad's own drinking was social, some of his income in the late 1920s, as well as some of his drinking pals, came from bootlegging. My sister remembered the time Dad learned that the police might be coming to our house with a search warrant. He loaded the supply he had in our little black Ford and told Mother to take us children, the liquor, and the car, and go. She did. As my sister related the story, once Mother got out of town, she had a great time dumping all the liquor out on the ground. She was laughing and having such a good time that Mary, who was nine at the time, got out and helped. Mother may have seen herself a latter-day Carry Nation, who thirty years earlier had wielded her hatchet in the saloons of Kansas.

After Daddy left for the sanatorium, Mother's only choice was to seek help from his family in Sherman, Texas. One of her half-brothers came in an open truck to haul us and our possessions south in the spring of 1929, when I was six years old. We were only a few years ahead of the Dust Bowl exodus, and, as we drove across Oklahoma towards Texas, we looked like a scene from John Steinbeck's novel, *The Grapes of Wrath,* with our furniture and belongings piled in the truck. My brother Bob rode in back with the furniture, holding onto our little black and white bulldog. Mary sat in the middle between Uncle Elbert and Mother. I sat in Mother's lap all the way.

When Dad was healthy and working, he'd gotten us railroad passes that allowed us to travel to Texas to see family. I remembered sleeping overnight in a Pullman car, eating in the dining car and, once, staying in a large, ornate hotel a block from the railroad station. We were always finely dressed. I remembered Mother looking beautiful and very much in control as she directed a porter to take our bags to the hotel.

Now, as we drove south in Uncle Elbert's truck, I remembered the red ants of Texas, the horned toad lizards and the wickedly pronged goathead stickers that stuck on shoelaces, socks, and bare feet. I remembered the hot dust that burned my feet and blew in my face. I remembered the water, its rancid smell and its taste like iodine. The anticipation of staying with grandparents I didn't know was not comforting.

Grandma Cantrell was stern and strict, a small, wiry woman who wore long black dresses and high-topped shoes. She had a never-healed sore on the bridge of her skinny nose. She was given to odd behavior. She bought ice cream for herself and wouldn't share it, telling the rest of us that she had to have it "because my bowels are hot." Once she ordered my mother to put a light bulb in a hanging light fixture "because if it doesn't have a light bulb all the electricity will run out." Mother never argued with her and did as she was told, probably thinking only of how to have her own home again.

Grandpa Cantrell was not large, but he had a sturdy build, like my daddy. With his long thick white hair and beard, Grandpa was an impressive-looking man, and he had gentler ways than Grandma. He was always tending his chickens or his garden or going somewhere in his open-sided Model T Ford, which he had to crank to get started. Like my daddy, he liked to get away from the house after his chores were done.

Our brief sojourn in Sherman was a time when my world expanded beyond our small family of five. It grew to include events and circumstances that I didn't understand and that were troubling to adults. It stretched me to take risks, to learn to do things I didn't know I could do.

One terrible event stands out vividly. I first knew something was happening when a neighbor excitedly told my mother that the courthouse was on fire. We could see it from her front yard, a cloud of smoke and flashes of flame.

From bits and pieces of comments from all the neighbors gathered there, I learned what was going on. A black man had been jailed on the top floor of the courthouse on an accusation of rape of a white woman. I didn't know what "rape" was; to me it meant only some sort of attack. A group of white men had set fire to the courthouse in order to get to the black man. I watched my mother standing on the lawn wringing her hands and repeating over and over, "That poor man, that poor man."

Decades later when I returned to Sherman to research family documents, I told the county clerk what I remembered. She suggested I read the official description of what had happened. It read:

Mother and her two daughters shortly after arrival in Texas in early 1930s.

> On Friday, May 9th, A.D. 1930, at the County Court House, in the City of Sherman, Grayson County, Texas, one George Hughes, Negro, and confessed rapist, was being tried in the 15th District Court. An angry mob formed on the Court House lawn and demanded that this negro be turned over to them.
>
> At, or about, 2:30 P.M. this mob set fire to the Court House. The City Fire Department responded promptly to the call but the mob would not permit them to put water on the blaze. The fire hose was cut in several places.
>
> Within a short time after the Court House was set on fire the entire structure was a mass of flames.

The county clerk told me that the victim had been brought into the trial on a stretcher, which had inflamed the mob. The vigilantes reached the black man, lynched him, and then dragged his body through "black town" behind a car.

❧ ❧

One experience I had in Sherman made me feel very brave and rewarded me with my first feelings of pride and self-esteem. I got onto a bicycle that belonged to an older boy. It was so big that my feet barely touched the pedals, much less the ground. To get me started, one kid on each side held the bicycle and then gave me a shove. I had to ride up a small incline to the next street, turn around in the intersection, and go back down the hill, where the kids waited to catch me. The tricky part was timing my arrival in the intersection when no cars were there.

As I pedaled awkwardly up the hill I could hear the kids hollering, "Don't stop, don't stop." They knew that if I did I'd fall off, getting a good scraping from the road's hard-packed dirt. I didn't stop. I turned around in the intersection and went flying back down the hill. I rode that bicycle over and over up and down the hill, and I never did fall off.

By summer my grandparents' two-bedroom house had become uncomfortably cramped. Dad hadn't been released from the sanatorium, and there was no word when he would be. Uncharacteristically, Mother was so dispirited that she went to bed for two or three days. Shortly after that we moved to Wichita Falls, where Grandpa Higgins, Mother's father, had a shoe repair shop just north of the Wichita River on busy Burnett Street.

Grandpa Higgins had moved out of my mother's life after his first wife died shortly after giving birth to her. Since then he'd been widowed twice more, and all his children were grown. Grandpa lived in the back of his shoe shop. When I saw his little apartment, I hoped we weren't going to try to squeeze four more people into that space, but somehow we did. Mother and Grandpa hung wire across the one room in various directions and then hung bed sheets over the wire to give everyone a bit of privacy. Maybe because the crowding got to be too much for them, Grandpa and Mother soon took an apartment over an A&P store. That was in a slightly more respectable location, and Mother finally got her Kansas furniture moved in.

Shortly after we moved, Grandpa Higgins decided to marry for the fourth time. His intended was a woman in Minnesota with whom he had corresponded through a lonely hearts club. They decided to marry by telephone, with a minister on each end to make everything legal. The local newspaper provided a telephone and a reporter bearing a wedding cake. Soon after the ceremony Grandpa moved back to his shoe shop in anticipation of his bride's arrival. She showed up with a few small children in tow. She'd not told Grandpa about the children. I wondered what he'd told her about himself. The lady was short and wide, a startling contrast to Grandpa, who was over six feet tall and skinny as a rail. She didn't stay long in Texas, but the attention given the long-distance wedding was intriguing relief from the dreary life we were enduring.

It was in that apartment over the A&P store that I learned the stark fear of being without food. One day we all arrived home from school to find Mother gone. That was disturbing. By suppertime she still hadn't come home, and my twelve-year-old sister thought it was her duty to fix supper. All she could find was a little lard and some flour.

Calling on her resources, Mary made biscuits and water-based gravy. I began to wonder what we were going to do if Mother didn't come home. I guessed my sister would have a plan, but I wasn't sure. The biscuits and gravy would be temporarily satisfying, but I wondered how long the meager food supply would last. If for some reason Mother didn't come home I hoped our relatives would help us, but I wasn't sure of that, either. I certainly didn't want to live with any of them.

While we were eating our paltry supper, Mother came in with bags of groceries she had gotten at the Salvation Army. We were so happy to see her and to know she was all right. She explained she'd had to go to many places that day to find food, and then had to wait a long time to get it. She said the groceries were a gift and a blessing.

❧ ❧

My daddy had gone to the sanatorium when I was in the second grade. In the summer after my third-grade year we learned he would be coming home.

Mother started looking for a house—she knew Dad wouldn't be able to climb the stairs to our apartment. She found one that would do, but she had no money for the rent. She convinced the landlord that Dad would be there soon and then we would be able to pay the five dollars a month. The landlord may have been easy to convince, for the house was not in a desirable part of town and he hadn't been able to rent it at all. Landlords didn't want their houses to stand empty, as many did during the Depression, for fear they would be vandalized.

The two-story house sat on a dirt street a block from busy railroad tracks and an eight-story flour mill with six tall grain elevators. A big open field stretched to the railroad tracks. A block away stood the black, sooty buildings of a foundry. The noise and the dust didn't bother me at first, but it wasn't long before I grasped the relationship between the flour mill and Mother's newly developed asthma, especially when the wind blew from the north. And it wasn't long before I made the connection between where we lived and our financial situation. We didn't speak of it, but we were on the wrong side of the tracks.

The previous occupants had left an upright piano in the living room, and Mother managed to fill the house with music from time to time. She played hymns—"Amazing Grace," "Rock of Ages," "The Old Rugged Cross," "In the Garden," and others from the Methodist hymnal she'd borrowed from the church. It was good to see Mother happy again with her expectation of Daddy's homecoming.

On the appointed day my brother and sister and I waited on the front porch, gazing anxiously up the street. Finally we saw Grandpa Cantrell's Model T Ford approaching, its sides open in the summer heat. We could see Daddy sitting upright in the front seat. We ran down the street and jumped onto the running board and threw our arms around him as he sat in the car. He tried to hug all of us at once. It was an ecstatic reunion. With my daddy's arm tight around me, I peeked into the backseat and saw his crutches lying there.

Awkwardly, he maneuvered from the seat to the running board using his strong arms and hands. His legs and feet were almost useless. His movements were painfully slow and deliberate, but there was no point in trying to help him. There was nothing anyone could do short of physically carrying him. Finally, he planted his two crutches firmly and pulled himself up to a standing position. Then, slowly, he moved step by step toward the house.

While fighting back tears, I was happy to see my daddy and have him put his arm around me once again, feel his shaven face and smell the pipe tobacco in his shirt pocket. But it hurt to see him so helpless. Young as I was, I knew Dad would never work again. He would never walk again without crutches or canes. Our mother stood, smiling and brave, managing her emotions as best she could.

My parents never discussed it in my presence. My mother told inquiring neighbors that Dad had contracted polio, which was better for everyone at the time than the truth. Mother started taking in washing to support the family, working in our small backyard with her wash tubs and clotheslines. She turned to my older sister, Mary, for support and solace. They went to church together and became constant companions.

❧ ☙

When my daddy's beer was in the bathtub, things at home were downright unpleasant. Mother's silence could last a week. When there was beer, a poker game couldn't be far behind. It was 1931, Prohibition had been the law for eleven years, and America was in the stranglehold of the Great Depression.

If it hadn't been for Prohibition, Dad would not have gotten sick, and he would not have been hospitalized. That was my way of thinking. If it hadn't been for Prohibition, Dad would have been working instead of making bathtub beer. And if it hadn't been for Prohibition, he would not have needed two crutches just to move around the house.

Everyone looked for relief from the economic depression and the depression of the soul that accompanied it. My father was no exception. Neither Prohibition nor my mother's disapproval had curbed his desire for a "little toddy" now and then, and bathtub beer was better than nothing.

Occasionally Grandpa Cantrell sent Dad a few dollars, and then Dad would send me to the store for cane sugar. He always emphasized that it had to be cane sugar, because beet sugar wouldn't make proper beer. I worried all the way to the store about getting the right kind of sugar, and then I wouldn't ask the grocery clerk, because if he knew I needed cane sugar (or was it beet? I still can't remember), he'd know what I needed it for.

It didn't bother me that Dad made beer, and it didn't bother me that he drank it. It was just the double inconvenience of Mother's belief that drink was sinful and the fact that we couldn't let anyone know because it was illegal. And because Dad could not go up the stairs, he used the downstairs bathtub, which made Mother's silence even more impenetrable. We couldn't let neighbors or friends come into the house, and all of us but Dad had to use the upstairs bathroom.

One day Dad did manage to get himself up the stairs. He'd probably sat on the bottom step and lifted himself up backward with his arms, step by step. Once on the second floor, he said he was staying—he was going to live up there. The upstairs must have been rented out as an apartment some time in the past, because one of the rooms had a sink and a stove, so Dad could cook. There was a bed in one of the other rooms, and there was a bathroom where he could make his beer without Mother's reprisals.

He was satisfied. He had a place of his own where the neighborhood men could come up for poker games. We children took him food and anything else he needed. We brought his laundry down to be washed and then took the clean clothes back up.

Our mother was dismayed. My brother remembers coming home from school one day to find Mother standing at the bottom of the stairs with Dad's Stevens single-shot lever-action rifle in her hands. Dad called it his "varmint" gun. It was well-worn, and the shell ejection mechanism didn't work—it took pliers or a pocket knife to get the shell out of the chamber. Bob doesn't remember what Mother and Dad were saying to each other, but the gist of it was that Mother was demanding that Dad come down and live with his family. My brother wasn't worried that she would do anything with the gun, and Dad evidently wasn't either. But Mother would have her way.

She arranged to rent a smaller house next door that was owned by the same landlord, for three dollars a month, and we moved there. There were probably many reasons for the move. Mother's sense of obligation was so strong that she would have felt it was better to not pay the landlord three dollars a month than to not pay him five dollars a month. The smaller house also had a larger backyard for her wash tubs and clotheslines nearby. Perhaps most importantly for Mother, the smaller house would not allow Dad a separate place to live or a second bathtub for making beer, or a place to have poker games, either. We lived in that house for the next five years, still breathing flour from the mill and dust from the foundry.

Even with the occasional Salvation Army food, we seldom had enough to eat. Sometimes Mother had my brother catch one of the pigeons that nested under the eaves, and we'd have it for supper. There wasn't much meat, but it seasoned the dumplings or potato soup.

It was always a wonderful day when Uncle Bill and Aunt Tessie came from Goree. They brought fresh vegetables, eggs, milk, and butter from the farm. In the summertime, cantaloupes, watermelons, and tomatoes were a part of the largesse, and in the fall they brought sausage, bacon, and ham. When their car pulled up in front of our house, there were shouts of greeting and plenty of hugs for everyone. After the car was unloaded, Uncle Bill went to the barbecue stand a few blocks toward town for three or four kinds of barbecued meats. We'd all sit down for a big lunch. Then they'd go to town to do their shopping.

If it was summertime I could go back to Goree with them, and there'd be a flurry of putting my few clothes together. I knew I'd get to stay until the next time they came to Wichita Falls. Summers in Goree were a welcome respite for me. I could go to a different world for a few weeks. There, I had cousins, twin sisters my age, Aunt Tessie's and Uncle Bill's grandchildren. Their names were Dorothy Jane and Lois Elaine, but everyone called them Janey and Laney. We played under the weeping willow in the front yard, and spent hours pedaling the player piano in the parlor. When the adults couldn't stand the piano any more, they sent us out to churn, put lids on the milk bottles, set the table, or do whatever other simple task they could devise.

There were days when I was alone with Aunt Tessie. Once when I needed something to do I asked if I could go out with the hired people and pick cotton. She said she would talk to Uncle Bill about it. He consented.

I remember being up early, by daylight, with the long gunnysack laid out behind me between the rows of cotton. I was supposed to pick the cotton and fill the sack. The other pickers were all black people, including children my age or younger. I watched how they were doing it, and then I began. The cotton was soft but full of tiny seeds. Then I began to feel the sharp pricks on my fingers from the pod that held the cotton, and knew I had to be careful to get the cotton out of the pod without poking myself. I was far slower than the others.

We stopped for lunch at midmorning around a wagon that had brought sandwiches and water out into the field. I was more than ready for a rest. Someone gave me a sandwich and water, and I sat down to eat. All of the other workers went around to the other side of the wagon. That was a great disappointment. I don't know what I had expected—maybe that we would eat together, for the other children and I had exchanged glances but no one had spoken all morning. I sat and chewed my sandwich by myself.

We quit picking by about two o'clock. Uncle Bill stood by the weighing machine and paid everyone. When my bag was weighed he handed me a few coins without a word. That night after dinner, when I was helping Aunt Tessie with the dishes, she said that Uncle Bill had decided that I should not pick cotton any more.

I was puzzled and dismayed. I wasn't productive enough? The hired hands didn't want me there? Aunt Tessie wanted me to help her? Or did Uncle Bill think it wasn't right to have a member of the family in the field? I will never know. Yet I was proud to take the coins home to show Mother that I had earned my own first money.

❧ ❧

President Franklin Delano Roosevelt took office in 1933, when I was in the fifth grade. Mother and Dad hadn't voted because they couldn't pay the poll tax required by Texas law. But Roosevelt's election cheered them.

In 1933 Congress submitted a repeal of the prohibition amendment to the states for ratification. The measure was ratified. It was too late to help my daddy, but both the new president and the repeal were signs of changing times.

One of the first things the president did was create the Federal Emergency Relief Administration, which in turn created the Federal Surplus Relief Corporation. Its purpose was to buy agricultural surpluses that the farmers couldn't sell and give them to people who needed food. A commissary opened in the basement of the Wichita Falls city auditorium. People like us could go there and get food, but first a social worker had to visit us to determine our need.

I remember standing beside Mother while the social worker asked her questions about our names, ages, and income. When she finally said we qualified, Mother began to interview her, very diplomatically. She thanked her for her help, and then inquired how she had come to be the person hired to go to homes and make this important decision. Even in my child's mind I knew what Mother was thinking: "If she can do this, I can do it." Perhaps the information was not encouraging, for nothing ever came from that self-initiated interview, but it gave me another glimpse of my mother's resourcefulness.

The food from the commissary was mostly staples: flour, sugar, lard, canned meats, potatoes, beans. But there would be surprises from time to time—peanut butter, canned pineapple, and other treats. All four of us walked the fourteen blocks to the commissary to help carry the groceries home, mostly with the help of Bob's red wagon that we had brought from Kansas.

How grateful we were! Mother was creative with the variety and quantity of our new food. She would even make puddings and cakes occasionally. Peanut butter was a delicious treat, especially when she made peanut butter fudge. With the Karo syrup she showed off her talent at boiling a pan of taffy and pulling it in great dramatic motions. When it was set just right, she laid it on the counter and cut it into bite sizes with scissors.

The empty Karo cans served for all kinds of other uses, including my siblings' bright idea, one summer day, of using them as floats to help me learn to swim. They had learned in clean public pools in Kansas. My lesson was in a swimming hole carved out of Holiday Creek, where the sides were slick with slimy dirt and the water was a thick, murky mess. I wore two Karo cans, joined together by a sturdy string running through small holes pierced with a nail near the top rim, just under the ridge of the lids. The string was fitted across my chest. The Karo cans bobbed around on either side of my shoulders as I waded into the water, flanked by my brother and sister.

Mary and Bob gave me a shove and hollered, "Move your arms! Kick your feet!" About halfway across I felt the cans sinking from the water that had seeped inside through the nail holes. I grabbed Mary and pushed her under the water to stand on, and then I did the same with Bob, which they both deserved. A teenage neighbor boy, watching this unusual operation from the shore, came to the rescue of all three of us. They sat in the mud laughing about the failed experiment, but I didn't think it was funny at all.

⁂

Visions of Dad's walking again were with me always. I wanted to help. I'd begun to blame our poverty for his condition. If we just had money, I thought, he could go back to the sanatorium and finish the process of getting well. Not willing to accept that he couldn't be helped, I daydreamed of how I could get that money.

Mother accepted reality soon after Dad returned home, and it made her tougher. That toughness came through one day in the backyard; she was at her ever-present tubs doing a washing, Dad was on a stool tending his small garden, and I was sitting on the step just outside our kitchen screen door.

A stray chicken wandered into the yard, pecking at the hard ground. My parents' eyes met momentarily. Mother walked around the wash tub and slowly moved behind the chicken. In one rapid move she grabbed it, put its head in her right hand, and started swinging it around and around. I'd never seen her do that before, but she looked like she'd had practice. She'd learned it growing up in Goree, I guessed.

Maybe she married my father to get away from wringing chicken necks, to get away from the cotton fields and the dairy farmer's kitchen. Now she had to resort to a past she'd hoped she'd never see again. She had to do it to feed me, my brother and sister, and my father. And if anything was left, to feed herself.

The headless chicken flopped on the ground, its blood making dark spots on the small clumps of Johnson grass. Mother dipped up a pan of boiling water from the tub over the fire, doused the chicken, and deftly plucked it. In no time the poor curious chicken was on the stove cooking for our supper. Mother returned to her wash, humming "Amazing Grace," her way of giving thanks to her Lord for the good fortune.

That scene holds a lasting lesson for me. It taught me that, while hope and faith are helpful for peace of mind, a woman must be prepared to seize the moment and act quickly when an opportunity presents itself. My mother had abundant hope and faith, but she used her knowledge and experience to turn the opportunity to her advantage. She'd been prepared. I learned that day that there's no point in having a chicken stroll across my path if I'm not prepared to turn it into an opportunity.

Chapter 2

A New Deal, War, and Marriage

When I think back now on that little girl growing up in Texas three generations ago, I can discern some of the threads of influence that guided her to become the woman I am today, a woman who is, to some observers, an enigmatic mix of traditional and unconventional. It was never a puzzle in my mind. The protection I received as the youngest child gave me an understanding of the importance of home and family and emotional security. And yet I was given a surprising measure of independence, too.

Mother keenly wanted me to be more "ladylike." If that meant doing the domestic chores that go with being a wife and mother, I wanted no part of it. My older sister, Mary, helped Mother with all those tasks, and I never felt inclined to interfere.

Mary was Mother's second-in-command when it came to teaching me feminine manners. She'd tell me to walk with my toes pointed straight ahead and to hold my tummy in. She told me she didn't think it was fair that I got a permanent after the sixth grade when she'd had to wait until the eighth grade, and that I didn't know how to take care of my hair, anyway. She told me these things, she said, to make me want to pay more attention to how I looked. She said I would thank her some day.

Maybe so. For now, I found that even when I tried to be ladylike, it never came out right. One afternoon I played "tea" with my doll-sized china tea set Mother had saved from our Kansas days. After putting vinegar in the teapot and salt in the sugar bowl I invited my guest, a little girl who was visiting a neighbor, to drink it. She took one gulp and went away crying. I didn't mean to make her cry; I was only trying to make the tea party more fun instead of so prissy.

My brother was my best friend. We liked to do the same things—climb trees, build forts, and play ball with the neighborhood boys in the vacant lot across the street. Toward evening we'd have a game of kick-the-can or king-of-the-mountain in our front yards, where the coming darkness would help us hide. I didn't want to be a boy, but I thought they had more fun than girls—an attitude that may have helped when it came to working with men in my adult life.

I was allowed to explore my small world in my own groping way, which gave me a strong appetite for freedom and all its consequences. One day I wamdered down the block to the big green house at the end of the sidewalk, across the dirt road from the foundry. This house had the best climbing trees in the neighborhood. I swung myself up to a low branch and started climbing. I climbed higher and higher, until I could see buildings blocks away. I eased myself out toward the end of the limb and looked down, and a sudden dizzying light-headedness swept over me. The earth was undulating far, far below. The limb swayed, although there was not a wisp of wind. I squeezed my eyes shut to let everything settle down.

I was, literally, out on a limb. I understood clearly that no one would see me if I fell. I was eleven or twelve years old then, old enough to understand the idea of taking responsibility for myself.

I would have to go down the same way I'd gone up. By myself.

Gripping the limb tightly, eyes focused straight in front of me, I eased myself, inch by inch, back to the solid, reassuring trunk. My head cleared. My body steadied. I followed the trunk of the tree, limb by limb. Finally I reached the bottom branch and tucked myself into the curve where it grew from the tree. Then, with one last move, I swung from the branch with my hands and dropped to the ground.

Was it exciting to climb the tree that day, or was it dangerous? The answer to both questions, I know now, is "yes." I knew I would climb that tree again. I'd be more careful, but now I understood that the responsibility for my acts and resulting predicaments rested with me alone.

☙ ☙

At school, I got into tussles with other girls and got sent to the principal's office regularly. Once I wrestled my best friend to the ground and took her shoes off her. She walked home barefoot ahead of me and wouldn't speak to me. I left her shoes on her front porch and went home, hoping she wasn't mad at me. The next day I was in the principal's office again.

Looking back now, I realize that my insensitive behavior at those times revealed my feelings about the circumstances of our family. No longer having Mother's time and the activities we enjoyed in Kansas, feeling deprived and sad that Mother had to work so hard, I'd developed mean and tough edges. In Kansas I was precocious. In Texas I was angry that we were poor, that my father was crippled, and that my mother had to take in washing.

A snapshot from those days shows how I must have appeared to others. Standing apart from a group of my sister's friends, wearing a straight, waist-

Betty in Texas in
the 1930s

less dress, I am skinny and barefoot, expressionless, with straight hair parted more or less on the side and hanging to my neck.

One day a well-meaning woman showed up at my school, whisked me out of class, and took me shopping for a whole new outfit of school clothes—dress, slip, shoes, socks. It must have been a parents' project, but no other student was similarly singled out. When the woman returned me to school, everybody's eyes were on me and my brand-new clothes. They knew my parents couldn't afford to buy me these things. Instead of being grateful I was bitterly resentful.

Mother never let us wear clothes that were torn or had buttons missing. That was shameful, but it was fine to wear clothes that were patched and mended. Dad did his part, too, by keeping the tops of our shoes polished and broken shoe strings tied in such a way as to hide the knot. And he covered the holes in the soles of our shoes with cardboard cut to fit just right. I heard Mother tell a neighbor once that if she had only a nickel and had to choose between milk or soap, it would be soap. Cleanliness was next to Godliness in her mind. I don't doubt that she made that choice sometimes.

The only thing that kept me from feeling completely worthless was my parents' conviction that we were worthy. Mother told us that we were not poor white trash. Poor white trash didn't send their children to school, didn't go to church, and didn't take baths, wash their clothes, or make an effort to work. But sometimes her talk about being worthy made me even angrier. If we were doing everything we should, if we were so worthy, why didn't we have anything to show for it? For me, being angry was a way to take charge, feel in control, maintain a measure of self-esteem. I believed I had to stick up for myself, even when I was the aggressor. Poorness would not define me. I would rather be "that mean little girl" than "that poor little girl."

⨀ ⨀

Even in poverty there was tenderness and respect among our family members. No one spoke a harsh word except Dad, sometimes, who'd swear to himself about his limited abilities. As the first one home from school each day, I got to spend precious hours with my father. He taught me to play dominoes, checkers, and card games like solitaire and pitch. We even played poker when Mother wasn't around.

We couldn't afford to buy books, so I resorted to the Compton's Encyclopedia for Children that Mother had saved from our Kansas days. We often borrowed a newspaper from the only neighbor on the block who sometimes had one.

When my sister was in junior high school, she was invited to stay with a family who had an only daughter a few years older than Mary. The parents wanted someone to be company for their daughter, who was already in high school. In return they would provide food and clothing for Mary and a small allowance. Mother encouraged her to go.

Things apparently went fine for a while, but one night Mary showed up at home after midnight. She'd walked the two or more miles in the dark. As her story came out, my parents agreed she'd done the right thing. The daughter had gone out on a date and had been told to return at a certain time. When she came home late, her father met her at the door with his belt in his hand and began beating her. Mary grabbed as many of her things as possible and headed for the door. As she left, the daughter was running around the house screaming, her father chasing her with the belt. The mother was out of sight in her bedroom.

Mother and Dad were shocked, and so was I. They had never disciplined us physically. Mother said often, "There is no such thing as a bad child." From Mary's experience I learned that being raised in a poor family is not the worst thing that can happen to a person.

※ ※

Our family existed on the commissary food, the occasional bounty from Goree, and whatever food Mother could buy with her washing money, but we were still stuck with no way to pay for clothes, utility bills, or rent. In fact, the only utility we had was water. We had a wood stove in the dining room, a kerosene stove in the kitchen, and kerosene lamps for whatever light we needed after dark.

Mother always preferred prayer to crying, but once the water was turned off because she couldn't pay the bill. That night, sleeping between Mother and Mary in the big bed, I felt Mother's body shake with sobs. Soon she blew her nose, and then all was quiet for the rest of the night. The next day the water was turned on. I have no idea how Mother did it.

Mother did a lot of things that amazed me. She made bread in nice fat loaves, and sometimes even sourdough bread. When I'd started school in the third grade in Wichita Falls, my lunch every day had been two slices of Mother's bread. When we began to get commissary food a couple of years later, there might be margarine in the middle, or once in a while some sort of chopped meat from a can or a bit of peanut butter. My greatest challenge was to find someone who would trade their white bakery-baked, machine-sliced sandwich with lunchmeat in the middle for my sandwich.

One day I begged Mother for a nickel for lunch. Reluctantly, she gave it to me with a promise to buy soup, which was quickly forgotten when I saw the ice cream bars in the cafeteria. In the first class period after lunch, the sugar began to work on my empty stomach, I thought I would either pass out or throw up. After that I went back to the bread. When I was finally in high school I worked in the cafeteria for my lunch, and was mighty happy to do it.

≫ ≪

In May 1935, the first of President Roosevelt's proposed work programs, the Works Progress Administration, began. A Women's Division was set up under the WPA, and my mother went to work sewing dresses and shirts for the needy—a category which, of course, included us. She worked in a big room with dozens of sewing machines and cutting tables in the basement of the Wichita Falls city auditorium, where the food commissary was located. Her pay was twenty-nine dollars a month. She was relieved and happy to have a regular income, even though it meant that every day she walked fourteen blocks to work and fourteen blocks home. She saw the job as one more instance when her prayers had been answered and her faith renewed—one more instance of grace.

The head of the Women's Division was named Ellen Sullivan Woodward. Her work proved to be of great significance not only for poor people of the Depression but for the status of working women. Woodward created a jobs program for women in every state and the District of Columbia, with each state program directed by a woman. She insisted that men and women in relief work be given equal pay for equal work.

One day Mother came home from work and told us with great glee that all the women in the sewing room had received a raise. She would now be paid fifty-seven dollars a month. We were all ecstatic. I though we had become rich, and we had, relatively speaking.

Here was the long-awaited respite Mother had hoped and prayed for. No wonder people thought Franklin Roosevelt was a wonderful president. For many, he alone was the one who put food on our tables and put people to work. I began to understand that government is good when it helps its neediest citizens. At the time, I didn't know I'd have my own opportunity to vote my appreciation when I turned twenty-one and Roosevelt ran for his fourth term.

With Mother's pay raise we could go to town to shop on Saturdays. We could each buy a new pair of shoes at least once a year. Mother would sometimes splurge on ice cream sodas or a bag of candy, and we always went home with the Sunday *Denver Post*, which cost ten cents.

After Mary graduated from high school she went to work for a cookie company. My brother, still in high school, had a job as caddy at the municipal golf course on weekends. Mother, Mary, and Bob pooled enough money to move us to a new place, where we lived in one-third of what had been a big single-family house. Finally, we could begin to pay a small amount of rent. By this time Dad was staying in Sherman most of the time to help his elderly parents.

Mother took a new government-funded job at the city library. The WPA had added a Professional Projects Division to fund art, music, theater, and writers' projects; Mother's job at the library may have been under this new branch of the program, which some folks criticized because they thought it siphoned off money from the bigger, more labor-intensive public projects. Mother was proud to be helping to keep the library open during those Depression years. That job in a more peaceful, more intellectual environment, along with our better neighborhood, greatly boosted her self-esteem. Bob and I still walked thirty-six blocks to high school, but we had sidewalks all the way and didn't have to take the old shortcut down the railroad tracks any more. We no longer heard the trains switching and passing. We no longer looked out at the flour mill and its huge grain elevators, and we no longer lived on an unpaved street. Our move was a major step up, even if we lived in one-third of a house.

Our family's six years on Twentieth Street are imprinted in my mind, and they had a great influence on the woman I became. I watched my strong, determined, spiritually guided mother maneuver her family through years of hard times with only her hope and faith in a better future to sustain her. I'd been reluctant to invite anyone to that house after one girl referred to our street as an alley. The move to the new neighborhood raised my own self-esteem. Starting high school with a new, more respectable address was a sign we weren't living on the edge of nothingness any more. The hardships we'd endured were behind us, yet the memories and images from those years would last a life-time.

❧   ❧

I graduated from high school after the eleventh grade, which was as far as a Texas education went in those days. I was sixteen years old and unprepared for either college or employment. During the next two years I went through a series of menial jobs—clerking at a dime store, tending a soda fountain, answering the phone for a typewriter repair shop, typing specifications for an architect. Finally I got a job as receptionist and bookkeeper for a pediatrician, earning eight dollars a week. In those two years I learned about all kinds of jobs that I didn't want to do for very long. I spent everything I earned on clothes and cosmetics, and I developed an active social life with servicemen who were stationed at the new Sheppard Field Air Force Base a few miles from Wichita Falls.

We three siblings had lived through our childhoods with Mother's strict standards. As we became teenagers, these became more difficult to live with. Having been brought up Southern Methodist, Mother believed smoking, drinking, gambling, and dancing were sinful. While my sister had become an even more serious Christian and churchgoer than Mother, her views were different. After a disagreement with Mother about inviting her friends to our house to play records on the Victrola and dance, my sister's religious views trumped Mother's when she argued that dancing was simply an expression of joy and not necessarily evil. She met a young man named Marshall Wood, who became her steady beau. Two years later they married and moved to Virginia.

After my brother graduated from high school and was taking classes at Hardin Junior College, he began work as a draftsman for a real estate firm that was building houses on the outskirts of town. As his income increased, he, Mother and I moved into a new house, the nicest we'd had in Wichita Falls. Bob bought us new living-room furniture and our very first refrigerator.

One day Mother came home from work to find beer in the refrigerator. She scolded Bob and said he had to get rid of it. Dancing was my sister's issue; beer was his.

Bob: "Now, Mom, beer is legal. I am not breaking the law." Mother was silent. "You don't approve of drinking, but I don't drink very much." Silence. "Besides, I bought this refrigerator, so I will put whatever I choose in it, including the food I bought that's there for all of us." More silence, but you could tell she was thinking. She made no further objections to beer in the refrigerator.

My issue was shorts. As I matured I'd developed muscles along with other curves, and I was often surprised at my strength and resilient energy. I joined the church volleyball team. We wore shorts to play in, of course. But Mother forbade me to wear shorts to and from practice and the games. She wanted me to wear slacks, which were by then accepted attire for young women (although she'd had to overcome some resistance even to slacks), and to change into the shorts in the locker room. Furthermore, she insisted that the shorts I wore to play in had to be the old navy blue ones I'd worn for three years in my high-school gym classes. That made volleyball an extension of an authorized school activity in her mind, I guessed.

Mother had thought that Mary's dancing would lead to premarital sex and then to hell, and Bob's beer would lead directly to hell. I decided that I might go to hell for any number of reasons, but if so, it was going to be in shorts.

I tried to be patient with her. I pointed out that the one pair of shorts I'd already worn for three years was not going to get me through the summer. All she needed to do was come to the volleyball games to see that other girls wore different colored shorts and shirts, and they wore them to and from the games. My most convincing argument was that the games were church-sponsored and no one in charge objected.

The volleyball-shorts discussion turned out to be a warm-up drill for what came next. I was invited to join a girls' football team. There were only two teams in this so-called league, but our male coaches hoped girls' football would catch on after we played a few demonstration games. Remember this is Texas, and anything can catch on there as long as it's about football.

We practiced in shorts or slacks in a vacant lot full of dirt, gravel, and goathead stickers. I played in the backfield—I was one of the smaller players and I could run fast—but I got tackled a lot, and I always went home with bruises and scrapes and dirty clothes. It's an understatement to say that Mother's patience with me was severely taxed. She was beyond telling me that playing football was not "ladylike." She was steaming: "Betty Lucille, if you keep this up you will never be able to have babies." While that was dramatic and extreme, it was a poor approach to take with me, because I'd never given any thought to whether I'd ever want babies. Truth be told, I was becoming impatient with Mother, too, for trying to mold me into something like my domestic sister. As it turned out, she had little to worry about. Our games were so poorly attended that the coaches gave up trying to start something new in football.

※　※

In the summer of 1941 a recruiter from Texas Wesleyan College in Fort Worth interviewed me about attending the school. She told me I could major in physical education and become a teacher. I enrolled for what turned out to be a difficult year, even though I had the company of two friends from Wichita Falls. All three of us attended classes in the mornings and worked at Leonard's Department Store until seven in the evening and all day Saturday. From our eight dollars a week, four went for tuition and our dormitory room.

Betty as a freshman at Texas Wesleyan College, Fort Worth, Texas, 1941-42

The rest had to cover food, bus fare, and any other necessities. Food again became a major concern.

On December 7, 1941, Pearl Harbor was bombed by the Japanese. Young men began leaving Texas Wesleyan in large numbers to join the service. In January 1942, home for semester break, I met a serviceman from Sheppard Field at a girlfriend's house. Bill Rice was a nice-looking young man who had left his job as a bank teller in Oregon to join the Air Force. He had completed his basic training and was a drill instructor for the new recruits.

After returning to school, I learned Bill was continuing to visit my mother. She cooked Sunday dinner for him and he'd stay the whole day. I thought it was nice that Mother had Bill to keep her company—he probably missed his own home and mother. But then at Easter break, there he was; he and Mother both seemed to assume that he could come over whenever he wanted to, and that I, too, wanted him to be there. In all fairness, I never told him I didn't.

That summer I got a good-paying job at the telephone company as a long-distance operator, working the plug-in switchboards. On my days off Bill and I went to movies occasionally. He was quiet, reserved, a bit stodgy. I didn't learn a lot about him. I knew he had played saxophone in a small-town band and that he loved the big-band music of the era. He knew all the songs, singers, and musicians.

Mother clearly considered Bill a good catch. She told me he would be a "good provider," just what she had longed for over the years. After our lean times during the Depression and my hardships trying to make ends meet at school, that was important to me, too.

That summer he asked me to marry him. I couldn't think of a good reason not to.

Chapter 3

Hello, Oregon

After I'd made a commitment to marry, I had a little time to think. I'd miss Texas and my mother. But life had been hard in Texas. Maybe being married and living in Oregon, Bill's home state, would change all that. This would not be a butterflies-in-the stomach kind of marriage. It had more of the elements of an arranged union, with the benefits of security, maternal approval, and, ultimately, an opportunity to move away from Wichita Falls.

On September 25, 1942, my brother walked me down the long aisle of the First Methodist Church. As we were taking our first few steps, Bob said softly, "Are you sure you want to do this? I'll walk you out if you want to change your mind." Somehow it didn't surprise me that Bob said that. I knew he wanted me to continue college.

I paused for a second to ponder his words. In the feverish time after Pearl Harbor, young couples all over the country were marrying in great numbers, often after short courtships, just before the groom shipped out to some unknown destination. The heightened emotions had affected me, I knew, but practicality was also important. I had learned from my father that taking a risk could cost a person everything. But I'd learned from my mother that faith and hope were rewarded. She had been tested in the toughest of times and had ultimately regained a life filled with peace and self-respect.

It was a risk, but I also knew there could be much to gain.

Shaking my head, I whispered, "Keep walking."

ঌ ঞ

In the spring after the wedding, Bill and I visited his home state of Oregon on one of his few furloughs. We went first to Portland, where his mother often came from her home in Klamath Falls to be with an elderly aunt. As Bill and I were dozing off in Aunt Jo's well-appointed guest room, I heard the rain and a moaning sound coming through the slightly opened window. I roused Bill and asked, with alarm in my voice, "What's that noise?" His sleepy reply: "It's just the wind in the trees. You'll get used to it." Some forty years later I'd learn from a different husband that the sound had a name—a beautiful name. It is "soughing," as in murmuring, rustling, sighing; or, as the writer Robert Penn Warren put it, "a slow sad susurrous rustle like the wind fingering the pines."

Betty and Bill Rice

The next day Bill and I and his mother traveled by train to Klamath Falls. On our way to the train station that morning I noticed how clean and fresh the city looked. Windows sparkled. Lawns were carpeted with soft green grass, and flowers of every color grew on bushes as big as the mesquite trees in Texas.

The train trip from Portland to Klamath Falls took us through the Willamette Valley and over the Cascade Mountains. As we began the climb into the foothills, the tended fields gave way to trees of many varieties and shades of green, from chartreuse to deep blue. We began to see patches of snow, a rare sight for me. Before we reached the summit, my ears plugged. Bill's mother, who'd joined us in Portland, handed me a stick of gum and explained elevation and pressure to this flatlander.

A chill and a thrill swept over me as I looked out the window and saw the two engines curving to the left over a bridge that spanned a great divide in the mountains. My heart pounded as I studied the bridge's rickety-looking timbers. How could it possibly support the weight of our long train? I was afraid but compelled to look down. Snow covered the ground far, far below, except for a ribbon of water winding in and out of the trees. It must have been a big river.

I knew instantly that I wanted to live in this country. And we would, just as soon as the war was over.

❧ ❧

On the day in 1943 when I learned I was pregnant with my first child, I took the bus back into town from the doctor's office at Sheppard Field. I walked the dozen blocks from the bus stop to the Boys' Club, where Mother now worked, to tell her the good news. No longer would she have to worry that her late-blooming daughter would not be able to have babies. She would be proud that I was about to fulfill my responsibility and destiny as a female by having a child.

My sister wrote from Virginia telling me how happy she was for me. As the enforcer of our mother's strict standards, she'd told me I'd thank her some day, and now I guessed she was right, because things were turning out for me very much as they had for her. She had two children by then and was happy being a mother and housewife.

I recalled the time I'd gone to visit her in Virginia during those two years between graduation and Texas Wesleyan. We talked about a lot of things on those visits, including our memories of Kansas, before times got hard. Once she asked me, "Do you remember Mother being in the hospital?"

"I remember going to see her at the hospital, yes."

"Do you know why she was in the hospital?"

I told her I didn't know and had not been curious about it because Mother had only stayed overnight, so I had concluded it wasn't important.

"Well, it certainly was important, because we almost had another child in the family, and you would have had a younger brother or sister."

It happened when I was three, maybe four years old, Mary said. Mother was pregnant with her fourth child, and she started spotting or bleeding,

She didn't go to the doctor. Instead, she went to the barn, got out the pusher lawn mower, and began mowing a great expanse of weedy grass that lay between our house and the road. She mowed for at least two hours. When Dad came home he took her to the hospital. That evening we went to see her. The next day she came home, and there were no more children in our family.

Mary told me all this in such a matter-of-fact way that I had no emotional reaction other than curiosity about why it was important for me to know the details. At the time it seemed to convey the message that women were responsible for all things related to pregnancy. Now that I was pregnant and remembered the story, I would happily take that responsibility and produce a healthy, beautiful baby. I didn't know that I would look upon Mary's story in a different way many years later.

❧   ❧

After the war Bill and I moved to Oregon and settled in Klamath Falls, where he had a job waiting. Klamath Falls was not where I had wanted to live in Oregon. After Portland and the beautiful train ride we'd had over the Willamette Pass while he was on furlough, the brown hills that surround the town had been disappointing. And then he had taken me to Lakeview, an even smaller and more remote place, about one hundred miles southeast of Klamath Falls, where he had been working when he enlisted. On our drive back I had told him that I didn't want to live in Klamath Falls or Lakeview because Portland had literally stolen my heart. But here we were, living in the other side of the duplex where his parents lived and preparing to make Klamath Falls our home.

After a few days, Bill took me and our two-year-old daughter, Dian, to the bank where he would work. The setting was daunting, with its high ceilings, ornate columns, and barred tellers' windows. Small and uncomfortable in the formal surroundings, I sat in the chair next to the manager's desk holding our child.

The manager turned to stare at me for a bit, and then said, "Well, Bill, you sure got yourself a cute one—and a little Texas gal, at that." Turning to me again, he said, "Say something Texas, honey."

I felt myself stiffen. I'd heard from other Oregonians about the "Okies" and "Arkies" who had come to Oregon during the Depression. They were unwelcome, spoken of in disparaging tones, and I did not want anyone to think of me as a hillbilly. "You don't understand," I said haughtily to the manager. "I am from *north* Texas." I tried not to let a trace of Texas enter my response.

As the winter dragged by and those brown hills kept leaning in on me, I found myself longing for the expansiveness of Texas. How could I get my bearings without a horizon and a sunset? Klamath Falls and the quiet reserve of my husband's family took some getting used to.

Bill's mother and father were kind and modest, not politically active, but they were Republicans and conservative to their bones. Bill wanted me to try the Presbyterian Church. I soon learned that our church friends were Republicans, too.

With the political news of the coming 1946 spring primary, I announced that I wanted to register to vote. Bill asked, "How do you plan to register?"

"Democrat, of course."

"Oh my God, don't let my folks know," he cautioned.

Religion and political parties suddenly seemed to be linked. I registered Independent, rationalizing it as a way to prove my own independence. Then I found I could not vote for either the Democrats or Republicans in the primary. Oregon is a closed-primary state, where registered Independents can vote only in nonpartisan races and on issues.

I soon returned to being a Democrat. I adjusted somewhat to the new religion and Bill's Republican family, but I would not change my political party.

☙ ❧

It was impossible to ignore the dreary surroundings, but enjoying Dian and planning for a new baby helped. Mother came to Oregon when son John was born in early May 1947, declaring she'd left Texas forever. She wasn't sure she was going to stay in Oregon either, as she had already investigated the possibility of working for the Boys' Clubs of America in Chicago. She'd worked for seven years for the Boys' Club in Wichita Falls as receptionist, secretary, and hostess, den mother to the boys, and sometime arbitrator. The boys and staff loved her.

Bill and I bought a small, brand-new house, but after only a year, he was transferred to Lakeview. He was promised that the assignment would be for only one year. The little town sits at 4,000 feet between sections of the Fremont National Forest. We were assigned a house owned by the bank—maybe from a foreclosure—that had no insulation, no fireplace, and only a small grate floor heater in the hallway. We moved in during an ice storm on January 2, 1949, during one of Oregon's coldest winters on record. The temperatures were consistently below zero.

My memories of Lakeview reek with disappointment and physical discomfort. The two children and I made do by shutting ourselves off in the kitchen with the oven door open for heat, lots of toys and coloring books and a little phonograph that played nursery rhyme records. Sometimes Dian would scratch her ABCs into the ice on the living-room windows and practice writing her name.

I was angry with the bank for putting us in such a poor-quality house, and I questioned society's assumption that a wife and children should follow the husband when he'd only be in Lakeview for a year and we had a perfectly good, warm house in Klamath Falls. I made a conscious resolve to get out of that house and out of Lakeview as soon as possible and set our lives in a better direction. So far Oregon had not been my promised land.

Spring finally arrived, and with it morning sickness and signs of a possible miscarriage. When the doctor ordered bed rest for at least three weeks, I panicked, for there was no one to care for Dian and John. Then a young woman I'd met who had two preschool daughters made a remarkably selfless gesture by offering to keep Dian and John each day.

Delpha Plato had lived all her life around Lakeview and worked side by side with friends and family in farming and ranching. She was a talented horsewoman, a former rodeo queen, and a most attractive young woman. Delpha had a take-charge personality coupled with a colorful vocabulary. "Have those two little suckers ready for me to pick up by eight o'clock," she'd say, "because I'm too damn busy to wait around." When she came it was, "I'll get these two little bastards back by four o'clock, and you'd better stay off that fat ass of yours all day so I don't have to take care of you, too."

I worried about the language my children would hear, but I knew they would be well cared for. Delpha and I molded a strong friendship during these brief visits. Delpha sensed my unhappiness in Lakeview. She told me Lakeview was a man's town—if you ranched, hunted, drank, and swore, you'd enjoy it. Since she did all those things herself, she loved Lakeview completely and uncritically. Knowing Delpha helped me understand the town and the people better, and a time would come when she and I would share more pleasant tasks and responsibilities.

Finally, in September, Bill was transferred to Gresham, a suburb east of Portland. We settled in an unincorporated area of east Multnomah County. At last we were near the beautiful, clean, green city I'd visited with Bill after our wedding. Our stay here would be only a brief interlude, a teaser, but it would have a lifetime influence on me.

Our neighbors were an older couple whom Bill had known in Klamath Falls before the war. Helen and Milas Winningham immediately accepted us as family, and when daughter Jo was born in November of 1949, it was a major event for them as well as for us. Helen and Milas were practicing Christians in the best sense; they helped people in every way they could. As Helen and I visited over coffee and shared family activities, I knew she was teaching me, subtly and patiently, to enjoy my children, to appreciate every day and love every task. Helen was my role model and mentor long before those terms became commonplace.

The coming of Delpha and Helen into my life, so close in time but so different from each other in age, experiences, and attitude, had a profound effect on me. Lakeview hadn't changed me, but Delpha's selfless act of helpfulness had. And Helen had added to that growing awareness of who I wanted to be.

When the news came that Bill had been designated coordinator for all the bank branches in Eastern Oregon—from Hood River to Ontario and south to Bend, Lakeview, and Klamath Falls, a job that would require us to live in LaGrande and him to travel from Monday through Friday—I was torn between my desire to live in the Portland area and the new adventure that was a significant promotion for Bill. We'd go, of course, and make the most of it. But we'd return to Portland; I was sure of it.

Chapter 4

Daring Decisions

Fall days in LaGrande, eastern Oregon, are gorgeous, with warm sunshine and a touch of crispness. One particular day in 1955 was exceptionally glorious. With my five-year-old daughter at afternoon kindergarten, her three-year-old brother napping at the home of a friend, and the two older children, a second-grader and a sixth-grader, at school, I walked across the campus of Eastern Oregon College to the main administration building.

A smell of sawdust and cedar oil, a combination I remembered from my schools in Texas, met me at the front door. Confident in a stylish dress, nylons, high heels, purse, earrings, and short white gloves, I found my way to the second-floor sociology classroom.

Hesitating briefly inside, I took a quick survey. This was just like the rooms at Texas Wesleyan—blackboard, teacher's desk, and rows of chairs with an attached desktop that required a little turn and a wiggle to get into. Students were gathering, but there was still a choice of seats. After taking one far enough back to view the room, I took a pencil from my purse and opened my notebook as the slightly built, cheerful-looking professor came in. "Good afternoon, students. Welcome to Eastern Oregon College and Sociology 101," he said.

As he gave information on our textbook and other preliminaries about the class, I wrote it all in my notebook. Writing was awkward with my gloves on, but I staunchly continued. Other students, younger than I and dressed more casually, looked at me quizzically. I made a mental note that I'd dress more like the other students the next time I came to class, but for now I could at least remove my gloves. As I did, the glances drifted away.

Taking the gloves off that first day in a college classroom after fourteen years perfectly symbolized the audacious decision I'd made. It was a casting off of the traditional and conventional, baring my knuckles for hard fights that were sure to come. Given my personal circumstances—four children, two not in school yet—and society's attitudes in the 1950s, the decision to go to college was a big step away from my genteel, white-gloved life. It was seen as frivolous by some of my women friends. It was, as I would learn, unacceptable to my husband. But it made perfect sense to me.

⚜ ⚜

When we first moved into our two-story rental house in a tree-lined neighborhood in LaGrande, I didn't know that in a few years this would be considered the *perfect* house in a *perfect* small town for our *perfect* family in the *perfect* 1950s. At least, that's the way social and political commentators would view the 1950s, not because we were perfect, but because that was the way we thought of ourselves. There was status attached to the notion that women stayed home and raised children while the husbands worked on building careers that would provide handsomely for their growing families. I settled into being the perfect wife and mother, both as a challenge to myself and to make sure the children had a good home. My domestic talents improved with a self-imposed routine. Each day had its special task—wash, iron, bake, mend, clean, shop, then go to church on Sunday. Each season had its own schedule—spring cleaning, summer canning, fall holiday cooking and celebrations, winter household organizing, painting, and preparing for spring cleaning.

The weekly and seasonal schedules gave an aura of importance to housework. It was something like running a business. Because Bill was traveling, I assumed responsibility for the children and the house, including our coal-fired furnace, that friendly monster in the basement that had to be fed and cleaned out every day, and in return kept our big house cozy and warm.

I made women friends through the Newcomers' Club, bridge groups, church groups, and a women's day at the nine-hole golf course. These women were fine company, always sharing recipes and tips on child-raising and home decorating, giving me a sense of community. There were Cub Scout duties and PTA activities, and I served a couple of terms as president of the elementary school PTA and co-coordinator of a high-school activity night. These reminded me that once upon a time I'd started out to be a teacher.

By the time Randy was two years old, we'd decided four children were enough, and Bill had a vasectomy. I had recurring thoughts of how I would support the children if something happened to their father. Not an idle worry, as he was traveling on mountainous two-lane highways every working day of the year. I'd had a taste of a good life in Kansas as a small child; now my own family was starting the same way, but I knew well how fast that could change.

With growing children there were growing expenses. Bill's transfer to LaGrande had been a nice promotion, but pay raises were few and small. Yet the image of a banker's family was supposed to be one of prosperity. I wondered how much more I could cut from our food budget for school supplies, music lessons, and adequate clothing for everyone. Each summer I canned every kind of food I could buy cheaply, pick myself, or gather from surpluses of friends

The banker's wife ready for church, a tea, or a PTA meeting. La Grande, 1954

and neighbors. One friend shared her raspberries with me, another her apricots. I went to Milton-Freewater to pick tomatoes. A farmer let me pick peas for a small charge, and he always added squash, corn, and cucumbers to the bounty I took home. He frequently went into the field with me just to talk. Once he said, "I sure never thought I'd see a banker's wife picking peas."

"Well," I responded, "You've never seen this banker's wife before."

Bill brought apples, pears, and cherries from Hood River and peaches from Ontario, which I canned while they were still fresh from the orchards. Batches of sweet chunk pickles and bread-and-butter pickles gave the kitchen a spicy aroma. I let the jars of jams and fruit sit on the kitchen counter for a few days to admire my handiwork and enjoy the mingling of the beautiful colors, like strings of crystal beads, before storing them in a dark, cool corner of the basement. It was equally satisfying to see the containers of frozen vegetables in our newly acquired secondhand chest freezer.

My canning and freezing often kept me in the kitchen past midnight. I was proud of myself for that contribution to the family and for the money it saved in groceries, but concerns about providing for my family grew. How could I do more?

As they look back on those times, many women have expressed feelings of confinement and stultification. Some have even described the feeling of being trapped or caged because they had no role other than wife and mother, and they saw no possibility of expansion of themselves, nothing to allow even minor diversions, and certainly no exit without dire consequences. I didn't feel so desperate. That was probably at least in part because I made the day-to-day household decisions, and Bill's absence on weekdays and evenings gave me more freedom to pursue activities of my own. Even so, I was alone four nights a week after the children went to bed, and I couldn't play bridge every night. I turned to homemaking projects to help me feel productive. Without having done any sewing before, I made slipcovers for the old blue sofa and chair Mother had left us. Then I started mending nylon stockings—that had been a big thing during the war, when women couldn't buy new hosiery. After that I made earrings from small artificial flowers, pine cones, and colorful materials.

Maybe I wasn't feeling the acute uselessness that other women later reported, but all that experimenting meant that I must have been searching for ways to use my energies and fill up time.

Sometimes my friend Helen Winningham came to mind. Helen, a tiny woman with wisps of graying hair around a face that rarely showed signs of makeup, had a kindness and compassion about her that was so overwhelming I sometimes felt I was in the presence of a saint. Once she said, "If I'd been a man, I'd have been a minister."

"Well, you still can," I'd replied, not really believing it myself. She sighed and said, "My dear, it's all right. I have a good husband, wonderful daughters, sons-in-laws, and grandchildren. I can't ask for anything more." In Helen, such resignation was admirable, but I knew I would never be able to accept limits on my life so unquestioningly.

Delpha Plato, my tough-talking friend in Lakeview, was also often in my thoughts. She'd managed to make a life for herself by adopting men's ways—riding, cussing, hunting, and doing the equivalent of ranch-hand work. She was comfortable with such a role, but it wasn't one that suited me.

With the aid of history and reflection, I now wonder how I would have answered the questionnaire that Betty Friedan sent to her Smith College classmates in the mid-1950s, which revealed that many of them "were restive and unfulfilled in their traditional roles." As Friedan interviewed more women, she began to call this phenomenon "the problem that has no name," and in 1963 she published her findings in *The Feminine Mystique*. While my life-changing decision preceded the book, it probably was motivated, in large part, by the conditions Freidan described.

❧ ❧

I told myself that returning to college would be a smart move for the sake of the family. I could become a teacher, as I'd wanted to do earlier in my life. I could bring in a salary to help provide for the increasing costs of the children and the household. I turned my mind to the practical realities. A state college was just minutes from our house, and daughter Jo would be going to kindergarten on campus in September. From managing a large family and working with community groups, I knew how to organize my time. From my efforts to provide food for the family, I'd developed imagination, and I'd found I had an amazing amount of energy.

On the Monday before classes started at Eastern Oregon State College, I went to register. The registrar thought it was "cute" that I wanted to take classes while Jo was on campus in kindergarten. When I told him my major in

Texas had been in physical education, he said, "That's out. We don't want any heart attacks in the gym." I was thirty-two.

I'd not shared my plans with Bill. I didn't see any reason to tell him until after I'd enrolled. Friday evening, when he returned from his week's travel, would be soon enough. Schoolbooks would have to be explained, and I would need to study.

I knew he wouldn't like my decision. This was not the image of the banker's wife he carried around in his mind. I was sure he would regard my going back to school as a negative reflection on him as a provider and as a career banker. But I knew it was more than that. It was a threat to his unconscious desire to exercise control over his wife, not unusual in the male psyche in the 1950s, and condoned and promoted by much of the culture of the time. I would simply tell Bill about my decision to go to college in a matter-of-fact way. "Oh, by the way, I registered for classes at Eastern Oregon College this week." It would be as good a method as any, and maybe the best.

Bill arrived home as usual around six o'clock on Friday evening. After the children were in bed, I told him what I'd done. He didn't say a word. Not then, not on Saturday and not on Sunday, no words about my decision or about anything else, for that matter. He talked to the children but not to me. After the children were in bed Sunday evening, he looked up from the newspaper he was reading and casually said, "I see here that a WAC (Women's Army Corps) recruiter will be in town this week. I hope you won't do anything foolish."

᙮ ᙮

I liked my courses and my professors. Although I made an A on my mid-term exam in sociology, I got a D in U.S. history. As Dr. Johnson handed me my paper he said, "Would you like to talk about this?" In his office after class he said, "I know it's hard to get back into a school routine and studying, but I think you can do it." So few words, but they were the only encouraging ones I'd yet heard, and they lifted me onto a new plane of determination. After discussing the test, we talked about a term paper required for his class. He thought I should write on pioneer women of the Northwest. Another surprise, but I recalled his comment in class that in the cemeteries along the trails to the West, graves of women and children far outnumber those of men. That was evidence, he told the class, that women were more important in settling the West than history recognized. I received an A on both the paper and my final exam.

Toward the end of the school year Bill informed me he'd be transferred back to the Portland area. That was where I had always wanted to live, and yet we'd had six good years in LaGrande, and I felt a part of the community. My feelings about wanting to go to Portland and wanting to stay in LaGrande to go to school were colliding.

In telling Dr. Johnson about the move, I said, "I guess this means I won't continue school because I can't afford any of the private schools in Portland." Regret must have sounded in my voice.

Dr. Johnson handed me a final surprise. "You must keep going to college," he commanded. "There is a brand-new state college in Portland. I don't know its name, but you must go and find it."

We moved in August of 1956, driving west across Oregon with our three younger children, plus a dog and a cat, headed for The Dalles, where we would pick up Dian after her swim meet. The car was a furnace. The hot wind blowing through the open windows gave little relief. The children sat in the backseat with the dog, Poochie, who normally acted like he'd escaped from a circus because of his love for climbing trees and ladders. Now he lay on the floor panting in misery, with no sign of the circus about him at all. The cat, McDuff, got carsick from the curves over the Blue Mountains. We almost lost him on Cabbage Hill, east of Pendleton, when we stopped to let him throw up, and he ran away and Bill had to chase him down. After that, he was either in a coma or resigned to his fate and was passed around, limp as a rag doll, from lap to lap. Thank goodness the children had been willing to leave Doc, our big white rabbit, with a neighbor in LaGrande. We didn't think he would adjust to life in Portland. The rest of us would do just fine with the move. Bill would be manager of the bank in Gresham, the same bank where he'd worked before in the small town a few miles east of Portland, and the children, still young enough to adjust to change well, would be in new schools.

There was a moment of distraction from the searing heat when we stopped at Celilo Falls to watch Indians fishing from their platforms in the Columbia River. It was the last time we would see them fishing in that ancient way. The platforms and the wild river surging through the rocks would be inundated the following year, when The Dalles Dam, then under construction, began backing up water.

We retrieved Dian from her swim meet, and Randy moved to my lap in the front seat. As we drove farther west through the Columbia River Gorge, the children began to count waterfalls. Portland was just down the road.

❧ ❧

As we were settling into the new Portland house and getting the three older children into their new schools, I went in search of the new Portland State

College, which was housed in the former Lincoln High School in downtown Portland. The staff, eager to help, scheduled all my classes on Mondays, Wednesdays, and Fridays; that way Randy would need child care only three days a week. Because my education continued to stretch us financially, I inquired about student jobs and landed one in the library working fifteen hours a week for a dollar an hour. I would have to work two evenings a week.

The prospect of spending evenings away from home added to my already strong guilt feelings. Guilt was my punishment for not being at home. In the 1950s, a woman who worked when she had a working husband, or as in my case went to school and worked as well, had to suffer some consequences to prove it was wrong.

The worst of it was the worry about harming Randy. I'd found care for him with an older woman who looked after two or three other children in her home. She seemed like a good substitute mother, but I watched my son closely for signs of suffering. One day as I was driving him home, he showed me a picture he had made, an ugly glob of black and brown finger paint. A very depressing sight. I was concerned, even apprehensive. Certainly it was evidence he was in immediate need of psychological counseling, which I had learned about in a child psychology class.

With hesitation I asked, "Uh, what is it?"

In his Moms-are-sure-stupid voice, he answered, "It's a big mud puddle."

Well, sure. Of course it is! What else? I worried less about Randy after that.

֍ ֍

This time, when I walked into my first classroom at Portland State, I was not a timid, out-of-place older student, but seasoned and confident. My courses were loaded with social science subjects—western civilization, geography, psychology, political science, and one required general science course.

In the fall of 1957, as a full-fledged senior, I was again thrust into an unforgettable classroom situation that tested my hard-won confidence. It was the first meeting of the Portland State College Forensics Team for the fall term. A speech professor the year before had suggested that the forensics team would be an easy way to add needed credits. On entering the classroom only thirty minutes earlier, I had been greeted warmly by the professor and students. Now I stood at the podium looking out at a group of strange faces. I knew that professor had lied—there was no way this was going to be easy.

Professor Ben Padrow, better known by this group as "Coach," had started the class by pacing at the front of the room as he spoke with clipped efficiency.

"Let's get started. No time to waste. So little time, so much to do. I have here, in this box, news clippings containing two or three sentences each. I will now instruct you on how we will proceed." Ben Padrow, whose small physical stature was packed with energy, spoke rapidly in staccato style and poured his deep voice into drawn-out words he wanted students to remember. He had a reputation for being fervent, impassioned, even evangelistic, but, as I was to learn, he was compassionate and respectful, too.

I thought, *Okay so far.*

"Our exercise today is called M-PROM-TOO speaking. M-PROM-TOO speaking is very easy. We do it all the time with friends and family. It is talking about a subject for a brief period of time, two or three minutes, without interruption, in the course of which IT IS HOPED," a long pause, "the speaker says something worthwhile."

I began to feel a little uncomfortable.

"Now, I will ask each of you to come to the box, pick one of the clippings, and walk to the front of the room as you read the sentences. When you arrive at the podium you will speak IN-TELL-I-GENT-LY for three minutes on the subject you have just read. Very simple."

The more experienced students were called on first. They seemed stimulated by the exercise. I, meanwhile, was swamped with apprehension. My only thought, more of a prayer, was to draw a topic I knew something about.

My turn came. I picked a clipping. It was about the Middle East. At the podium I read the clipping aloud as other students had. Then I blurted, "I don't know anything about the Middle East. I can't possibly say anything."

Professor Padrow leaned back in his chair, put his feet on the table, took a drag on his cigarette (professors, and students, too, smoked in the classroom in those days) and said, "Now, I know you will think of something. We'll wait."

With that the students relaxed as one or two started writing, including the professor. Others picked up papers or books to read as though they were in for a long wait. A few fiddled casually with their cigarettes. I guessed they'd seen this before. I stood there. No one spoke. I wondered if they could hear my heart pounding. Obviously, I was not going to sit down until I said something. "Think, think," I scolded myself. "What do I know about the Middle East?" I forced my brain back to my class on western civilization. We'd talked about the Middle East, hadn't we? What did I learn?

I began to talk. The students listened attentively. The teacher called time at three minutes. I haven't the faintest idea what I said, but I'd done it! I'd learned to dog-paddle, if not swim, in that pool of speech sharks. I'd be one of them before the school year was out.

Another Portland State professor influenced the direction my teaching would take in his own very different way. With his stout build and shaved head, Marko Haggard looked like a professional wrestler. He taught politics and government, not from the textbook but from everyday political life. He began each class with an anecdote or "editorial" on a current event, much as he did years later as a political commentator for a local television station. He admired a few politicians and was open in his disdain for the rest. He encouraged his students to get involved in political campaigns and to observe government in action, especially the goings-on at the state Legislature.

From Haggard I began to feel a strong attraction to politics. I learned that inquiring minds are a required attribute for citizens in a free society. His regular critiques and analysis of politics and government—and to him there was little that was not political—sometimes seemed extreme to me. But from his influence I came to see that up until now I had lived with little information about the world around me.

Learning was electrifying. Sparks of ideas, information, theories, and insights charged around in my brain. It felt to me like a key clicking into a lock. I'd unlocked the door that was right for me, and I had to open that door and walk through. I'd just as soon do nothing the rest of my life but go to school. It was as close as I've ever been to a spiritual experience.

I soaked up every drop of learning from my classes, collecting materials I could use when I became a teacher. It was exhilarating to know I would soon be able to help others in their learning. And from Haggard I found the courage to question not only my own beliefs but the actions of our government, and I came to look upon that as a duty. I began to know I wanted to teach political science and government.

My assigned readings were critiques of modern society, books like *The Organization Man, The Hidden Persuaders, Madison Avenue USA* and *The Lonely Crowd*. I understood what these writers were talking about, because I was living it. I had my own "organization man" at home, and mine was the very suburban family the advertisers studied for marketing purposes. This placed me in a different position from most of my classmates, who saw the writings as a merely theoretical exercise. The sociological and political analysis of the decade since the war gave my own life new meaning. I began to see that we were all conforming to a social ethic held in place by families, communities, and businesses, where no one dared to be different. I began to feel I'd had a narrow escape.

I dragged my books everywhere, like an extra appendage. They were with me at the girls' piano lessons, at John's violin lessons, at Little League games, at school programs, and at PTA meetings. I had books with me when I sat inside Timberline Lodge at Mount Hood and the children skied and played in the snow outside. I propped my books in the kitchen window so I could read while I washed the dishes. I taped notes on my bathroom mirror to review as I dressed. I kept my notes beside me in the car to read at stoplights. When I couldn't read, I tested myself mentally on how much I could remember. The mental game became more intense as exams neared.

Fall-term finals came just before Christmas, but I wanted to make the holidays as festive as ever. I baked fruitcakes and cookies, made candies, did the shopping, and decorated the house. During Christmas dinner, the relief I felt at this, the last ritual of the season, was interrupted by a sudden pain between my ribs. With the next bite there was more pain. I couldn't eat the meal I had worked so hard to prepare. I comforted myself, "With Christmas over and a week to rest before winter term starts, I'll just take it easy and be fine."

The doctor diagnosed an ulcer. It was my first physical ailment other than those related to pregnancy, and I felt a curious mix of impatience and pride. I hated being sick, and yet … that ulcer was a tribute to my intensity and determination. Ulcers were what successful men got from their hard work, and mine was the result of pursuing an education and maintaining a household at the same time. I saw it as confirmation that I was succeeding at both. The truth was that my body was paying a heavy toll.

Ulcers, the doctor explained, usually occur in people who are worried about their jobs, their marriage, or their financial situation. He asked me if I had concerns in these areas. I replied, "Would you believe all three?"

I passed the winter term on a diet of milk, soft-boiled eggs, milk toast, puddings, ice cream, and ulcer medication. The spring term of 1958 was a rewarding culmination of my educational efforts. For my student teaching requirement I taught a required social studies course called Modern Problems at a high school and came away with a tremendous amount of self-confidence. I was ready for my own classroom and my own students.

As for the worries that had caused the ulcer, I thought the work and financial worries surely would soon be solved. With my degree in hand in June, I would soon be teaching, and my monthly paycheck would be a bonanza. The marital worries were something else. I was sure that those were the basis for the pain in my gut. The closer I got to finishing my degree, the less tolerant Bill became about my schoolwork. I told myself, *Hang on, only six more months to go.*

In my last term I managed to win first place in a statewide contest in extemporaneous speaking. The title of my speech was "Modern Woman—Saint or Sinner?" I talked about how women have always labored in one way or another, and I pointed out that only women of the elite class had ever enjoyed the privilege of not working. I asked rhetorically, "How should society view working women in the 1950s?" I didn't really answer my own question, instead suggesting that society had changed dramatically since the war, and that attitudes toward women would undoubtedly change, too. Exactly how, only time would tell.

The judges liked it. The speech, of course, was a monologue about my own quandary.

After graduation I was hired at Reynolds High, a new school in rapidly growing east Multnomah County, teaching senior social studies and history. I was also appointed Dean of Girls, a job the superintendent created on the spot, and I'd be advisor to the International Relations Club as well as senior class advisor. And could I, by any chance, also be advisor to the Ski Club, the superintendent asked? Okay, but only if I could take my children along on the trips to Mt. Hood.

So much for time to teach students about the burning issues of the day! But, most important, I had a job that paid four thousand dollars a year. Ecstasy.

The only shadow in my life was the serious and growing alienation in my marriage. Bill had paid little attention to my job search, but when I told him I was successful, he said, "I accepted your going to school, but I don't want you to work. If you start working, the next thing you'll want is a divorce." That word *divorce* had never been spoken in our home before.

Betty's family celebrating with her at her graduation from Portland State College, 1958

I tried to explain. "But my reason for going to school was to go to work and help with family finances." The fact that I had loved school was an unexpected bonus. Nothing would be different when I began teaching, except that I would bring home a paycheck.

Was the paycheck the real problem, perhaps?

Bill began to tell friends and family that my "school thing" had been so I could get a divorce. I told him he should not say that. "It's just a joke," he said. But if it was a joke, why wasn't I laughing? And why wasn't he laughing?

I was getting sick of his jokes, I told him.

I asked Bill if it was he who wanted a divorce. "No, but I don't want you to work," was his repetitious refrain.

Giving up my work was not an option. With all the lesson plans that were in my head, aching to be shared with students, I had to teach. My college work and student teaching had been too exciting, too challenging and rewarding—I couldn't let them go.

Finally, Bill's "joke" became a self-fulfilling prophecy. I told him, "I intend to teach, and we cannot continue as we are."

Chapter 5

Can't Is Not an Option

I pulled the station wagon up outside Savage Memorial Presbyterian Church and made my way to Pastor Arthur Schwabe's office. He asked me to sit down, brought me a cup of coffee, and then regarded me gravely across his desk. Ordinarily Arthur had a smile on his face, and I expected we might have some conversation about my college work and teaching before moving into the topic for the evening. Today there was no smile, and there was no friendly warm-up to the more serious matter I had come to talk about.

I'd finally decided that there was no way around a divorce. Bill would not change his attitude, and I was not about to abort my new career path. I'd begun the process by finding one of the few women lawyers in town, Shirley Field. Hers was a familiar name, for she was a Republican state representative. She arranged to have the appropriate papers served on Bill, but he was refusing to move out of the house.

The wait for a trial date became interminable, and it was a stressful time. As the months went by, Bill grew more moody, even with the children. He was getting counseling from our pastor, Arthur Schwabe, and he asked me to go. I finally agreed, thinking I might be able to relate to the minister how Bill's depression was deepening and how his sullenness and lack of communication were affecting the family. In short, I was hoping this usually kind and religious man could help.

Pastor Schwabe launched right in. "Betty, you should delay the divorce," he stated bluntly and authoritatively.

Taken aback, I replied, "The trial will not be for a while, but I doubt it's possible for the marriage to continue."

His demeanor became threatening. Arthur was clean-shaven, with a smooth, rosy complexion. He looked more youthful than his years, with features that gave him a permanently pleasant appearance. Not that evening. He gave me a piercing stare, and his mouth drooped disdainfully. "You may think you're pretty smart with a college education," he said, "but as far as theology is concerned you're still in kindergarten. If you were my wife, you would not have gone to college and you would not be teaching."

I didn't understand what theology had to do with the situation, but I certainly did understand the direction his so-called counseling was going.

43

There was no point in attempting any communication with Arthur if that was his message. I stood up and left with no explanation or apology. I was shocked, disappointed, and perplexed at Arthur's attitude and words.

I was not taking the divorce lightly. I had made a bargain in marrying Bill. Ours was not a romantic marriage, but it was a sensible one. I had benefited greatly—I had been blessed with four healthy children and the opportunity to live in Oregon. We had shared companionship and mutual interest in raising our children. But that companionship had gradually disappeared as the children grew older. Once the divorce proceedings had begun I never doubted that it was the right thing to do.

❧ ❧

While waiting for the trial date, I turned to my next project. I wanted to start work on a master's degree in political science. Portland State College was too new to have any graduate degree programs yet. I would need to apply to the University of Oregon, but acceptance was far from automatic.

I approached Marko Haggard, my political science professor, who had taught at the U of O before coming to Portland State. He made a phone call, and when I met with the chairman of the department I was approved for admission.

The next step was to meet with an advisor. This part did not go so smoothly. As I sat down with Professor Lester Seligman, he asked, "Why do you want a master's degree?" I explained that I thought a master's in political science was a natural extension of my bachelor's degree. "Well, why did you want a bachelor's degree?"

This was not a question I had anticipated. I assumed a college professor knew the value of an education and wouldn't question a student's motivation in going to college. It frankly irritated me, and so maybe my answer was too flippant: "I was bored being only a housewife who did PTA work and played bridge."

Impatiently, and with a distinct edge in his voice, he said, "What's wrong with bridge? Why don't you like to play bridge?"

I shrugged my shoulders, thinking, *What kind of a question is that for an advisor to ask a prospective student? This man sounds like my husband.*

Seligman informed me that he would accept me as a student, but only for a reading and conference course. He assigned a book to read and review and a date to have the paper returned. After that he would assign another book for a review. I received an "A" on each of the first two papers. The conference part of the course never happened. I prepared my third review ahead of the deadline, but before the due date I received my final grade early—a B. I called to ask why. "I'm leaving for Israel," he told me, "and I assumed your last paper would be a B, so that is your term grade." What? This guy's a college professor and he can't average out grades?

After that I had a series of four or five so-called advisors, none of whom seemed to care whether I completed the degree work or not. I knew what credits I had to have, so I proceeded on my own to plan out a schedule whereby I could take a few transferable graduate courses at Portland State in the evenings, take two more reading and conference classes at University of Oregon, and take the remainder of the required courses in two summer sessions at the University. Plus, of course, the mandatory thesis.

❧ ❧

In December 1959 the court heard our divorce proceedings. My attorney, Shirley Field, and I had gotten along well. I'd hired her because I'd thought it important to have a woman lawyer because of Bill's suspicions of any man I came in contact with. I didn't know it then, but Shirley and I would later become political associates—not always on the same side of things. That day I learned she was a bulldog when it came to representing her client.

After the divorce was granted I was overwhelmed with pure, bald joy, tempered with confusion. Everyone knows divorces are awful. And I knew it would be hard on the kids. And yet—why was I so happy? Why did I feel such liberation and exhilaration? The burden of tending to the everyday needs of a person who placed unrealistic and ridiculous limitations on my life was lifted. I was free, free to learn and to teach without criticism and without constantly trying to justify my actions.

By the spring of 1960, I began to move easily into political activities. Marko Haggard's discourses in my classes at Portland State College had personalized the major figures in state politics, both Democratic and Republican. I found I was more interested in the Democrats: U.S. Senator Wayne Morse, Governor Bob Holmes, Congresswoman Edith Green, and U.S. Senator Richard Neuberger and his wife, Maurine, who both had served in the Oregon Legislature. The Democrats had captured a majority of seats in the Oregon Legislature in the fall of 1956. That had been a startling political event, because Republicans had controlled the House and Senate since the 1880s except for a brief period in the 1930s.

I first got involved at the local level, where I was able to watch candidates and elected officials in action. In no time at all I was appointed Democratic precinct committeewoman, because no one was serving in my precinct.

Naturally enough, my first political campaign centered around education. I'd begun attending meetings of the Lynch Elementary School District Board, as part of a group of parents who were concerned because one board member was accusing schools of failing to teach patriotism. There would be two open seats on the board in the May 1960 election, one each for a five-year term and a one-year term. Our parents' group knew we had to elect people who would not be intimidated by this disruptive—some thought dangerous—board member. Two men announced their candidacies for the one-year term. So did I.

"But, Betty, you're just divorced," someone said. "It will hurt your chances of election."

"Voters don't know that," I countered. "And what difference does it make, anyway? I'm qualified." It didn't make sense to me, but divorced women were not held in very high regard in those times. People tended to suspect a divorce was due to some fault of the wife, maybe even infidelity. So if the issue of divorce were raised in the campaign, the next thought in the voters' minds could be that I was not fit to be on the school board.

I tossed that possibility out of my mind, just as I'd rid myself of other strange notions about women. Not only was I a parent of children in the district, but I was a teacher in another district. I'd had courses in school finance and school administration and organization. I knew more about education and school board responsibilities than both of the male candidates together. And I knew I had the guts to stand up to the antics of the rogue board member.

On my manual typewriter I typed up a one-page fact sheet about my qualifications and had a few hundred copies made at a printing shop. Teachers from both Lynch and Reynolds school districts helped me distribute the fact sheet to friends and neighbors. The two men didn't appear to campaign at all. I won.

That same spring of 1960, the Reynolds District School Board renewed my contract, but assigned me to be a full-time dean of girls. I protested, not wanting to give up teaching. The superintendent said, "You have no choice; it's an accomplished fact."

I could not allow my teaching career to be pulled out from under me just like that, just as I was finally getting started after years of struggling. I went looking for other options. Two days later I interviewed with the superintendent of the Gresham School District and was hired on the spot to teach a full schedule of senior social studies, my true love, for the following year. I'd be at the new Centennial High School, where Dian's class had been transferred after its freshman year at Gresham. By the time I reported to Centennial for the teachers' workshop in late August, I had begun serving as a member of the

Lynch Elementary School District Board, and I was still working toward my master's degree.

⋟ ⋞

Soon after my election to the school board, a speech professor with whom I'd taken two courses at Portland State invited me to attend a performance of *The Fantasticks*. Then he invited me to go out on his sailboat, and later to a cocktail party at his home—which was a houseboat, as it turned out. Then he invited me to Salem for a political event.

Frank Roberts had just been elected chairman of the Multnomah County Democratic Party Central Committee after a bitter battle between the liberals, who supported him, and the conservatives who had run the party for years. I had participated in the Central Committee meeting and had voted for Frank, so I guess that made me a liberal.

By October we were seeing each other often, and my children were getting used to having him come to see us. I worried about whether having a man around was proper—not that I was a prude, but in 1960 it was unthinkable to live openly with a man you weren't married to. Frank never stayed overnight at our house nor I at his houseboat. Had I done that, I was sure Bill would have initiated custody proceedings on the basis that I was not a fit mother. I might have been recalled from the school board and fired as a teacher, too.

Frank was a nice-looking man, clean shaven with a good physique. He had a high forehead and wore horn-rimmed glasses. He had been divorced for more than six years and had two daughters the ages of my two oldest children, sixteen and thirteen, but he rarely saw them. It seems his divorce from their mother had caused an alienation from his daughters as well. With my optimistic attitude about raising children I was sure that could be overcome. Sadly, it never happened.

The best thing about Frank was his happy and outgoing approach to life. That was a tremendous and welcome change from Bill's dour moods. Frank's interests in politics gave a sparkling new dimension to my life. In late November, we decided to marry.

Why would I agree to do that after less than a year of reveling in my new freedom and independence? At the time, it seemed like another instance of the practical thing to do. Frank didn't want to spend another cold winter on his houseboat. He couldn't live with me unless we were married. I thought the children would benefit from association with an interesting, intelligent man. I certainly would welcome an adult in the household who brought with him energetic, informed conversations. Frank would never dream of limiting what

I wanted to do academically or politically. I knew I would have all the freedom I wanted, and with his blessing.

On the Friday after Thanksgiving we went to the courthouse late in the afternoon, found a judge, and were married. We hadn't taken time to think about a ring, but we did pick up the children and met Ben Padrow, my speech professor at Portland State, and his wife, Dee, at a Japanese restaurant downtown for some semblance of a wedding celebration.

And that was that. It was back to our teaching and our political activities.

⅌ ⅌

That same month, John Fitzgerald Kennedy was elected President of the United States. He was the youngest president in the nation's history, and his charisma was electrifying. His proposal for a Peace Corps demonstrated his belief in individual commitment for the common good, as well as a new approach to international relations. His election promised a new era of tolerance, and he issued a challenge to all of us to help make our country a better place to live. President Kennedy gave many of us a greater sense of purpose in our lives and a resolve to work for the causes we thought important.

Another political highlight of that year was Maurine Neuberger's election to the United States Senate after the death of her husband, Richard Neuberger. That gave Oregon a woman in the Senate as well as in the U.S. House of Representatives, where Edith Green had served since 1955. Both women inspired me. It was a heady time to be active in Democratic politics in Oregon.

Having Frank to discuss politics with at home was wonderful. In January he went to the State Legislature to serve as the bill-reading clerk in the Oregon House of Representatives, where a Democrat, Bob Duncan, served as Speaker. The reports he gave about the Legislature enlivened our discussions considerably.

In the summer of 1961 I completed the coursework for my master's degree. I'd already finished my thesis, and I began to think about running for the Legislature from east Multnomah County. My association with Democratic Party elected officials gave me confidence. "If they can do it," I told myself, "I can do it."

Frank had similar ideas for himself. He first looked at east Multnomah County, but I gently steered him in another direction. My base of support as a school board member and teacher was primarily in east Multnomah County, so a run for an Oregon House seat from that area was optimal for me. Frank was better known county-wide because of his teaching position at Portland

State and his work in the party. Because senators at that time were elected on a county-wide basis, the Senate was a better choice for him. By early 1962, we were running two separate Roberts campaigns, his for the Senate and mine for the House.

In March, the day after my formal filing as a candidate, I received a notice of "non-reelection" to my teaching position. I'd had two successful years at Centennial, and the notice was an unexpected, serious development. I arranged immediately to meet with Harry Thompson, the district superintendent. "The school board voted not to renew your contract until after the primary election," he told me. "If you are nominated in May, you will be given a leave of absence for the following school year. If you don't win the primary, your contract will be renewed." The east Multnomah district was heavily Democratic, making the outcome of the general election predictable from the May primary. The superintendent was able to make his decision based on that knowledge.

"But Mr. Thompson, the Legislature only meets from January until May every other year," I pleaded. "If I win, I only need a leave of absence for the half of the school year that the Legislature is in session. I want to teach the first half of the school year, and I need the income to support myself and my children."

His impatience was obvious. "The school board made the decision, and it's final. We do not want a teacher to teach only a half of the year and then go off to the Legislature." This was another "accomplished fact," like the one that had brought me to Centennial High School in the first place.

What a dilemma! If I lost the primary, I had a job. If I won, I would be without a teaching position every other year for as long as I served in the Legislature. It didn't take a mental giant to see that a new teacher would be hired in my place, and then there would be no position for me the following year. Again I went looking for other options.

The David Douglas School District had a statewide reputation for its progressive administration, and its board was made up of solid, straightforward businessmen who dealt boldly and firmly with the current rash of radical conservative groups. Those groups, primarily the John Birch Society and the Save Our Schools organization, had charged the board and the administrators with promoting Communism and brainwashing students, the same charges regularly being made by the school board member I was serving with on the Lynch School Board. I knew that David Douglas's administrators had faced them down, and I admired them for it.

I knew and respected Floyd Light, the superintendent, and Howard Horner, the principal of the high school, through the Multnomah County School

Boards Association. They could at least give me good advice. I first went to see
Howard Horner. When I told him about my situation, he said he thought the
board's decision was a short-sighted one. I became bold enough to say, "Well,
I guess I'm looking for a job, but I am still going to run for the Legislature."

The principal's reply still sings in my ears, "We'll take you—win, lose, or
draw." Floyd Light called later to tell me my formal application had been
accepted. "Come in any time and sign your contract," he said. "In the
meantime, don't worry. You'll be working for us in September, regardless of
the outcome of the election."

With a job assured for the fall, I turned to campaigning. Frank and I
each conducted reasonably good campaigns, but our time and volunteers
were thinly stretched. In the May primary, we both lost. I came in fifth in
a race that chose three Democratic candidates to run for three seats against
three Republican nominees in the general election. Frank was beaten by Ted
Hallock, a newcomer in elected politics but a man professionally experienced
in public relations and advertising.

The lesson I learned in that campaign was how tough it is to lose. I wasn't
prepared for the feeling of humiliation that comes with such a public defeat.
It seemed to me that everyone in the world knew and maybe they'd feel sorry
for me, which I definitely did not want. I didn't spend much time analyzing
the loss other than realizing I hadn't put the necessary effort into getting name
familiarity. I hated that the press portrayed Frank and me as a husband-and-
wife team. I had been elected to the school board on my own, but with the
name Betty Rice; I didn't need to be identified with someone else in order to
win an election. Later I reflected that being a politician's wife may have hurt
me in that particular legislative district. Many voters might have thought I was
not a serious candidate and feared that, if elected, I would not be independent
in my legislative work. That perception troubled me more than anything. I
knew I'd be my own person. The voters would have to learn that.

¾ ¾

I finished the school year at Centennial in June 1962 confident in the knowledge
that I had been a good teacher there, and I was looking forward to joining
the David Douglas faculty in September. My children were all doing well in
school. Randy had finished fourth grade; Jo would move from sixth grade to
junior high school; and John had graduated from eighth grade and would be a
freshman at Centennial. I'd had the unusual opportunity of teaching my own
daughter, Dian, in a senior honors class at Centennial. She was president of

the senior class, graduated as valedictorian, and achieved her college dream by winning a scholarship to Stanford University.

To help with her college expenses, Dian took a full-time summer job at the County Elections Division, and then she worked at Jim Dandy's Drive-In from six until ten o'clock on weeknights, till midnight on weekends. It was a grueling schedule, but she did fine—until one night when she came home late from the drive-in. She walked in the front door shaking with rage. "My boss is such a jerk," she snorted, but there were tears in her voice. "He told me I didn't know how to line garbage cans properly and then made me watch while he lectured me for twenty minutes on how the newspapers had to be placed just so," she said, making circles with her hands. She felt humiliated and demeaned.

"Honey, forget it," I said. "In September you'll be at Stanford University majoring in math, and that guy is still going to be at Jim Dandy's lining garbage cans. You've got to decide what's worth spending emotional energy on. Forget him. Go to bed and sleep well."

➣ ➢

As the end of summer approached, my mind went in search of the next project, the next challenge. My master's degree program was completed, and my campaign for the Legislature was over. I felt unoccupied.

I went to talk to Burt Wingert, the chairman of the political science department at the University of Oregon, about working on a Ph.D. I had become interested in behavioral politics as a result of my own political experience and the coursework on polling and public opinion I'd done in my master's program. For one of my courses my classmates and I had developed an opinion poll and taken it door to door. Our poll was not directed at predicting election outcomes, but at trying to determine how voters felt about politics in general; the "efficacy," we called it, that voters felt toward politics. Did they feel comfortable participating? Did they feel alienated? How often did they vote? Our poll asked these and other related questions.

After we'd completed our door-to-door work, the professor had our results key-punched onto three-by-seven-inch cards. Then we fed our cards into a marvelous new machine that could tabulate our results in a few hours. I was struck by the power of this mighty tool. The computer was so much faster than pencil and paper in generating timely information that would be critical in election campaigns. I knew immediately I'd found my niche—political science specializing in public opinion. I had to do more of this. I felt I could be a good college professor, able to continue my classroom teaching and do research as well. The only way there was to get a doctorate in political science.

So I went to see Burt Wingert with high hopes and grand plans. But when I asked his advice on how I should start my Ph.D. program, he gave me this stunning reply: "Betty, I can't let you do that. You're thirty-nine years old. By the time you complete a doctorate you will be forty-five, and you'll only have twenty years to repay the taxpayers of Oregon for their investment in your education."

I don't know what shocked me more, his twisted reasoning or the casual air with which he made his remark. It was well known that there had never been a woman professor or Ph.D. candidate in his department. I knew my age was not the real reason.

Had the building collapsed on me, I would not have been more surprised, or more crushed. I don't remember what I said, if anything, or how I escaped his presence.

⁂

On the hundred-mile drive back to Portland from Eugene, I stacked up in my mind the many times a man had told me, "You can't." Just in the past seven years: I'd been told by a male registrar that I couldn't major in physical education; by my husband that I couldn't teach; by a male minister that I should never have gone to college; and by a male academic advisor that I should be happy being a housewife. Twice I'd been forced to shift jobs to another school district—once to be able to teach rather than be a dean according to a male superintendent's decree. Once I'd been fired when I ran for public office, just because another male superintendent had disliked the idea.

I had dealt with all the obstacles that had been thrown in my path. But none felt so final as the door Burt Wingert closed and bolted as I stood there, on the threshold of desire and opportunity. I felt I could go no further. The blockade was too high, too wide, and too powerful. Driving back to Portland in the summer heat, I was simmering, and not from the weather. I swore. My anger and disappointment prevented any rational dialogue with myself. What was it I had told my daughter a few weeks earlier about conserving one's emotional energy? After fifty miles, exhausted from the rage that had consumed me and anticipating my arrival home and being with my children—always a welcome relief and satisfying experience—I became calmer, more reasonable.

I am not defeated, I counseled myself. *I cannot become brittle and bitter.* Resolve and determination—some might call it "grit"—took over. I made myself remember the men who had supported me in my life. My father, who told me I could run faster than any kid in the neighborhood. My brother, who urged me to go to college instead of marrying. Dr. Johnson at Eastern Oregon College, the first to encourage me to continue my education. Ben Padrow and Marko Haggard at Portland State College, who had been consistently supportive and challenging and had accepted my return to college as a natural event. The men I'd taught with in high school, who had treated me as an equal. Howard Horner and Floyd Light, who had demonstrated great faith, not only in my teaching abilities, but also in my personal integrity. And my husband, Frank Roberts, who'd supported my run for public office.

With those better thoughts in my mind, I began to think of what my options were. Could I go over or around Burt Wingert? I didn't think so. Could I wait awhile and try again? I was too proud and too impatient for that approach, and I feared the answer would be the same. Could I change my plan and take a new direction? Maybe. At least, the question was intriguing, especially since I would be free to decide the direction. The thought sent my mind along several possible pathways.

Portland State College had no doctoral programs, and tuition at private institutions was beyond my means. But there was a night law school in Portland. Now there was a possibility. I wasn't sure I actually wanted to practice law. I wondered if any institution of higher education would accept a law degree as a qualification to teach college political science. I guessed I'd have time to find out. But then, being a lawyer might not be so bad. It was not my original plan, but lawyers probably did interesting work, and obviously they got paid more than teachers.

I would visit the law school right away. My academic background, I thought, should be adequate for admission, but I wasn't sure about the "problem" of being a thirty-nine-year-old woman.

⊱ ⊰

The Northwestern College of Law occupied the second and third floors of a building on Southwest Park Avenue just off Burnside in downtown Portland. The rest of the building housed the telephone company. The second floor was reached by a set of wide, dirty, well-worn wooden stairs. The small valleys in the steps on the left side and the right side, close to the handrails, were testament to the many feet that had trudged those steps over God knows how many years.

As my spectator pumps made their own mark on each step, I wondered what awaited me at the top of the stairs. I had become a veteran at seeking admission to colleges—Eastern Oregon, Portland State, the University of

Oregon twice—the second petition had been forcefully rejected. That still stung, but it had brought me to these stairs. Reaching the top, I braced myself for the obligatory routine. Why do I want to go to law school? Why isn't being a housewife sufficient? (Or now maybe it would be, Why isn't being a teacher sufficient?) And, by the way, don't you think you're a little old for this?

A woman said, "Hello. Can I help you?"

"Yes, I'd like to inquire about the law school."

"Do you just want information or are you interested in attending?"

"Both," I said as I thought, *Well, we're still on topic.*

"That's good," the woman said. "I'm Dorothy Cornelius. I'm happy to talk with you, but Judge Gantenbein will be the one to discuss admission with you."

I was taken through a doorway into another sparsely furnished office where Judge John Gantenbein sat behind his desk. He stood up as I entered, shook my hand, and asked me to have a seat.

It was another extraordinarily warm August afternoon. The sun slowly made moving patterns on the walls and floor. A barely perceptible breeze came from strategically placed fans, which hummed sleepily. Judge Gantenbein's demeanor was friendly and cordial. When I told him I wanted to go to law school and needed information on tuition and class schedules, he said, "Yes, of course, but I need to ask you one question."

Here it comes, I thought.

"What is your educational background?"

Surprise! One question and it's the same question he would ask any applicant. I told him I had both a bachelor's degree and a just-completed master's degree and that I was a teacher of senior social studies.

With a happy expression he said, "Ordinarily most of our applicants must take and pass an entrance test, but with your degrees that won't be necessary. Classes start in just a week, so you will need to talk to Mrs. Cornelius to get registered. She will give you the information on tuition, classes, and books. She will also show you our library and the classrooms."

As Judge Gantenbein stood and offered his hand again he said, "Welcome to Northwestern College of Law, and good luck." That meant I was accepted, I guessed. But it felt too easy. I'd come all prepared to argue for the admission of a woman, and an older woman, at that. And now I'd been deprived of the opportunity. As I descended the stairs I let out a long breath.

Driving through downtown, reaching the end of Broadway just short of the curves that dropped down to take me across the Ross Island Bridge, right at the corner beside Portland State College's Lincoln Hall, waiting for a stoplight to change, I had one last thought of Burt Wingert. "To hell with you, Mr. Chairman." In my mind, I flipped a finger south toward the University of Oregon. "I am going to be a lawyer."

Chapter 6

Learning to Campaign

Describing one's first year of law school is difficult, except to say there is no other learning experience—really no other form of torture—like it. Reading case after case after case, then reading textbooks that set out rules of law, variations on those rules, and exceptions to those rules, often in a language as unfamiliar as any foreign language, turned many of my classmates' dreams of being a lawyer to nightmares. Our freshman class dwindled rapidly.

On the first night there weren't enough desks for everyone; some of us sat on plain chairs or stood at the back of the room. Mr. Cairns, our contracts teacher, casually said not to worry about it. There'd be enough desks the next time we met. He was right, not because there were more desks but because there were fewer students. Many would drop out along the way, including one who sold his second-semester course books to me, saying, "If all those judges can't decide what the law is, I sure as hell can't."

I never thought of quitting. I hadn't begun law school just to see if I liked it; I had begun law school to complete it.

Driving home after that first meeting with Judge Gantenbein, I'd mused about the next four years. I would be in class three nights a week. The work required would be enormous. It wouldn't be a first-class legal education: Northwestern was a night law school aimed at working people like me, who could not otherwise hope to become lawyers. It was a make-do school, what we'd call in Texas a "hard-candy" law school. No frills, no extras, no soft centers for those who taught or those who learned. The library's few dusty books were nowhere near adequate. Fortunately we had access to the Multnomah County Law Library in the county courthouse. The restrooms were famously disgraceful, "two of the filthiest ... north of Nogales," as one of my classmates wrote in an article about the school. Northwestern's faculty were practicing lawyers or judges. That might not be such a bad thing, I reflected. We might not be treated to all the law's theoretical fine points, but the experience gathered in that school promised a rigorous practical curriculum. This was going to be a serious four years.

My evidence teacher would be Tom Tongue, whose place I would take, years later, on the Oregon Supreme Court. George Joseph, with whom I would serve on the Court of Appeals, taught conflict of laws; Bob Jones, with whom I

Law student Betty Roberts, Northwestern College of Law, 1963-64

would serve on the Oregon Supreme Court, taught mortgages and insurance. George Van Hoomissen would become a Circuit Court judge, presiding over many of my family law cases, and he would go on to serve on the Court of Appeals and the Supreme Court. These men were tough, practical teachers, and they welcomed any student who was willing to work hard.

☙ ❧

I was still a member of the school board, having been elected to a full five-year term when my one-year term expired. Law school had been underway for only a few weeks when an issue was raised at a school board meeting that would test me in many ways. The member of the Lynch school board who had accused teachers of not teaching patriotism introduced a proposal requiring all teachers to lead students in the flag salute each morning. This board member—who was a member of the John Birch Society, a radically conservative group whose members believed America was being overrun by Communists—thought former President Dwight Eisenhower was a Communist dupe, and he believed Communists, or their dupes, were taking over the schools and government. Requiring the flag salute would counteract the Communist threats, he told the board. He wasn't clear on exactly how it would accomplish that purpose.

The same board member also proposed to lower the women teachers' salaries and raise the men's salaries because, according to his thinking, women worked because they wanted to, while men worked because they had families to support. I teased him with a bit of Marxism, saying, both humorously and sarcastically, "Why, I didn't know you believed in the theory of 'from each according to his abilities, to each according to his needs.'" I hoped other board members recognized this core doctrine of Karl Marx's *Das Kapital*. He sputtered. That proposal went no further.

The flag salute issue was not so easily averted. I knew the board couldn't force children to recite the pledge of allegiance: in 1943 the United States Supreme Court had found that requiring the flag salute in public schools violated the freedom-of-religion provisions of the U.S. Constitution. I assumed most citizens understood that and believed it. I drafted an alternative proposal that would recognize the importance of patriotism and encourage teachers to teach it at every opportunity. After I talked with two other board members, the three of us agreed to support this strategy and oppose the proposal for a mandatory flag salute. We had the three-to-two majority to end the issue with a compromise.

On the night of the hearing more than four hundred people showed up. Many were in military uniform, and many carried American flags or Bibles. They appeared to be mostly from outside the district, and they were clearly there to support a mandatory pledge of allegiance. But with our alternative proposal, I felt reasonably confident that the board could lay this issue to rest without too much fuss.

One after another, the uniformed men rose to speak in favor of the mandatory pledge. There were a few in the audience, a former student of mine and at least one parent, who were brave enough to speak in favor of my alternative proposal, but they were soon shouted down. The various speakers and others in the audience became threatening in their language toward anyone who supported the compromise proposal. The theme of the evening became "Get the Communist teacher off the school board." That would be me.

In closing the debate our board member gave a performance that Jerry Falwell and Pat Robertson would have envied. With a Bible in one hand, loosening his tie and tugging his shirt collar open with the other, he paced back and forth before the audience, condemning educators for being "soft on Communism" and vowing he would protect the children in the Lynch School District.

It was an amazing and frightening speech. I listened to the angry words directed at me, but I did not feel afraid. I knew I was legally right. Instead, I watched with awe, intellectually detached. The meeting was a living laboratory of the propaganda techniques that my students were learning about in my classroom, and I wished they could hear and analyze them now. Those arguing for a mandatory salute used American flags and military uniforms to stir patriotism, Bibles to signify their righteousness and invoke the infallibility of their belief. With their accusatory rhetoric, they skillfully cranked up the atmosphere to inflammatory levels. Civility had vanished.

The debate continued for three hours. Finally, a vote was taken on my compromise motion. There was one "Aye"—mine—and three "Nay" votes. The chairman, one of the men who had helped me draft the compromise proposal, abstained, saying he was only there "to referee." Mine was the only vote against the mandatory pledge when we voted on it next.

I was dumbfounded. When the meeting was over I saw my two former compatriots being confronted by their wives. One of them had tears in her eyes. She questioned her husband repeatedly, "How could you do that? How could you do that?"

So there you have it. Free speech in one of its noisier, more chaotic moments. Maybe I was too inexperienced to expect that reason and compromise would carry the day, or that my colleagues would keep their word. One hopes that, even in democracy's most raucous times, the reason and tolerance that people of goodwill bring to the process will overcome the rancor and meanness. Not so that evening.

People told me I had been courageous. If so, it was unconscious, and my action didn't deserve such a description. Courage was the firm resistance shown by the thousands of citizens accused by Senator Joe McCarthy and his Congressional Un-American Activities Committee of supporting Communism in the 1950s—they had lost jobs and the respect of their communities. By the 1960s, "closet Communist" battles had seeped into school boards all over the country, initiated by fearmongers like our board member, who applied the McCarthy tactics well. I knew I was in good company in taking the position I did.

As I walked to my car, a voice replayed in my head, the voice of a woman saying to her husband, "How could you do that? How could you do that?"

The issue was kept alive with front-page stories and letters to the editor in *The Oregonian, Gresham Outlook, Portland Reporter,* and the Parkrose-East County *Enterprise.* Even the *National Eagle,* an anti-Communist, pro-Christian publication, printed its own version.

As a result of this controversy, the John Birch Society filed a complaint with the David Douglas school board demanding that I be fired. After Superintendent Floyd Light briefed the board on my background and good performance in other teaching positions and affirmed his support for me, the board refused to take any action. They understood the tactics, for some of them had been accused by these same people of being Communists.

The flag incident was my first public battle over civil liberties. I appreciated the lesson in how to withstand public pressure with composure and dignity.

More important to me personally was that the incident proved I was tougher than the men who caved in. Most surprising to me was how calm I felt in the midst of irrational turmoil.

When the new policy handbook came out, the compulsory pledge was not in it, and no one raised any question about it.

※ ※

With the fall of 1963 came the beginning of another election season. Defeated in 1962, I saw the 1964 election as a second chance. What beauty we have in our democratic form of government! Our system is generous with second chances—the grace of "try, try again." It's the rare politician who can boast of never having lost an election; in fact, losing is often seen as a badge of courage. There is no shame, only an opportunity to learn and work harder next time. Politics spoke my language: achievement through hard work and perseverance—that grit again.

At that time the whole of east Multnomah County outside Portland was one big district from which three representatives were elected. For lack of any official name for this election method, we generally referred to it as "running in a pack." In the 1962 primary I'd come in close behind the three who'd won on the Democratic ticket. Supporters had encouraged me not to be disappointed, but to look ahead. Still on the school board, still with good name familiarity from the 1962 campaign, I found it an easy decision to run again. But what about law school? I would never give that up. I'd have to do both.

The only way to win would be to campaign better than all the other Democratic candidates. I'd begin by gathering signatures to file by petition, rather than by declaring myself a candidate and paying the filing fee. This strategy would legitimize the campaign at a very early stage. Most importantly, it would begin to get my name into the minds of the voters long before most other campaigns began.

At that time Multnomah County had five legislative districts. One was all west of the Willamette River, and three were east of the river inside the city limits; these were designated as north, east central, and south. The fifth, my district, was outside the city limits and covered the area called east Multnomah County. It was the largest geographically, running all the way from the city borders at about Southeast 92nd, slicing down from the Columbia River on the north to Clackamas County on the south, and extending to Hood River County on the east.

The demographics of the east Multnomah County district were complicated. Developers were rapidly turning small family farms, orchards, and berry fields into suburbia. New schools had to be built for these new communities; my own school board was building at the rate of one school a year all the time I served. Supermarkets were being located strategically with smaller businesses huddled around a large parking lot, harbingers of the mini-malls and super-malls that would eventually cover the landscape. Lloyd Center, located in Portland just east of the river, had opened in 1960 as the largest covered mall in the whole country. Farther east in my district were five small incorporated towns. Of these, Gresham was the most populated and the most commercially and politically significant.

The district was heavily Democratic, which meant that elections were almost always decided in the primary. I needed to locate the neighborhoods where the most Democrats were clustered so I could maximize my time collecting signatures door to door. From the county registrar I obtained maps of each precinct and lists of the registered voters who lived in them. Armed with the petition on a clipboard and a small flyer that introduced me, I began appearing on doorsteps. I needed five hundred signatures, but there was no point in stopping there, since the objective was not just to get the required number but to meet as many voters as possible.

This detail of getting a campaign started may seem unimportant in my story as a politician, but, in truth, it may be the most important. In my 1962 defeat I had violated one of my own personal rules: always be prepared when an opportunity presents itself. The defeat showed me that winning takes more than desire and interest; it requires diligent, persistent work.

ﾟ ﾟ

On November 22, 1963, a few days before our school's Thanksgiving holiday, my senior social studies students and I were in a large, theater-like classroom at David Douglas High School, watching a film. The principal's voice came over the public address system—an unusual event in the middle of a class period.

I turned off the projector, and we listened in the quiet, pitch-black room to the wrenching news so many across the country were hearing, the news that would shape my students' generation. In a voice heavy with grief, Mr. Horner said, "I am so sorry to have to tell you that President John Kennedy was shot in Dallas, Texas, and the announcement has just been made that he is dead."

The intercom clicked off. From the darkness came gasps. Sobs. A fist slammed on a desk. Someone gave an agonized "Damn." I turned on the lights and faced my students. Girls had their arms around each other, and some students sat with their faces in their hands or their heads on their desks. Some stared straight ahead as if in a trance.

There was nothing more to say. Classes were dismissed so that students and teachers could talk to each other informally or go watch the televisions that had been hastily set up in the auditorium and gym. Later, television screens would show Vice President Lyndon Baines Johnson being sworn in as president on the airplane that carried Kennedy's body back to Washington, D.C. The sight of the president's widow, Jackie Kennedy, still in her blood-splattered pink suit, standing beside Johnson as he became our president, is etched into my memory.

The assassination of the president sent waves of disbelief and mourning throughout our country. President Kennedy was a political idol to most young people. He instilled in them a sense of hope, not only for our country but for the world, and he challenged them to work with him to make that hope a reality. I'm sure many of them feared that his death would be the death of their own dreams and goals. For who now would lead them? Who now would inspire them?

For me, the president's tragic death instilled a greater sense of purpose and an even stronger commitment to my campaign. All of us would have to be more resolute and strong in carrying on the work John Kennedy had laid out for us.

❧ ❧

Campaigns in my early days in politics were far simpler than they are today, but they still required a cadre of volunteers who pitched in to do whatever was necessary. The most effective campaign method was trudging from door to door handing out brochures and planting yard signs in the lawns of supporters. My house served as campaign headquarters, with a map of my district covering the dining room wall. The garage was the lawn-sign construction site.

I braced myself to confront the issue of the mandatory pledge if it came up in my campaign. Amazingly, no one mentioned it—no candidate, no one in the audiences I spoke to, no one we talked to on doorsteps.

We did one thing that had not been done in legislative races before: we bought six billboards and scheduled our campaign ads to appear in mid-April, one month before election day. When the ads first appeared, I was shocked to see my name in huge, bold print. They looked pretentious—but they were necessary if my campaign was to lead the others.

Studying had to wait until late at night. Strong coffee and mustard and pickle sandwiches kept me going as I briefed cases and read law books until one or two o'clock in the morning. Even with my hard studying, my law school grades were sagging. Time was delicately balanced between home, children, teaching, law school, and the campaign. The family had to stay well. There was no time for illnesses or unexpected events. Every working mother knows that refrain well.

Nevertheless, I learned that even the best-prepared woman can't control everything. The first interruption of my plans came when Dian announced her intention to marry a fellow student at Stanford. The wedding would be in mid-April—one month before primary election day. Dian and Glen took the responsibility for planning the wedding, which would be in Klamath Falls, halfway between Portland and Sacramento, where his family lived.

And then—another whammy. A few days before the wedding I received the sad news that my father had died of a heart attack while working in the garden at my brother's home near Chicago, where Dad lived in the guest house. The funeral would be held the same weekend as Dian's wedding. I was faced with the choice of celebrating a new life for my daughter or mourning a life just ended. I chose the wedding.

After a full weekend of wedding activities we all headed back to our respective homes, and Dian and Glen returned to Stanford to finish the semester. It was a relief to get back to the familiar feel of the campaign. *But please, please,* I silently willed, *don't let anything else happen to get us off schedule.*

❧ ❧

Finally election day came. I voted on my way to school, and then the wait began. It was customary, after the polls closed, for candidates to tour the television stations to get the latest election results. The stations posted returns on a large board. If the results looked good, candidates would want to be interviewed. By 8:15 p.m. the first returns showed me topping the ticket of nine candidates. I stayed there the entire evening. I felt the euphoria that every candidate feels when a winning tally is posted. I had won! My high was a great festival of sensations—pride in myself for the endurance, immense gratitude to the volunteers who'd worked in the campaign, thankfulness to the voters for supporting me, and relief that it was over.

Elected with me from east Multnomah County were Ross Morgan, an incumbent, and Howard Willits, a newcomer like me. Feeling a little giddy, I elatedly greeted Morgan, my new colleague and friend, at one of the television stations and congratulated him on his win. His reply was a stern lecture about using billboards, saying, "It will run up the cost of campaigns." That brought me back to reality. "Well, it worked," I said, only momentarily chastened.

I saw State Senator Vern Cook that night, too. He had told me early in the campaign, "You will lose some friends by being involved in politics, but you will gain many more." That was true. When I saw him on election night, he said, "When you win, you can afford to be gracious." I would certainly try.

It was a fortuitous time to embark on a political life. Not only would I have a ringside seat to the upheavals and reforms that were about to occur in our state and society, but I would be in the ring myself. On reflection, there were signs in Oregon's 1964 election and the 1965 legislative session that the state and country were on the cusp of change. The campaign and the session would turn out to be practice runs compared to what would follow.

❧ ❧

The State Democratic Convention was held in Coos Bay shortly after the primary. There I met Bob Straub, a state senator and former Chairman of the State Democratic Party, who was running for State Treasurer against a one-term incumbent. Straub was enormously well liked, but many Democrats thought he couldn't win, both because he was running against an incumbent and because he was not noted for being a good campaigner—that was the opinion of both Frank and Ben Padrow, my speech teacher at Portland State. I didn't agree with them. Although Straub had a slight stutter, he had many positive qualities that made him a good candidate. He was a graduate of a prominent eastern university and a successful businessman, with interests in timber, ranching, and construction, all of which gave him good qualifications for the State Treasurer's office.

Straub and his large family lived unpretentiously on a farm outside Eugene. His supportive wife, Pat, was an organic gardener who often cooked on a wood stove. He embodied ruggedness and individuality, and once voters became acquainted with him they would be convinced of his devotion to Oregon. The more I learned about him, the more politically interesting he became. I thought his qualifications, lifestyle, and family demonstrated the values that Oregonians most cherish. But Straub was not well known in the Portland metropolitan area, and he would have to campaign hard there. The press probably would not cover the Treasurer's race with any fanfare because the office was of little interest to most voters. I was sure these drawbacks could be overcome. Tall, gangly Bob Straub was not charismatic, but he would be accepted by the voters if they got to know him. I was sure of it.

I called Straub with ideas for increasing his name familiarity and visibility in Multnomah County. Where better than my own East County district? I suggested he spend time at the Multnomah County Fair, where he and his children could show off their prize cattle. This followed an Oregon tradition established by U.S. Senator Wayne Morse, who had entered his prize bulls in fairs all over Oregon for years. Pat could enter her cooking and garden produce as well. The whole family would love it, I said. Straub agreed to do it.

Because two of Straub's campaign themes were the need for jobs for young people and the need for more parks in Oregon, I suggested that a youth jobs project at a new park along the Sandy River in my district would be an ideal place for a news conference. The appearance at Oxbow Park attracted good television and newspaper coverage for him and a little bit for me, which I appreciated, but I'd already won my most important election. I hoped some of the goodwill voters had shown me would help him.

On Labor Day weekend Straub invited Frank to Eugene for a campaign strategy session. When I prepared to go along, Frank said, as tactfully as he could, "Um, you're not invited." I was silently furious and lectured myself about expecting to be included. Men were the candidates, and their wives kept out of sight as much as possible or were given menial tasks. Men took responsibility for raising money because it was assumed women did not have the proper contacts—read, "influence." Too, there was the assumption that if a woman asked a man for money it implied a *quid pro quo* of a sexual nature. Men were the candidates and planned campaigns, while women typed and stuffed envelopes. Men bathed in the glory of winning and holding office, and women supplied the applause.

This was not a new revelation. I just thought it didn't apply to me any more. Wasn't I a candidate? Hadn't I raised the money for my campaign? Was I still to be treated as inferior to men in planning campaign strategy? I didn't know who I was angrier with—Bob Straub for not including me, or Frank for not telling Straub I'd be there, too.

To work off my indignation, I took eleven-year-old Randy to the State Fair in Salem. Straub, apparently, wasn't showing his cows at the fair, at least not in person, and I didn't bother to look for them. The carnival atmosphere of the fair and Randy's company helped me calm down. The best attitude in politics is "get over it." I resolved to immerse myself in my own campaign, my teaching, and my law studies. I was entering my third year in law school; now that my campaigning was over, I planned to make better grades.

❧ ❧

My exclusion from the Straub campaign meeting represented only the most recent of the growing number of evenings and weekends when Frank and I went our separate ways. Our time together had been further diminished by Frank's efforts to improve his relationship with his two daughters, who were by then twenty and sixteen. My hope that we could overcome their long standing alienation had not been fulfilled. From time to time Frank called them to try to arrange to take them on the boat, to dinner, or to a movie. He was usually rejected out of hand, and if I were to be included the refusal was even more adamant. They would never come to my house. After four years of marriage I had never met Frank's daughters. It was an unsettling situation.

I pondered our growing separation. I began to see that Frank and I had little in common besides politics. He was an accepting person, supportive of my teaching career and my political ambitions. Still, the marriage was not right. I was ashamed to conclude that I had married Frank for much the same reason I had married Bill. It had been the practical thing to do.

Everyone has seen marriages fall apart for some unspoken reason. Often the parties themselves can't explain it. The one thing I could specifically pinpoint was that I had not been single long enough to adjust to that new status and to give more serious thought to whether I should marry again, especially with the obligation of four children to raise. On the other hand, Frank had been single for many years and in those years he had developed a lifestyle of bachelorhood, unhindered by family obligations, that fit his independent, free-spirited nature.

I scolded myself over and over for making a second mistake. But then I reasoned that the two marriages weren't the same. My eighteen-year marriage to Bill had given us four wonderful children, and we had made a good home together. Those bonds were not a consideration with Frank. I had no relationship with his children, as I had hoped I would, and we owned no property jointly. As I prepared for my first session as a state legislator and began looking forward to the 1965 session, I knew it was only a matter of time before my marriage to Frank would end. But all that could be put on hold for the time being.

Chapter 7

Rookie Legislator: The 1965 Session

January 11, 1965, was cold and clear; there was an unusual dusting of snow on the ground in Salem, the state capital. As my three younger children and I walked toward the white marble building, the gold pioneer standing tall atop the dome glistened majestically. The Capitol building and legislative chambers were not new to me. I'd testified on education bills, and I'd visited there when Frank was on the House staff. But now, as a brand-new legislator, I found it all more inviting, more awe-inspiring—the state seal in the center of the rotunda, the soaring space of the dome, the broad marble steps leading to the Senate chambers on one side and the House chambers on the other.

This was the children's first visit to the Capitol, and I assumed the role of history teacher. The huge murals surrounding the rotunda walls portrayed Captain Robert Gray's entry into the Columbia River and Lewis and Clark's expedition at Celilo Falls. That panel also featured Sacagawea, the teenage Shoshone woman who guided Lewis and Clark on the journey, and York, the first African American to come to the Pacific Northwest. Another panel showed the arrival in 1836 of the first white women to come to the Oregon Territory. The women in the murals welcomed me as a participant in Oregon's history, as did the state's motto, "She Flies With Her Own Wings." As we turned to walk up the stairs to the House of Representatives, I knew I'd never match their achievements, but I'd give it a good try.

Newspaper accounts of the opening ceremonies of the Legislature included a picture of me with my handsome, well-mannered children. The photo appeared in the state's largest newspaper, *The Oregonian*, but—true to the times—in the society section. The reporting now seems quaint if not outright silly. Representative Fritzi Chuinard "complemented her soft powder hair with a deep pink knit suit, accented with a purple orchid," while "red-haired Rep. Juanita Orr ... wore a businesslike two-piece black wool dress," and Rep. Katherine Musa "wore a tailored taupe dress, complementing her becoming streaked hair."

As for me, "Rep. Betty Roberts wore a flattering cream suit, accented with a single rose..." although "what Mrs. Roberts ... wore was probably the least of her concerns ..." because, the reporter pointed out, my children sat with me at my desk on the floor of the House of Representatives during the opening ceremonies. I was proud of them, and they of me.

⚹ ⚹

When I started my campaign for the House of Representatives, the Democrats were in control. But on election day, as I was winning from a heavily Democratic part of the state, the Republicans were sweeping the Democrats out. They became the majority in the House, thirty-two seats to twenty-eight. The implications of this had struck me full force during freshman legislative orientation in December. As the majority party, the Republicans would nominate and elect one of their own as Speaker; this session it would be Monte Montgomery from Eugene. The Speaker has the power to name committee members and chairmen and to determine the assignment of bills to committees—all of which heavily influences the success or failure of specific proposals, and, in turn, the success or failure of individual legislators.

There were six other women serving in the House, four Democrats and two Republicans. Only one woman, Alice Corbett, served in the thirty-member Senate. All had served previously. Two were unmarried. None had children at home.

Grace Peck, a Democrat and a legendary figure, had served many terms in the House, dating back at least to the 1940s. She was a large woman with a flamboyant manner of dress—large-patterned, brightly colored dresses, ample jewelry, and heavy makeup, especially bright red lipstick. She was noted for the candy jars covering her desk, and also known for her staunch Catholicism. Grace was regarded as the political patron saint of people in prison and mental institutions for her frequent visits and regular reports to the Legislature on the status and welfare of the institutionalized.

Juanita Orr, a Democrat, had been a county assessor and a county clerk, but both these offices were bureaucratic in nature, with no policy-making involved. In the Legislature she rarely expressed views on issues. Fritzi Chuinard, a Republican and the wife of a well-known Portland physician, represented Portland's upscale West Side. She, too, was quiet and without any apparent passion for issues. Katherine "Kitty" Musa, a Democrat, was the wife of Ben Musa, the Senate President. While quite capable as a legislator herself, she was prone to object, or even cry, when negative remarks were made about the Senate in general or her husband in particular. None of these women would seem to be a role model for me. I had run for the Legislature to work on important issues, and to do that I would have to be more aggressive, more persuasive, and more visible.

The remaining two women, Beulah Hand and Shirley Field, stood out as well-informed, intelligent, and aggressive legislators. Beulah, a Democrat and tough partisan fighter, impressed me immediately. Shirley Field was recognized as a young Republican leader with great potential. She had been my lawyer and my friend during my divorce from Bill. Now that we were both in the Legislature, she saw her role as my partisan adversary. While her lawyer's training had made her capable in debate, she had a reputation for turning personally vindictive.

Shirley and Beulah each provided her party a tough, outspoken woman. While I was intrigued by their forceful confrontational styles, I knew they made enemies. I hoped not to do that. Comfortable working with men and confident of my ability to match their legislative skills, I would rely on the male legislators to help me learn about issues and the process. I was as ambitious and competitive as any of the men. I presumed we were all in politics because we wanted to be in a position to make decisions on public policy. My aggressiveness may have been tempered by the fact that I had children and domestic responsibilities. From this personal standpoint, I had much in common with the male legislators' wives, many of whom worked for their husbands as secretaries. That had its benefits, because my acceptance by their wives made the men more comfortable working with me.

Few women had served in the Oregon Legislature prior to the 1950s. By late in that decade, however, the number of registered Democrats in the state had grown significantly as the population increased and the economy expanded following the war years. In the early part of the 1950s the Oregon Democratic Party began to flex its muscles, recruiting outstanding and influential leaders. But it was hard to find men who could afford to leave their jobs long enough to serve in the Legislature. Legislative pay was low, six hundred dollars for a two-year term, with no reimbursement of expenses. Men were usually the only wage earners in their families, and even if they were politically motivated, most could not afford to give up jobs to be legislators. The Democratic Party began to recruit women, and the number of Democratic women serving in the Legislature increased dramatically between 1950 and 1960. In 1957, five women had been elected, the most ever to serve in a single session. In 1959, that number doubled to ten, all but two of them Democrats. The presence of women in the Legislature was of more than historical interest; it had a powerful practical payoff. Women helped the Democrats gain control of the House in 1957 and retain it until 1965.

I read Betty Friedan's *The Feminine Mystique* during the 1965 session, more for myself than for ideas on what needed to be done legislatively. While the feminist movement was in its germination stage, it was not yet felt at the Oregon Legislature. Official recognition of the changing role of women in society had come when President Kennedy established a Commission on the Status of Women and named Eleanor Roosevelt as the chairperson. Oregon Governor Mark Hatfield, a Republican, followed the president's lead and established an Oregon Commission for Women by executive order. In 1963, Congress passed the Equal Pay Act and, in 1964, the Civil Rights Act. The latter was originally introduced to prohibit discrimination on the basis of race, and Congress added prohibition of discrimination on the basis of sex. These events sparked considerable public discussion on the rights of women.

Yet women as a group were not organized and did not have a unified political agenda. We were still thinking individually, as we did in our isolated roles of wife, mother, and homemaker. We would not begin to think collectively until we had experiences beyond the home and the opportunity to communicate with other women about our mutual concerns. It did not occur to me then that women should be organized or have an agenda. In a newspaper interview I was quoted as saying I felt more women would go into politics because it is "an extension of community work in which they are already involved." My thinking had gone no further.

❧ ❦

Beverly Steffen was my secretary. She'd been my loyal campaign worker who had covered precincts with me in rain or shine, any day of the week and at any time. She worked beside me at our "office" on the floor of the House of Representatives. Beverly was married and had two sons in school, but her political activities always came first, and apparently with no objection from her husband. She had a nice figure and dressed appropriately, but always wore a wig. Curiosity finally won out when I asked her, "Why the wig?" With a shrug of her shoulders, she replied that it was simple—a wig was so much easier than always worrying about her hair. Bev would be my secretary for four sessions—eight years—riding to and from Salem with me and being with me in the precincts with every election. The experiences we each had in the Legislature in our separate roles was a fine reward, I thought, for all the hard work we had done in the campaigns.

Legislative work came easily for me, with committee meetings scheduled as my college classes had been—Mondays, Wednesdays, and Fridays or Tuesdays and Thursdays. I was usually back home in Portland when the children got home from school and in time to brief a few cases for law classes.

At first I found myself observing the Legislature from a thoughtful distance, more as a student and teacher of political science than as an active participant. I saw legislators and lobbyists working in much the way textbooks described the political process. Those moments of detachment gave me a sense of security that was near smugness. But before long I felt myself in the thick of it, and the Legislature became a living laboratory for the study of sociology and psychology as well as politics. From time to time I could recapture the analytical detachment, but in those times it was as if I were a spectator to my own life. I realized that clinging to my perceived objectivity would not help me become an effective legislator. I had to get into the muck with everyone else.

Out of those observations came essential lessons in political survival. Who associated with whom? What were the real roles of staff, especially those who worked for legislative power brokers like the Speaker, the President of the Senate, and the committee chairmen? What were the relationships between legislators and lobbyists? Information that flowed through the Capitol grapevine led to speculation about who knew what, how quickly they knew it, and who their sources were.

All this time, I was developing in my mind a formula for success in the Legislature. Patience was important. I had very little patience then, and I didn't want it very much—I was afraid it might turn into passivity. Persistence, of which I had an enormous amount, would be useful. By far the most necessary tool was influence, or to use a bolder word, "power." Of that I had none. Achieving power would take time. Power came, first and foremost, from being in the majority party, then from seniority in the Legislature and from holding committee chairmanships. Having none of these for the time being, I had to make the most of my position in the minority party, with zero seniority, and no committee chairmanship. Nevertheless, I tackled issues, mostly related to education, with all the zest I could muster. I introduced bills for the Oregon Education Association on sick leave and teacher tenure, and one for myself that would reestablish funding for kindergartens.

The Legislature had funded kindergartens until 1957, when the formula for the distribution of state money for education was drastically altered. I'd written my master's thesis on the interest groups involved in that change. Now I took it as a personal mission to convince other legislators to reinstate funding for this crucial part of children's education. How could they fail to see the importance of kindergartens once they had the facts?

My bill passed from the Education Committee, on which I served, to the Ways and Means Committee, where it was dismissed without serious consideration.

After my testimony, one committee member said, "Representative Roberts, if you can come up with a way to pay for this we might be interested in your proposal." I suggested that funding was the responsibility of the committee members hearing the bill. This didn't sit well with the chairman, who said, "Well, if that's the way you feel, maybe you should get yourself appointed to this committee." He was saying the kindergarten bill was dead, but I took his insincere, snide suggestion as a very good one. I'd work on doing just that, becoming a Ways and Means Committee member, knowing that it would take a while.

Another bill I introduced on the suggestion of a constituent would compensate victims of crime, a new idea for the times. It fared no better than the kindergarten bill. While it was given a well-attended hearing in the Judiciary Committee—supporters included Dean Seward Reese of the Willamette Law School—its fate was indefinite postponement. There was some satisfaction in knowing that I was identified as the sponsor of both the kindergarten bill and the victim-compensation bill, that the hearings were well attended by supporters, and that both bills received good press coverage. That would have to do for now.

I did not fully appreciate it then, but it is clear to me in hindsight that the 1965 Legislature provided an early glimpse of an old era dying and a new one being born. Two issues from the 1965-66 session stand out as indicators of things to come: the growing revolution in race relations, and the increasing demand for accountability in government. The yet-to-come upheavals over the war in Vietnam, the soon-to-break environmental and consumer-rights issues, and the huge public sympathy for the civil rights movement—along with the shock and anger at the violence employed against it—would change the way citizens saw their government. Yet even before those cataclysmic events, change was in the air.

On the race-relations issue, a bill to fund a model school program was assigned to the Education Committee, on which I served. It would make funds available to the Portland School District to improve the education of disadvantaged students. The bill was an outgrowth of a report titled *Race and Education*, from a study commissioned by the Portland School Board on how to improve the education of black elementary-school children.

To my surprise—and this is an indication of my naiveté—both the NAACP and an association of ministers from Albina, Portland's black community, opposed the bill. Their representatives testified eloquently that the bill was simply an attempt to avoid integration by setting up a compensatory system. The Albina Ministerial Association, made up of thirty-two ministers of predominantly black churches, testified against the bill and issued a printed statement summarizing their concerns. Their testimony pointed out that the study committee had been advised to address the subject of integration, yet the report failed to make recommendations to support integration. Instead it had come up with the model-schools proposal, for which there was federal funding. The controversy over the bill was rooted in the growing nationwide unrest with long-tolerated discrimination practices. Oregonians bragged about living in one of the first states to pass civil-rights legislation affecting racial minorities. In 1959, soon after Mark Hatfield became governor, the Legislature had passed a law that prevented discrimination on the basis of race in public accommodations. It would seem that Oregon was trying to move in the right direction.

With that goal in mind, I proposed that legislators respond to the concerns of opponents by including a preamble stating the Legislature's continuing commitment to civil rights. I drafted a simple statement: "It is the intent of this Act to provide funds and means by which disadvantaged children may receive education that meets their particular needs, and in so far as this Act affects minority groups, it is intended that it contribute to the elimination of the racial isolation of children so that all may fully share in America's political, cultural and economic life." The NAACP and the Albina ministers felt the preamble did nothing, because, no matter what it said, the bill provided that funds were to be used in their schools without any effort at integration. They were right. When I read that statement now, I hear its patronizing tone, and I understand why it fell flat and may even have been offensive to those citizens seeking real integration. In 1965, I felt it was better than nothing. The preamble was defeated in committee and on the House floor.

The House passed the model-schools legislation by a good majority, after legislators spoke about how they were not opposed to integration and how they "had one, or more, Negro friends." One legislator reported that he had even tried to rent a house to a black person but found no one interested—implying that the blame for segregation was on the black people themselves. I began to see the complexity of the issue and wondered how real integration could ever happen, not only in schools but in the workplace and our neighborhoods and churches.

The other issue portending things to come was the growing demand for accountability in government, particularly in the legislative process. Lobbying was an aspect of lawmaking that had remained largely in the shadows. It was still accepted practice for lobbyists not to reveal the identity of their clients unless they chose to, and they were free to buy drinks and food for legislators without any reporting requirements. In the days when legislators were paid only six hundred dollars for a two-year period, relying on lobbyists was often necessary, or so I was told by legislators who had served then. That was not the case in 1965—we were paid two hundred fifty dollars a month and twenty dollars a day in expenses. But lobbyists still bought plenty of food and drinks for legislators, as I would find out personally.

Three weeks into the session the Democratic caucus initiated a proposal that would require lobbyists to register and to identify their clients. Members of the caucus saw this as a way to publicly embarrass the Republican majority— although they were hardly blameless, having done nothing about the issue during past sessions when they were in power. In any event, I was assigned to make the motion on the proposal and to speak on it. Being a first-termer, my credibility wasn't tainted yet.

In keeping with House rules, the proposal was drafted and circulated one day before it would come to the floor, alerting both the Republicans and the lobbyists about what the Democrats were up to. That day Herb Hardy, a law partner in a well-recognized Portland firm and a longtime lobbyist, came to my desk. I had not met him, but I'd been told of his country-boy manner in dealing with legislators. His first remark was, "I don't know how to talk to a lady legislator." That struck me as typical of his "aw-shucks" approach, but an inappropriate way to begin a discussion.

My response was all business. "There are other women legislators whom you certainly must have spoken with before."

He mumbled, still in a shy manner, "Yes, but this is a personal issue because it's about my work as a lobbyist."

"But Herb," I said, "many of us see this as a public issue, and, therefore, an appropriate matter for the Legislature. So why don't you talk to me the way you would to any other legislator on any kind of legislation?" I couldn't believe Herb was so obtuse as to truly think that the identity of his clients was a personal matter. But I listened as he tried to convince me the proposal was not needed because, he said, lobbyists were willing to share information about their clients if asked. Lecturing like the teacher I was, I said, "Herb, that is not adequate for people who have an interest in legislation but have no direct access to lobbyists. Besides, legislators shouldn't have to ask for the information."

The Republicans were not about to let the Democrats either embarrass them or take credit for opening up the legislative process—the Republican leadership, indeed, favored the proposal. The next day, when it was to be voted on, I made the motion and said my piece. Then a Republican moved to refer it to the Rules Committee; debate followed, and ultimately, it was referred to the Judiciary Committee.

It was back on the floor very rapidly from Judiciary as a Republican proposal. By February 7, 1965, *The Oregonian* reported that 165 lobbyists had registered and identified their clients. That small opening salvo for reforms would go far beyond the lobbyist registration issue in later sessions.

And, damn, I'd missed my opportunity to ask Herb whom he worked for. But the news article revealed his clients to me and the rest of the world: "Safeway Stores, Oregon Food Council, and Oregon Cemetery Association."

⚓ ⚓

Beverly had taken to staying in Salem at least one night a week, and she told me that there was a side to my fellow legislators that I should know about. She told me that Chuck's Bar and Restaurant and the Velvet Horse Lounge in the Marion Hotel were gathering spots for legislators and lobbyists. The Prime Rib Restaurant was an upscale spot for dinner, and The Ranch was a late-night place for drinking and dancing. I asked Beverly, "Who pays for all the food and drinks?"

"Darned if I know," she said with a sly smile and deep chuckle. "Drinks just appear and if I order food the waitress says it's taken care of."

"But Beverly, it must be the lobbyists who pick up the tab," I suggested. "Who are they?"

She named five or six very rapidly, paused, added a few more names of people who, she said, were around now and then.

"Do the legislators pay for their own food and drinks?"

"Never noticed," she said, becoming impatient with my questions. Beverly was enjoying those evenings, and was obviously sorry she had told me if I was going to interfere with that pleasure.

Finally, I agreed to go to the Velvet Horse Lounge, but only for an hour, so I could get back to Portland for dinner with my children. We slipped into the red velvet–upholstered booth closest to the door, joining a couple of reporters and a lobbyist. We were greeted warmly, and a waitress quickly took our order. I dug in my purse for a five dollar bill and laid it on the table. Our drinks came, and my money stayed on the table.

I looked around the room at the huge portraits of women in various postures, mostly reclining, with long, transparent, discreetly placed shawls as adornment. At the same time I was looking at the other booths and tables to see whom I might know. A few more legislators and lobbyists wandered in. Some sat down in our booth, ordered a drink, asked how things were going, asked whether we were staying down for the evening, and then went on. All the while my five dollar bill stayed in front of me.

When the hour was up, Bev and I prepared to go. I asked the waitress for a check. She said "Oh, that's been taken care of." I had a passing thought of leaving the money on the table, either as a tip or just to help me believe I really had paid for my own drink. But I assumed the tip had been "taken care of" as well, and only I would know of my self-righteous gesture.

Early in the session I'd been approached by a veteran legislator from Eugene, Keith Skelton, who'd told me, "If I can be of help in any way, let me know." Keenly aware that I was a novice, I found that a thoughtful offer. Sometime in late February, he asked if I ever stayed in Salem in the evening. By then I knew he was a lawyer and a professor in the business school at the University of Oregon, was married and had four children the same ages as mine. I explained I had responsibilities at home and law school classes. His reply: "Well, if you ever can, I'd like to take you to dinner." I considered it a business invitation, an offer to join him and other legislators or lobbyists to talk about legislation. Later, when I agreed to have dinner with Keith, one of the most controversial issues of the session was shaping up as a major battle between business and labor. It was an important revision of the workmen's compensation law, and Keith was the lead legislator supporting it.

He had served in the Legislature in 1957 and 1959, then lobbied on behalf of the insurance industry for a major change in the laws governing workmen's compensation in the 1961 and 1963 sessions. The proposed revision had not passed then, and he had run again for the Legislature. Many suspected his primary motive was to work the legislation through from the inside, still speaking for the insurance industry, which wanted to be able to provide private insurance to businesses for workmen's compensation coverage. Relatively uninformed on the issue, I had decided, based on my own instincts and trust in others who opposed the legislation, to stick with the Democrats and the unions. When I finally accepted Keith's dinner invitation, I asked him not to lobby me on the bill.

Our dinner was anything but private, with lobbyists and legislators randomly joining us at our table throughout the evening. Nor was it for any "business" purpose. Drinks miraculously appeared. I never knew whether Keith paid for our dinner. He and I talked mostly about law school and the courses I was taking. He again offered to help if I was having any difficulty with specific courses. As I had requested, he said nothing about the workmen's compensation bill, and that impressed me. A few years later Keith told me he never intended to lobby me on the bill because he already had all the votes he needed. He said his interest was more personal.

Keith followed through on an offer of help for my law school studies. As a professor in the subject area, he gave me a one-hour lesson in negotiable instruments, one of law school's most disliked topics, at lunchtime one day while we sat on a bench on the Capitol grounds. He made the subject much simpler by helping me organize the material and by using examples I could understand. He was a good teacher.

༄ ༅

I wasn't getting very far very fast on any significant proposals, and I couldn't point to any particular successes, but I was having a great time learning the process while either butting heads with or learning from the more experienced legislators. While I was pursuing my own interests and attending my own committee meetings, countless issues were playing out with other legislators and in other committees.

That session the Legislature considered everything from what was called the "full crew" law for freight trains to a major revision of the Oregon Constitution. We debated bills on allowing mineral and oil exploration off the Oregon coast, allowing breathalyzer tests for persons suspected of drunk driving, and the redrawing of congressional district boundaries after the 1960 census. I had a hand in the redistricting; the plan I submitted was chosen by the House Republican caucus as the proposal they would support. The publicity that accompanied the Republican's acceptance of my plan was sheer freshman luck, I guessed, or else the least of all evils from their standpoint. Getting involved with issues that were new to me was a tremendous learning experience and kept me from being identified as a person with limited interests.

Late in the spring the Elections Committee, chaired by Representative Bob Packwood, was considering a major reform of the process for electing legislators. The bill would require that each legislative position in districts with two or more senators or representatives, such as Multnomah County, be assigned a number. Candidates would have to file for a specific position rather than "running in a pack," as I had done in my recent campaign. It meant there would be a face-off of candidates, rather than the automatic election of the three highest vote-getters in a district. This reform would have the effect of increasing direct competition among candidates, which would help voters know the candidates better. It passed both the House and the Senate and would be the method used in the next election cycle.

As the session wore on, I felt more and more accepted by male and female legislators alike. If there was a slight, I was too busy to dwell on it, or I chalked it up to my freshman status. I never felt I was treated unequally as a woman, probably because other legislators never knew when they'd need my vote. Therefore, one incident surprised me. After a morning session when I had made an exceptional effort in arguing for a bill, a Republican legislator from a small town west of Salem came by my desk as we were adjourning for lunch. "Tell Frank he wrote a great speech for you on your bill," he said.

My first thought was disbelief. *What nerve this guy has!* Letting a little annoyance creep into my voice, I said, "What makes you think Frank had a role in what I said this morning? I don't think he even knows about my work on this bill."

"Well, it was a good speech. Frank is a speech teacher. I just thought ..." his voice trailed off as he headed for the second-floor lunchroom.

I didn't want to think of his comment as a deliberate putdown. On the other hand, why would he assume that Frank influenced my work? Given the precarious condition of my marriage, that was ironic. The incident was a dramatic example of the persistent problem women had in trying to establish an identity that was not limited by custom or attachment to a man.

❧ ❧

On a Friday in mid-May the session adjourned for the last time, *sine die*— literally "without a day" on which we were ordered to return. We were not scheduled to meet again until the next regular session, eighteen months away, although a special session to deal with congressional redistricting was already being discussed. With mixed feelings I packed my few personal things from my desk to take home.

I had begun the session cautiously, telling myself that, if I was underestimated, it would give me time to learn while no one expected much from me. In hindsight, I realized my learning period had not lasted long. I had made my mark as a freshman legislator who was "a quick study," as one newspaper reported, and ended the session recognized as a lawmaker who was willing to work hard and take tough stands. In fact, the reporters covering the Legislature included me with other "most outstanding freshmen." It was a good beginning. I hoped I had fulfilled what *The Oregon Voter*, a conservative publication, had said about me before the session, "... those who enter floor debate or committee argument with her should be prepared."

As I left the Capitol building, it was sad to say goodbye to my colleagues and the House staff. It was especially hard to say goodbye to Keith Skelton. We'd developed a unique relationship. We'd shared our histories and found we both were having marital difficulties, but we respected each other's family obligations and never expected time or attention from the other. Both Democrats, we often voted differently, but we never questioned each other about legislation. I felt a strong attachment to Keith, and he seemed to feel the same way toward me. As he and I parted at the end of the session in mid-May, we admitted our mutual dismay at not being able to have an opportunity to see each other, or even to talk, for that matter. As I left the Capitol I knew I would miss him.

Driving to Portland on that last day, I shifted my thinking to what lay ahead. The summer months would be catch-up time, and then I'd be back in my classroom at David Douglas in the fall. After that, a reelection campaign in 1966. And law school to complete, and the bar exam to study for. Dian would graduate from Stanford, John from high school, and Randy from junior high school, and Jo would finish the tenth grade, all in the next year.

And Frank and I would have to accept the end of our brief marriage. We'd hardly seen each other during the session. He never came to the Legislature and was on his sailboat most weekends.

When I told Frank I thought a break would be best, he did not seem surprised, only disappointed. I was disappointed, too. Political creatures that we were, we talked about the effect a divorce might have on my reelection and on what he might decide to do in the future. We agreed he would file the necessary papers as the petitioner. I would file no response, and he would take the divorce by default. It would be as simple as possible.

Frank had been patient and good-humored about suddenly becoming a stepfather to four lively children, but I knew he'd had doubts about what he was taking on. He saw himself as, first, a speech professor; second, an ardent sailor; third, a politician. "In sailing, as in life," says the writer Richard Bode, "momentum is a valued commodity, the secondary source of power that keeps us going long after the original source has disappeared." I think Frank at first saw his marriage to me as adding to his political momentum. I was working on a master's degree in politics, had been elected to the local school board, and had many contacts in the community. Not that that was Frank's primary motivation, but our marriage would be an asset for him if he ran in east Multnomah County. When we both decided to run for the Legislature in 1962, it was with great delicacy that I preempted the choice for a House seat, while he then ran in the more difficult race for the Senate. While neither of us had won, my identity as a candidate for the House was well established. Two years later, in 1964, I had won with his unquestioning and important support. I was exceedingly grateful for that.

With the divorce, he would regain his independence and personal autonomy. He could choose to live anywhere and run for public office anywhere without bumping into his wife's political activities. He could think of it like a sailor— as taking a different tack and changing directions. He'd be making a transition and building momentum again. He seemed to be at peace with our mutual decision, and he would remain a friend to us all.

Chapter 8

Seasoned Legislator, New Lawyer

After a welcome and relaxing Christmas vacation in Mexico after the fall 1965 semester in law school, it was good to get us all home and back in school again. *It's all downhill from here,* I thought. One last semester of law school, the bar review, the two-and-a-half day exam—and I'd be a lawyer. The second semester of my high-school classes would be devoted to cramming as much information as possible into my departing seniors. My life was just the way I liked it, organized and predictable.

Then wouldn't you know it? Just when everything is running sweetly and we're coasting along, there's a sudden, surprising interruption that throws everything off kilter. That's how I felt when the children's father filed a lawsuit for a change of custody of the two younger children. I searched my mind for some basis for the action and concluded it was Bill's way of bringing pressure on me to agree to a reduction of his already-meager child support. Or did he think my divorce from Frank somehow made me a less fit mother? Whatever the reason, I had no alternative but to get a lawyer and counterclaim for an increase in child support. The legal proceeding was a time-consuming mental, emotional, and financial strain I could ill afford. What a stupid move he'd made! Just before the case was scheduled for trial, he abruptly dropped his petition, but I wasn't about to drop my counterclaim, which I suspected was his hope. The court awarded an increase in child support for the two youngest children.

By this time the end of my last semester of law school was near, and I was looking forward to getting final exams behind me. It had been a long four years, yet it had passed in a blink. Only one other woman had survived the grueling course—Nancy Carter, with whom I shared a double desk in the third- and fourth-year classes. Only twenty-two of the original one hundred freshmen remained, although another twenty or so had joined us as transfers or returning students. We were the first class to graduate with a new school name and affiliation: Northwestern School of Law, Lewis and Clark College.

While I studied for the bar exam, Dian and Glen were in Hawaii training for a Peace Corps assignment in South Korea. John, along with his friends, was investigating options for military service. If he enlisted for three years, he would train for specific duties. If he waited to be drafted, he'd have two years'

81

enlistment, but he'd get only basic training and then be sent for combat. Either way he would end up in Vietnam. He chose to enlist for three years with the Army, studying and working in communications. John and I had talked about the possibility of his being a conscientious objector, but we knew he was unlikely to meet the religious requirement. I assured him of my support if he went to Canada to wait out the war. His answer: "Mom, I can't do that. All my buddies are going in. I can't let them down."

By the time the bar exam came in July, everyone in the family was off in different directions—Jo had gone to my mother's in Chicago and then on to Virginia to my sister's family, and Randy was at sports camp. John was in basic training at Fort Lewis, Washington. In spite of all the distractions, I thought I was fairly well prepared.

The exam was held in the cafeteria of Salem High School. I lugged all my papers, books, and outlines to a motel room about a dozen blocks from the school and holed up there for the two and a half days of the exam.

Monitors distributed each essay problem by turning it upside down in front of us; the timekeeper told us when to start. The typewriters began slowly at first, picking up noisily as more began to write. I chose to write longhand because that's the way I'd taken all my exams in law school. I wrote more or less in rhythm with the typewriters, trying to cover every angle of the legal issues as they flashed through my mind. Then came a sharp "Time!" and the typewriters were abruptly silenced, almost as an orchestra concludes a piece when the conductor brings his baton down. I never knew thirty minutes could pass so quickly. At noon on the third day, I climbed into my trusty station wagon and headed home. For better or worse, I'd taken and completed the bar exam.

August passed quickly. I spent days on the ski boat with Jo and Randy and their friends. We often camped on Lemon Island so we could ski early in the mornings when the water was calm. By this time Keith's divorce proceedings were moving along, and he had rented an apartment in Eugene. He came to Portland on weekends, often with his younger son Tom. In the midst of our leisurely summer, a few thoughts still gnawed at me. What would happen to John after basic training? How would Dian and Glen fare as part of the first Peace Corps group to go to South Korea? Had I passed the bar exam?

I would not know the answer to that last question until the first Monday after Labor Day. Nancy and I agreed that as soon as she knew the results she would call my high school and leave a message to call her. When the message came I walked to the office phone with intense suspense. Nancy had passed the bar exam. I had failed.

While disappointed, I felt strangely resigned. It was not final, not like when Dr. Wingert rejected my request to work on a doctorate in political science. I simply needed to let the time pass and work to make the outcome different next year. The events of this year—fighting the custody suit and getting through the many graduations, worrying about the new adventures waiting for Dian and Glen, and my serious concern for John—all these had taken their toll. I felt the same disappointment I'd felt after my first election defeat. I hadn't been prepared.

I had missed a passing score by less than one point. That was within the range permitting a challenge, but I had no intention of challenging the grade. I felt proud that I had been able to do as well as I had done, had kept my mind on the law amid all the distractions. This would be a practice round, I decided. The next opportunity to take the bar exam would be the following summer. I'd be there.

With everything else that had gone on that past spring, the primary election had been only a minor bump in my life. I had no Democratic opponent—that's what one stellar campaign will do. There was only one major decision facing me: whether I should continue to use the name Roberts or return to Betty Rice, as I had been known when I first won election to the school board. I had come to be known in the school district as Betty Rice Roberts. Political advisers thought retaining Roberts was imperative because the name was well known to voters. At first I felt troubled by this idea. When Frank and I were married I'd thought I had to change my name according to custom, but it was the election, not the marriage, that had permanently established my identity as Betty Roberts. In the end I decided that the voters had, in effect, named me, and so I would keep that name.

That decision was unexpectedly empowering. I knew male legislators who had been married two, three, or even four times, and none had ever had to make a decision about changing his name. With my unchanging name I was, in that respect, as powerful as any of them. I would never have another name, and some years later I would help change the law to empower other women to choose whether to keep a birth name or a prior married name, or take a new married name.

I won the general election in November with little campaigning. On Thanksgiving Day we had dinner with Private John Rice in the mess hall at Fort Lewis, Washington. He was to leave soon for communications training.

❧ ❧

The opening ceremonies of the 1967 Legislature were even more impressive and grand than those of the previous session. The gallery of the House chambers was packed, and the House floor was a sea of people. A crowd was gathered around the television sets outside the House chambers. Then the parade of elected officials began. First the senators walked down the center aisle, followed by the Supreme Court Justices, then the statewide elected officials, and finally the outgoing Governor, Mark Hatfield.

Ordinarily the newly elected Governor, Tom McCall, would follow, but not this time. Instead, McCall's mother, Dorothy Lawson McCall, marched down the aisle, carrying herself like the well-bred Bostonian she was, escorted by an Oregon National Guard officer in full-dress uniform. She exuded the air of a true matriarch at the proudest moment of her life. Some thought her presumptuous, but I thought, *Now, there's a real mother.* She would not let her son's finest hour pass without her own display of support. After being announced by the Sergeant at Arms and escorted into the chambers by four legislators, Thomas Lawson McCall proceeded down the aisle, shaking hands and speaking to legislators as he moved toward the front of the chambers and the podium.

The Republican success in regaining control of the House in the previous session had been largely the work of Bob Packwood. He had traveled the state teaching campaign strategy to Republican candidates. His efforts had paid off even more handsomely in the 1966 election by widening the margin between the House Republicans, who now numbered thirty-eight, and the twenty-two Democrats. Packwood readily shared his ideas with anyone regardless of party, as he confidently proclaimed, "Give me a district with five-percent Democratic majority and I'll elect a Republican every time."

His personal appearance was nondescript, but Bob was a consummate political junkie and a hard infighter. He felt the challenge even more keenly if the playing field were tilted a little against him, because it gave him more personal satisfaction, as well as more political respect and clout, when his candidates won. I respected his knowledge and admired his successes. I didn't know then that one day I'd see his campaign strategies up close and personal.

The Senate, despite its majority of Democrats, was once again under control of a coalition of Republicans and conservative Democrats from the coast and southern Oregon districts, effectively giving Republicans control in both houses. Both *The Oregonian* and the *Oregon Journal* were critical of the eleven Republicans in the Senate who had again agreed to deliver enough votes to make Debbs Potts—a conservative Democrat from Grants Pass who thought, talked, and voted like a Republican—President of the Senate in the new session.

The newspapers complained that Portland suffered under the coalition Senate leadership and that Tom Mahoney, the only coalition Democrat from the Portland metropolitan area, did not adequately deal with issues of concern to his constituents. Republicans were admonished to "improve their record by refusing to join in the kind of ineffective legislating, which the coalition so often had represented." The "ineffective legislating" was code for the practice of holding bills in committee in order to put pressure on legislators to vote a particular way rather than considering the legislation on its merits.

No woman served in the Senate in 1967. Alice Corbett, who had been in the Senate for two terms, ran instead for county commissioner in Multnomah County. There were only five women in the House. The female incumbents were myself, Republican Fritzi Chuinard, and Democrat Grace Peck. Shirley Field and Beulah Hand had run for the Senate and lost. Two new women, Marva Graham and Connie McCready, both Republicans, were positive additions. I readily accepted them as capable colleagues. It was a compliment when a lobbyist told me Marva was the Republicans' answer to Betty Roberts. Connie, a former newspaper reporter who was married to an editor at *The Oregonian*, exhibited a good sense of humor—a quality lacking in the women of the previous session.

Frank had successfully run for an at-large House of Representatives position covering all of Multnomah County. I congratulated him on his win and welcomed him to the Democratic caucus, while noting a sense of pride on his part, and relief on mine. We were both in the Legislature, but neither of us would be encumbered by the other's presence. While some may have thought it odd, particularly because Keith and I continued to be together publicly,

Betty Roberts on the floor of the House of Representatives (Photograph by David Falconer, from *The Oregonian*, January 15, 1967)

Frank and I were at ease with our friendship and independence—a status that was returned to us by the divorce.

One of my first important tasks was to figure out how I was going to juggle my legislative work with studying for the bar exam in July. Not passing the exam the first time was no failure, only a setback, but this time I had to be successful. The best time to study would be evenings; the best time to mentally review would be on the morning commutes to Salem. Beverly, my secretary, who'd never learned to drive, would hold my outlines while I recited them to her. I told her, "You'll have to be sure I don't miss anything." As it turned out, Bev was quite a taskmaster, making me recite the outlines meticulously. It was often amusing because she didn't understand what the words meant; she just made me follow the script as she enjoyed her cigarette and coffee during our morning commute. Sometimes she would stumble on a Latin phrase, such as *res ipsa loquitur*, and ask what it meant. That gave me an opportunity to explain in lay terms, deepening my own understanding. Often she would chuckle in her deep voice and say, "Well, I'll be damned. Why don't they just say so instead of making it so hard?"

I was assigned again to the Education Committee, where I would try to get the kindergarten bill passed again, and to the State and Federal Affairs Committee, this time as Vice-Chairman, where Bob Smith, Republican majority leader, was again Chairman. In reality a Vice-Chairman has little power. Bob Smith and I got along fine, so long as we respected each other's roles in our own parties. I teased him some about letting me take over when he couldn't be there. He said, "Sure, just like having an alligator baby-sit my children." Then he said, more seriously but teasing right back, "Betty, if there is ever a time when I can't be here, there will be no committee meeting."

I was assigned also to a new committee, Planning and Development, where Chairman L.B. Day assigned me to chair a subcommittee to consider a proposal to create a Sea Grant College at Oregon State University. My work on that proposal was extremely satisfying and ultimately successful. The proposal had both environmental and economic significance and, with the professors from Oregon State working with us constantly, it was a great learning experience.

The major goal was to get state funding, demonstrating Oregon's commitment to the program to the decision makers in Washington, D.C. Once approved by our subcommittee, the proposal went back to the full committee for approval. Then it had to go before that awesomely powerful Ways and Means Committee for a hearing. I led off the testimony there, explaining why the proposal was important for the whole state of Oregon and urging Ways and Means to provide the necessary funds. The proposal was finally passed by both the House and Senate. I was delighted to have my fingerprints on something so important, evidenced some twenty years later by a ceremony at Oregon State University recognizing me among others as a Sea Grant Pioneer.

One of the most volatile of the bills to come out of that session was the famous "beach bill," which would preserve public use of the Oregon beaches. It all started when some coastal property owners, taking advantage of deeds that read that their property extended "to the high tide mark," barricaded off a portion of dry-sand area that had traditionally been in public use. The bill expanded on an earlier law that provided for public ownership of beaches between low- and high-water lines but still allowed for private ownership of the dry-sand area between the high-water line and the vegetation line. The Highway Commission, then the custodian of state parks, introduced legislation to clarify the public's use of the beaches.

House Bill 1601 was both complex and controversial. Coastal legislators opposed it, along with a few inland Republicans, but it was strongly supported by both Governor McCall and Bob Straub, our Democratic State Treasurer. Debate on its many amendments prompted heated political battles. Representatives Lee Johnson, a Republican, and Jim Redden, a Democrat, worked hard to achieve a compromise. And the governor took his famous walk on the beach to see for himself the setback lines for zoning.

In the end the Legislature passed the bill, which guarantees public access to the state's beaches and establishes an easement on all beaches between the low-water mark and the vegetation line. In the governor's view—and mine—this was a proposal for all the citizens of Oregon and for the future. With its passage the stage was set for Oregon's active efforts on environmental protection, which would become stronger as environmental legislation was introduced and debated in future sessions.

There was little concrete activity on women's issues, but seeds were being sown. One bill in the Ways and Means Committee proposed independent funding for the Governor's Commission on the Status of Women, which operated out of the governor's office. It did not pass. Another, which particularly caught my eye, would allow counties to offer family planning services to women on welfare. This bill was an odd sign of the times. Its primary purpose was not to benefit women, but to benefit the state, to save taxpayers from supporting more children on welfare. Nonetheless, it was recognition that more effective birth control techniques for women were now a legitimate part of family planning efforts.

The birth control pill had made its debut in the United States in 1960, only seven years earlier. And it had been only two years since the United States Supreme Court had said, in *Griswold v. Connecticut,* that a state's prohibition of artificial contraceptives violated personal privacy rights.

The family-planning bill was introduced by Representative Joe Richards of Eugene, who was a board member of Planned Parenthood. It included a provision that permitted County Health Division employees who objected to birth control on religious or conscientious grounds to refuse to give out family-planning information. Welfare recipients also were not to be forced to use family-planning services. Other language in the bill stated, "County employees engaged in the administration of this Act shall recognize that the right to decisions concerning family planning and birth control is a fundamental personal right of the individual." The significance of this important precedent was not lost on me, for I believed a woman should have a choice in matters of family planning. Making it a "personal right" was an idea just dawning on women. I was glad the bill passed, but I could not then foresee the relevance of this idea to the future debate, nor the debate's potential explosiveness.

There were few other bills explicitly addressing the needs and concerns of women. During the session, Harold Hughes, a reporter covering the legislature for *The Oregonian*, wrote an article headlined, "Dedicated Male Hunts In Vain For Legislative Bills Giving Aid To Women." He wrote, "It is easier to find a woman wearing a below-knee skirt at the Oregon Legislature than it is to uncover a bill that gives aid and comfort to females." Citing a child-protection bill of mine that would prohibit females under the age of eighteen from performing as go-go dancers, Hughes opined that the bill would discriminate against women. He missed the purpose of that bill by a mile.

Among other bills he deemed discriminatory was one that would have prohibited a woman from using "Mrs." and her husband's name on a ballot for election, and another that would have prevented the wife of a governor from succeeding him in office. To my mind, neither of these was a "women's bill" as such. The first was intended to prevent voter confusion. The second would deny voters the right to make their own choice. In contrast, Hughes gave Governor McCall credit for seeking funding for the Commission on the Status of Women, rather than continuing it in the governor's office, where it had no permanent life of its own.

Another newspaper item, "Prejudices Gone, Women's World Improving," quoted a member of the Governor's Commission on the Status of Women who reported that there was an increase in the number of jobs available to women, but concluded that a woman's success in getting one of those jobs "depends on her level of education." The commission member thought it was wise for women to continue their education "not only for personal enrichment, but to withstand the mounting stresses and tensions of our times toward the end of maintaining sound mental health." This was all well and good, but my experience had shown me a more practical reason for education than personal enrichment or mental health. Women needed to be educated to work outside the home so they could help support the family and develop some measure of financial independence. I thought the commission was espousing a version of the attitude of my children's father—that while it may be acceptable for a woman to get an education, it was not acceptable for her to use that education in a financially productive way.

The commission's report confirmed something I was observing on my own. The growing awareness of discrimination was bringing out feelings of ambivalence on the part of women and women's advocates. The Governor's Commission's first report, in 1965, had stated, "... the law generally does not need implementation or change," but it went on to point out that there was "discrimination against admission of women in many fields," and that "lack of adequate training keeps many women in work far below their potential."

The 1965 report strongly criticized the business community for discriminating against women in offering promotions and for maintaining the policy of not hiring both husband and wife in the same firm even when both were qualified, a policy that held also in education, particularly higher education, and in government. The commission was also troubled by the fact that businesses did not offer training programs for women equal to those for men, and that they often hired widows, divorced women, and single women who were heads of households before hiring married women.

The same report recommended changes in insurance rates and inheritance laws and an increase in the minimum wage from $1 to $1.25 per hour. It also called for distinguishing women from minors in labor legislation, on the grounds that their interests and needs were different and thus required different laws and policies. None of those proposals was addressed in the 1967 legislative session.

I had my own ambivalence. At times I was critical of women for not being more assertive, for not pursuing an education, and for allowing themselves to be, in my perception, dependent members of society rather than contributing members. I was smug in my belief that if I could do it, other women could do it, too. Still, I had to admit it had been hard to buck the obstacles that I had repeatedly encountered. And I realized that not many women had had a mother like mine, who learned to work and support her family and then learned how to progress into other jobs, giving me a good example to follow.

During this session, Senator Ted Hallock introduced a bill that would decriminalize abortion and allow the decision to be made by a woman and her physician without any other conditions. In addition, a request was made on the floor of the Senate for an investigation into an alleged "travel package" whereby a woman could travel to Japan for an abortion. The request was apparently for the purpose of determining whether there was any criminal activity involved. Senator Hallock's bill did not receive a hearing, nor did any committee take up the investigation request.

On the national level, the National Organization for Women had been founded in 1966, with Betty Friedan as its first president. Its stated objective was to provide a mechanism with which women could pressure government to adopt laws and policies to redress inequities in the law and affirm women's legal rights. While there was no local NOW chapter yet established in Oregon, there was discussion about the need for women to organize to challenge unfair laws, of which archaic abortion laws topped the list.

Senator Hallock's bill was ignored in the Oregon Legislature, but Colorado passed legislation that year decriminalizing abortion. Other states took up the issue with various proposals in their legislatures, and court cases challenging restrictive criminal statutes became regular news. My interest heightened. I had a feeling this issue was not going to go away.

❧ ❧

The challenges and pleasures of the legislative session were abruptly interrupted in May, when John came home on military leave with orders to go to Vietnam. I had known it was inevitable, but confronted with reality I became frightened. The United States had sent more and more troops to Vietnam, and by 1967 the troop level there had reached a half-million. We were in a full-scale war.

The most ardent and disruptive of the many antiwar protests were occurring on college campuses. These student demonstrations, often accompanied by the burning of draft cards and American flags, galvanized the public into factions for and against the war. I was firmly planted among those against, as I had been ever since I'd studied the U.S. involvement in Southeast Asia with my high school students. It was incomprehensible that my son could be going to war. My worst fears had come to pass.

Understandably anxious and frightened, John wanted to have a private medical check-up because of stomach problems and an old football knee injury. He saw a doctor in Salem, who discovered nothing serious enough to merit reporting to John's superiors. He would go to Vietnam. There was no one to help, no appeal to be made, no action to take, no way to protect my son. Helplessness tore at my insides. John would be at war for thirteen months. At best he would return with bad memories; at worst—I couldn't think about it.

Family and friends gathered at the Portland Airport to see John off and wish him well. I wondered if I would see him again. He gave me a last hug and said, "Mom, don't worry. I won't kill anyone."

My wonderful, peace-loving son to the end, I thought. Through tears I said, "Don't say that, John. You must do what you have to do to come back." I wanted to take his place on the plane.

The night before Memorial Day he called from a military staging base in Oakland, California, to say his unit was leaving the next morning. How ironic that my son left for Vietnam on the day set aside nationally to honor the men and women who died in our country's wars. Was that an omen?

A Memorial Day service was scheduled in the Oregon House. I asked the Speaker to excuse me for that period of time and sat on a bench on the Capitol lawn, trying to control my fear. I wondered about mothers with sons in Vietnam and mothers whose sons had already died. How could a mother bear that? I was sure I would hate my country if John did not return from that unnecessary and dishonorable war. How could Communism in a small Asian country be a threat to the power of the United States military and economy? Communism, in the context of the Vietnam War, was not worth my son's life.

My emotions turned from fear to anger to rage and finally to frustration, as I realized there was nothing I could do. Still, I hoped that in some mystical way my thoughts helped John control his fear and gave him strength to face whatever lay ahead. I could only repeat in my mind, "*Come home. Come home. Come home.*"

Dian and Glen wrote often, describing their primitive living conditions in South Korea. The winter had been bitterly cold. Their house had two rooms— a bedroom, heated by placing hot coals under the floor, and a dirt-floored kitchen. There was no indoor bathroom. They had the help of a Korean woman who put the coals under the bedroom floor, prepared their breakfast, shopped for food, and cooked and served their dinner.

Glen and Dian both taught physics, Glen in a boys' junior college and Dian in a girls' high school. While Glen was accorded all the privileges of a Korean male, including dinners out with other men teachers, Dian, as a woman, was not accepted in those kinds of settings. I admired them for their courage and was proud of their dedication, but I wondered how their harsh existence would take its toll, and how they would endure. I worried about them as much as I did about John. It seemed to me the height of incongruity, or hypocrisy, on the part of the United States—that my daughter and son-in-law were in the Peace Corps in one Asian country while my son was fighting a war in another. I would live with that paradox for months to come.

≫ ≪

The legislative session dragged on over the issue of property tax relief, becoming the longest in history at that time. I had done everything I could for the issues I had worked on. Some had passed, but many more were dead, including the kindergarten bill and the criminal victims' compensation proposal again.

I turned my thoughts and energy to the bar exam and to making arrangements for the care of my two children still at home. Jo, soon to be a senior in high school, was trying to find work for the summer. Randy, fifteen, would go to athletic camp at the University of Oregon in Eugene, where Keith could keep an eye on him. I'd arranged to rent the apartment Keith had occupied during the legislative session. With careful scheduling, it would all work out.

The Legislature was still in session when the bar review began. I asked the Speaker to excuse me for the final days, promising to appear if my vote should be needed. After the review course began, I never went back to the Legislature that session. Somehow they managed without me.

I was the only woman taking the review course, and the only woman of the 208 applicants taking the exam that year. I had the best teacher in Oregon to tutor me for six weeks—Jena Schlegel, counsel to the House Judiciary Committee, whom I'd met through Keith. Jena was recognized as an outstanding lawyer. Just a few years earlier she'd made the highest score on the bar exam of all that year's applicants. She'd expected that the Supreme Court, which certifies successful candidates to be sworn in as lawyers, would post the scores of the exam publicly, as they'd always done. But that year they changed the policy and decided not to make the scores public. Jena and I wondered whether it was only coincidence that the practice stopped when a woman made the highest score.

Jena was a tall, slender, dark-haired woman with large brown eyes that revealed her outstanding intelligence as they exhibited an assurance of not missing a thing. She had grown up in Oklahoma, not far from my hometown of Wichita Falls, Texas, giving us a common background that made us instant comrades, although she was a good ten years younger. During breaks in our work we talked about our experiences in Oklahoma and Texas. Both of us had grown up poor and had worked hard to educate ourselves. We shared stories about how people in Oregon thought either that we had rich daddies with oil wells, or that we were stupid hillbillies. It was hard to say which stereotype we hated most.

Jena told me that if I passed the bar she would cook me the best black-eyed peas and okra I'd ever had. How could I miss with that as an enticement?

This time, as I finished the exam, I knew I'd done well. More important, I knew the law far better than I had the year before. I would be a good lawyer. Triumphantly I packed my car and drove to Eugene to join Keith in a small celebratory cocktail party with a few of our lawyer friends from the Legislature.

In September the official word came. Jena and I celebrated with black-eyed peas and okra, complemented with meatloaf, cornbread, garden-fresh tomatoes, and iced tea. The two of us congratulated each other and shared good laughs about our work together. We were in a profession few women had yet explored. We were cocky, exhilarated by the possibilities that lay ahead.

By then Keith had bought a house in Portland so he could establish the required residency in order to run for the legislature from Multnomah County the following year. His law practice was easily moved as his clients were mostly insurance companies, and he transferred his teaching to Portland State University. This was all very nice for me—so many personal and professional possibilities to contemplate.

                           ✻ ✻

The idea of running against Senator Tom Mahoney, who would be up for election in 1968, had been in the back of my mind all during the 1967 session. Mahoney, the coalition Democrat from Portland, had used strong-arm tactics in trying to get a sales tax passed, and he was noted for his arrogant and abusive attitude toward constituents and lobbyists. His gamesmanship in the final days of the session caused many Democrats, and some Republicans, to long for someone to run against him. It had to be someone who could win, for if Mahoney beat a well-known and well-financed opponent, he would be meaner than ever in the 1969 session.

I researched Mahoney's record at the polls and found that he was not popular with the voters, having received, as a rule, barely enough votes to be elected as one of a group of winners in the old multi-member districts. He had lost a couple of races, but had returned to win again in the next election. This would be the first time Mahoney would have to run under the numbered-position election system that had been instituted in 1965. He could no longer hide in a pack. Democratic Senator Bud Lent, who had served with me in the House in 1965, thought I could beat Mahoney and encouraged me to run against him.

Like my campaigns for the House, this election would be decided in the May primary because of the large Democratic registration in the county. I'd need to recruit many more volunteers for this larger race, and I'd need to raise more money. That would be difficult—lobbyists knew that if they contributed to a campaign against Mahoney and he won, he would make them pay dearly in the next legislative session.

I was excited by the prospect of beating Tom Mahoney, but I needed to reexamine my ideas about taking risks. I would have to give up my sure seat in the House. It would be a hard campaign, but winnable if I could apply the same energy and strategy to the entire county that I had applied to my east Multnomah district in the 1964 race. In 1968 I was staring into the tantalizing eyes of opportunity. The Senate race was the chicken wandering into the yard. I could seize the Senate race, wring the heck out of it, and make it mine. Or, to use another metaphor from childhood experience, I knew I could climb this tree to the top, and I knew I could climb down safely if I had to.

If I lost, I would be out of the Legislature. That was a disappointing prospect, but if I made a good showing I'd be a viable candidate for the next election. And I'd still have a fulfilling life ahead of me, teaching and practicing law. Finally, no matter what, my kids would still love me, and Keith would still be my friend and lover.

So what was there to lose? Only an election.

Chapter 9

Severing Past from Future

The year 1968 began, for me, with prodigious optimism buoyed by motivation and political ambition. My physical stamina, fueled with mental drive, seemed limitless. My campaign for the Senate was taking shape, although I hadn't officially announced yet. I had moved from public school teaching to Mt. Hood Community College, where I taught political science and business law. College teaching gave me a flexible schedule, which allowed this new lawyer to take a few cases, working out of a home office that consisted of a desk, typewriter, and telephone in a spare bedroom.

Our two Peace Corps volunteers would be home from Korea by summer, and John's duty in Vietnam would end about the same time. Keith had bought a bungalow on Mt. Tabor and was putting together a campaign for a House seat from Multnomah County. He'd transferred his growing law practice to Portland and was teaching at Portland State College. I expected 1968 to be a banner year.

Then, with unexpected swiftness, all that sureness and predictability changed to uncertainty and worry.

We were barely into January when the North Koreans seized a Navy ship, the USS *Pueblo*. The press speculated that it was the opening act to an invasion of South Korea by the North, or a diversionary tactic against the United States' involvement in the Vietnam conflict. I wrote to Dian and Glen pleading with them not to be martyrs by remaining in South Korea if they might be in danger.

A week later the news reports were even more unsettling. The North Vietnamese military, joined by Viet Cong guerrillas, had begun a massive offensive in South Vietnam, using some eighty-four thousand soldiers to attack dozens of villages and towns including Saigon. The invasion began on January 30, the beginning of the lunar New Year. While it proved to be a defeat for the North Vietnamese in military terms, the Tet offensive was a psychological blow to Americans who'd been lulled by upbeat propaganda from the Johnson administration. The most shocking news was that the Viet Cong had invaded the American embassy in Saigon.

John's last letter had come from Saigon. If he was in Saigon, he was in the thick of the battles. I wrote to him saying that I was worried and begging him to please write as soon as possible.

A letter from Dian gave a measure of assurance. The State Department had briefed them on evacuation plans, and they had no intention of staying if the North Koreans pushed the conflict further. Weeks went by, however, with no letter from John. I was glued to the evening news, trying to understand where the North Vietnamese were moving and where the battles were occurring. The scenes of battle, and of the dead and wounded on both sides, were too vivid. I worried, prayed, and hoped. Finally a letter came. John's unit had left Saigon three days before the offensive and "headed north." I suppose he thought it was some consolation for me, but going north! I knew what was north.

So began my 1968, a year that *Time* magazine would describe twenty years later in this way: "Like a knife blade, the year severed past from future." *Time's* hindsight analysis was accurate for those of us who lived it—it was a politically turbulent, potentially troubling year, a year that would bring a presidential election in which the major issue would be the U.S. involvement in Vietnam, and that would reveal the fault lines in a civil-rights movement that had turned against the peaceful approach of Martin Luther King, Jr. and promoted Black Power—and violence—instead.

My Senate campaign was a good distraction. I'd been undecided about whether to spend money for a poll, which was rarely used in legislative races in those days. But there were so many unknown factors in the race that I decided that the money would be well spent.

The polling report was not encouraging. It showed Tom Mahoney beating me in every category—gender, age, education level, and income. What support I had came from twenty-one- to thirty-four-year-olds, singles, college-educated people, voters with high incomes, and teachers and ministers.

Significantly, more women favored Mahoney than me. The report said:

> One of the political myths that is frequently espoused by both
> amateurs and experts is that a woman who is running against a man
> can expect to get a larger percent of the female vote. Although this is
> generally untrue, the nature of the office sought has a dramatic effect
> on the female voter. A woman running for the local school board or
> even the city council can expect a large percent of the female vote
> just because she is a woman. However, partisan offices such as the
> legislature often bring about an opposite reaction ... Betty Roberts
> runs almost even with Thomas Mahoney among male voters, but loses

badly among female voters. It is interesting to note that a large number
of female voters remain undecided.

Mahoney's strongest supporters said they knew his name and that he was
more familiar to them, while mine said (contradicting the polling numbers)
that more women were needed in public office and that I was more concerned
about issues. Our work was laid out for us.

Fifty-eight percent of the voters were undecided. Among the 14 percent of
interviewees who were judged to be opinion leaders, I held a wide lead, with
57 percent to his 14 percent; 28 percent of this group remained undecided.
That told me we would have to make the campaign important to those opinion
leaders and pick up a large number of the undecideds.

On filing day, another woman, Virginia Grant, filed for the same Senate
position. I was told she had been recruited to take women's votes from me.
That was not too troubling, for if women were not going to vote for me because
I was a woman, they were not going to vote for her, either. If Mahoney was
behind this, I thought, he might have outsmarted himself this time, because
Grant was identified with the same people in the Democratic Party as he,
and she would generally appeal to his voters. I welcomed her as an additional
distraction for him.

Workers from my previous campaigns pitched in again for the race, and
the Portland Teachers Association provided many more. Our goal was to
walk every precinct in Multnomah County, targeting only Democrats who
would be most likely to vote in the primary election. This meant covering five
separate House districts, so there was five times as much work to do. To raise
money I spent hours calling lobbyists and other potential donors. A group of
women campaign volunteers worked for weeks planning and carrying out a
gigantic two-week rummage sale in a rented storefront at a busy intersection
in east Multnomah County. The sale paid off handsomely in both money and
publicity. It would be the rare male candidate, I thought, who would ever
think of holding a rummage sale.

To begin reaching opinion leaders, we sent a letter, signed by a few well-
known businessmen, to members of the Portland City Club, an all-male
organization that concerned itself with civic issues. The letter quoted disdainful
remarks Mahoney had made about the City Club and described legislation he
had opposed that had been favored by the club.

Mort Winkel, a lawyer and Democratic Party activist, came up with an
attention-getting strategy. He suggested we get the facts about Mahoney's
failure to pay his federal and state income taxes for many years. That was

common knowledge among more experienced politicians, Mort said, but until then I hadn't known it. Mort's research revealed that Mahoney had failed to pay over forty thousand dollars in taxes between 1949 and 1963, that the federal government had filed liens four times, and that the state had issued warrants fourteen times and garnished his Senate pay on two occasions.

Armed with that official information, we scheduled a press conference just twelve days before the election. We'd made large posters listing the years and amounts of Mahoney's unpaid taxes as visual aids for the cameras. I said, "Mr. Mahoney has not only refused to share his tax obligation with his fellow citizens, but he has placed an additional tax burden on them because of the cost to the federal and state government in collecting his." Voters began writing letters to editors, which kept the issue alive until election day.

※ ※

While my campaign was going forward and the reports from my children in South Korea and Vietnam indicated they were still as safe as could be expected, national events were becoming more disturbing. On April 3, 1968, the civil-rights leader Martin Luther King, Jr., was shot to death in Memphis, Tennessee. He had gone there to support a garbage workers' strike. For many of us, the implications of the tragedy were beyond dismaying. A voice of reason in the civil-rights movement had been silenced. The reaction was rioting and the burning of neighborhoods in the black sections of major cities all over the country. That made for more horrifying news and pictures on the television screen every night as police officers moved in to try to quell the violence by using their own violence.

While King's death was a shock, I can't say the explosive reaction was unpredictable. There had already been violent confrontations between demonstrators and police in the streets and on college campuses. As the war wore on and the expansion of civil rights stalled, more young people were taking up the cause for civil rights and against the war. My own beliefs put me on the side of the demonstrators ideologically. I shared the frustrations that came with the feelings of powerlessness against authorities that continued to send our young people to war and, at the same time, did so little to promote fairness and equality between blacks and whites.

The presidential primary was also keeping Oregonians preoccupied with national politics, especially the ongoing war. The North Vietnamese offensive had been a psychological blow. We were tired of the war, and more and more people were seeing it as unwinnable. Support for President Johnson's reelection had diminished, giving encouragement to other potential candidates. Senator

Eugene McCarthy from Minnesota saw the opening and, running as an anti-war candidate, made an amazing showing in the New Hampshire primary by winning 42 percent of the vote, coming in just behind President Johnson. Seeing that Johnson could perhaps be beaten, Robert Kennedy declared his candidacy for president.

On March 22, Congresswoman Edith Green announced that she was backing Robert Kennedy. As *The Oregonian* reported on March 23, "Much of the heartland of the Democratic political establishment in Oregon has moved into the Robert F. Kennedy camp." I loved the anti-war, poetry-writing Eugene McCarthy, but his issues and support were not broad enough to win the nomination, much less the general election. Kennedy was the answer for those of us who wanted to throw our hearts and souls into beating President Lyndon Johnson at the convention and taking the election in November.

On March 27, Robert Kennedy appeared briefly in Oregon for a speech at Portland State University, where throngs of people gathered to chant their support and to demonstrate against the war. The police were out in full force to try to control the exuberant crowd. The polls at that time showed Kennedy over Johnson by 44 to 41 percent and Nixon over Johnson by 41 to 39 percent, together showing a large anti-Johnson vote in both parties.

Then came a thoroughly unexpected development. On Sunday, March 31, President Johnson made two stunning announcements: he intended to de-escalate the war, and "I shall not seek, and I will not accept, nomination of my party as your president."

In contrast to Eugene McCarthy, who had visited Oregon regularly during the primary, Robert Kennedy had not seen Oregon as crucial except as it might affect the California primary. He had not come back since his visit in March. When he did, in the last few days of the campaign, McCarthy's strong showing in Oregon appeared to anger him. And he was not pleased with the treatment he received in southern Oregon, where crowds heckled him unmercifully on his gun-control position. His reception in Portland was more friendly, but when Keith introduced him at a rally, Kennedy's demeanor appeared, to those of us who were backstage, to be one of fright, exhaustion, and barely controlled anger.

≫ ≪

With election day nearing, I knew my campaign was going well. As we knocked on doors and talked with voters, it was clear that Mahoney's questionable payment of taxes was helping us. Voters knew I had been the one who'd raised the issue.

Late on Friday afternoon, only three days before the election, local pollster Warren Waterhouse called me. He said that his latest poll showed I would beat Mahoney on Tuesday. He also said that "the boys," meaning the men who met regularly at a downtown restaurant to play cards, "are betting on you." He didn't mean they were supporting me. I thanked him for the information and said I'd wait for the voters to give me the real answer on Tuesday. I knew that if, in fact, people were making bets on the outcome of the race, that meant it was close. That weekend I received several contributions from lobbyists.

After the polls closed the early returns showed Mahoney ahead, but as more precincts were reported I began to edge up. East Multnomah County usually reported late, and that was my stronghold. Finally, the vote tally gave me the edge and I stayed there. It was close; I won by only 1,285 votes out of some 112,000. Virginia Grant had taken almost fourteen thousand votes. I silently thanked Mahoney for getting her into the race. I had spent $8,374 and Mahoney $9,654—a lot of money then.

Eugene McCarthy won the Oregon primary, Keith won his primary race for a House seat, as we had expected, and we were both elected delegates to the Democratic National Convention.

A week after the primary election I sat propped up in bed, watching the returns from the California primary on television. I anticipated a good night's sleep as soon as I learned the outcome. When it was announced that Kennedy had won the primary and that he would soon be addressing his campaign workers, I had to watch a little longer. It was, indeed, a happy time for all of Kennedy's supporters, who were celebrating at the Ambassador Hotel in Los Angeles. Kennedy's victory speech was exciting, and I knew we had a great candidate to support at the convention. And when he said, "And now it's on to Chicago!" I could have jumped out of bed and started the trip right then.

The camera showed him leaving the stage and then—pandemonium.

The celebration turned to shock. Then to anguish. Then, within seconds, to mourning. The televised scene of Robert Kennedy's assassination remains as indelible in my mind as the scene of John Kennedy's assassination in Dallas only five years earlier. It could not be happening again. But it was. Tragically, it was.

The impact of the assassination on the country, and on Democrats in particular, was staggering. It had a devastating effect on the mostly college-age young people who had traveled from state to state on behalf of the campaign. The charismatic Kennedy was their idol. He spoke about more than just the war. He spoke of gun control, protection of the environment, decent wages and living conditions for migrant workers. But his appeal extended beyond his position on the issues; he challenged our country to live up to its ideals. For the young people particularly, Robert Kennedy's death galvanized their commitment to change. Many of them would put themselves forward in his place to work for those changes through their own political careers.

The Democratic National Convention would go on without the only candidate who could have given Hubert Humphrey, Johnson's Vice President, a challenge for the nomination. Indeed, many felt Kennedy had had the nomination in hand with the primary victory in California.

≫ ≪

As Kennedy supporters tried to make sense of how to proceed at the convention, Keith and I were making plans for our own future together. It had been three and a half years since we met. We'd talked of marriage and how it would affect our children and ourselves. I'd had time to think about whether I wanted to be married again. Now it was decision time.

Dian and Glen would be home from Korea in July, staying with me while they looked for jobs and a place to live. John would be home also, before going on to an assignment in Germany. Ann, Keith's college-age daughter, was living with her father for the summer. They would need a place to stay when Keith began his planned remodel on his Mount Tabor bungalow. There would be a lot of people living very close together in my small three-bedroom house. All that prompted Keith to give me a greeting card that pleaded, "If you won't marry me for myself, please do it for the children." Given the circumstances that made sense, but this time I wanted to marry for love, not convenience.

I had not wanted to marry again until I had established myself as an autonomous, self-sufficient woman. Now I'd done that, and if I married, it would have to be for the joy of being with this man, and for no other reason. When Keith and I met I was a high school teacher, a school board member, a state representative, and a law student; now I was a college teacher and a lawyer and had just won a crucial campaign for the State Senate. Keith certainly could have no illusions that I would be anything other than my own decision maker.

Looking at my first two marriages, I knew this one would have to be different. We'd have to invent it. My first marriage had imprisoned me. The second one had shown me what a marriage could be when both partners have lives centered on similar interests and on work they enjoy together, but it also taught me that even a cordial side-by-side mutuality was not enough. More was needed.

Betty Roberts and Keith Skelton married on
June 15, 1968. Shown here some years later.
(Photograph by Claudia J. Howell, from *Oregon
Journal*, May 25, 1978)

For Keith and me, the children had to be an integral part of our marriage. That was promising as we watched our eight children interacting with respect and civility. We were attracted to each other physically, and we accepted each other; these are even more important requirements in midlife marriages. We shared the loving care that each of us put into our homes, and we willingly accepted responsibility for, and found joy in, life's everyday tasks. Keith and I saw ourselves as two whole people who understood and embraced every aspect of our separate lives, but who knew that combining our lives could be even more satisfying.

I told Keith that I would not change my last name ever again for any reason. Maintaining my independence meant maintaining my separate identity. It was important that when legislators, lobbyists, the press, and friends learned that we were married, they should know that I would keep the name Betty Roberts. Keith agreed.

A Unitarian minister married us on June 15, 1968, with Ann and Jo, our daughters, as our official witnesses, and our only guests, Ross and Shirley Morgan and Poly and Betty Schedeen, long-time political allies.

We mailed a letter to hundreds of colleagues and friends, as well as news reporters and lobbyists, announcing our happy event and stating our decision regarding my name. The letter included an explanation of the legal authority—an Attorney General's opinion cited in an opinion from Legislative Counsel—that allowed me to continue to use the name Roberts. We received many congratulations on the marriage, but our decision regarding my name met resistance. The first challenge came from the Oregon State Bar. Within a month, I received mail from the Bar addressed to "Betty R. Roberts Skelton." I did not conceal my anger when I called the secretary and asked him if he had read the Legislative Counsel Opinion attached to our letter. He said he had, but that it was not within his authority to recognize it. When I protested, he suggested I sue the State Bar. His arrogance called for action.

I wrote a letter to members of the Board of Bar Governors enclosing the Legislative Counsel Opinion. The letter concluded: "Since I intend to continue to be known as Betty Roberts in my political office, and all political activities, as well as in my teaching at Mt. Hood Community College, it would seem that to require me to use the name Skelton in my law practice would only accomplish what we wish to avoid, that is, confusion on the part of my clients and colleagues and perhaps some suspicion of misrepresentation. Since Mr. Skelton is also a prominent public figure, an attorney and a teacher, it would appear to be less of a problem of clear identity if I continue to use the name Betty Roberts in my legal practice also." I ended the letter stating that the board should consider the fact that "Mrs. Abe Fortas, the wife of a United States Supreme Court Justice, is an attorney in Washington, D.C., where she practices under the name of C. E. Agger. This seems to be a fairly significant precedent."

We won this battle, but there would be others. The Registrar of Elections called to say that I would have to be registered to vote in the name Skelton for the 1968 fall general election. I sent the Legislative Counsel Opinion to the Registrar, but he was adamant that he would not issue me a voter registration card unless I agreed to use the name Betty Roberts Skelton as a voter. I would be on the ballot as Betty Roberts, but if I wanted to vote for myself I had to register using the name Skelton. The rationale of that arrangement, if there was one, escaped me.

I gave in temporarily. I had more pressing matters on my mind. Dian and Glen had arrived home from Korea emotionally exhausted, and Dian was recovering from amoebic dysentery. We were heartily glad to see them. And John's return from Vietnam brought not only the happiness of a family reunion, but relief and thankfulness that my children were home and out of harm's way.

❧ ❧

In mid-August we headed to the Democratic National Convention in Chicago. The Republicans had just convened in Miami, nominating Richard Nixon for president on the first ballot. Oregon's Senator Mark Hatfield had been touted as a favorite choice for vice president, but Nixon chose Spiro Agnew, former Governor of Maryland, instead.

Being on the Democratic platform committee along with Senator Wayne Morse, I headed to Washington, D.C., for the committee's first meetings. We would then move on to Chicago for the committee's final deliberations and the convention itself. Keith, Ann, Dian, and Glen would join me in Chicago.

By this time Senator George McGovern had announced that he was willing to be a candidate for president. He had the support of Robert Kennedy's key advisors. These men hoped to pick up former Kennedy supporters and make McGovern the compromise candidate over Hubert Humphrey and Eugene McCarthy.

Senator Wayne Morse and Betty Roberts

For his part, Humphrey was firmly tied to the administration's views. His position on the Vietnam War was to "see that the Democratic platform does not repudiate the policies of President Johnson." That did not sit well with those of us who had been Kennedy supporters, and certainly not with the McCarthy camp, who proposed language in the platform on ending the war in Vietnam. Protestors carried signs that said "Dump the Hump" and "End the War Now." By the time the platform committee met in Washington, the press was reporting that Humphrey had enough delegate votes to reject the McCarthy plank on ending the war. The platform committee was indeed controlled by Humphrey supporters, but Kennedy's supporters had joined forces either with the McCarthy people or the McGovern people, and between them these two camps made a significant minority voice. They challenged much of the language and many of the positions taken by the majority. Finalizing the platform language on Vietnam was postponed until the committee's final meeting, which was to be in Chicago just before the convention began.

At one of the platform meetings in D.C., while Secretary of State Dean Rusk was testifying, a man came in the side door near where Senator Morse and I sat at the end of a long row of tables. The man, evidently an official of some sort, walked to the back of the hearing room and started across the room toward the center. Senator Morse leaned over to me and said, "Something's up." Just then a news reporter came to Senator Morse, and, touching him on the elbow, said, "Senator, the Russians have invaded Czechoslovakia." Morse nodded and watched the official walk up the center aisle to where Rusk sat at the witness table and lean down to whisper in his ear. Secretary of State Rusk, without any perceptible concern in his voice, said, "Mr. Chairman, with your permission I need to be excused." Amazing, I thought, that Senator Morse knew what had happened before the Secretary of State did. More amazing than that—I knew, too. The Soviet Union's invasion of Czechoslovakia was one more in the long series of crises that marked 1968.

No one was prepared for the atmosphere of distrust and violence that gripped the city of Chicago as the Democratic delegates arrived. As we neared the city center, we saw well-armed police with riot gear stationed on every corner. Rather than welcoming the delegates, the city was combat-ready, prepared to silence anyone who showed any inclination to protest. And yet the young people came, they protested, and they were beaten and arrested.

In a story in *The Oregonian* on Sunday, August 25, headlined "Democratic Convention Scene Has All Qualities of Nightmare," the columnist David Broder wrote that "bullet proof glass and barbed-wire fence are designed to protect the delegates from the world, but they also seal them in and create a mood of enforced captivity that does little to ease building tensions." Broder said that Kennedy people were "there as mourners" and that "the curse of Vietnam haunts the Democrats' hopes and troubles their conscience." He concluded that Humphrey was the party's "sacrificial offering to the angry forces raging in this convention, this city, this party and this land."

On Monday, the newspapers reported that growing numbers of Yippies, members of the Youth International Party, along with hippies and war protestors, were gathering in Lincoln Park and Grant Park, which lay along the shores of Lake Michigan a few blocks from the delegates' hotels.

The great division among the delegates became clear in the very first session on Monday night, as the Credentials Committee's report on seating delegates was challenged repeatedly. The same contentiousness was present on Tuesday night, when the Rules Committee made its report. When the debate on the platform plank on Vietnam was postponed until Wednesday, it was becoming ever more obvious that the convention was progressing the way the Humphrey supporters wanted it to. In the meantime, there were rumors that Senator Ted Kennedy of Massachusetts, the youngest of the Kennedy brothers, had accepted a draft to become a candidate, and that State Representative Julian Bond from Georgia, a young black man who was a rising star in the Democratic Party, would become Ted Kennedy's nominee for vice president.

On Wednesday the convention voted to include the Humphrey position on Vietnam in the platform, rejecting unilateral withdrawal of troops and requiring Hanoi to show some sign of good faith before bombing of North

Vietnam would be halted. On receipt of that information, the young people poured into the streets in protest. Harold Hughes, reporter for *The Oregonian*, wrote that he "witnessed the wild battle that raged in front of the Hilton Hotel during the afternoon and into the night." Some police wore gas masks and unsheathed their bayonets. "It was a fearful melee of tear gas, gashed faces, cracked skulls, hundreds of arrests, injured and exhausted police who sought to protect the Democratic headquarters and open the main artery, Michigan Avenue, in downtown Chicago."

Many of the delegates were being intimidated and threatened, too, and they were angry. Often the microphones of those challenging the Humphrey platform provision on the war were turned off so the delegates could not hear the other side of the debate. It was well known that Chicago's hard-line mayor, Richard J. Daley, had orchestrated the police department's brutal suppression of the protests. He also had people interfering with the convention's audio system and instructing the band to play when any demonstration broke out on the convention floor. The press complained of not being able to cover the convention. Some reporters were forcibly ejected from the hall, prompting CBS's Walter Cronkite to threaten a press boycott of the entire convention.

After returning to our hotel that evening, we learned that many young people had been arrested, and that lawyers were needed to represent them. We went to a meeting where hundreds of young people were being instructed on how to deal with the police force's violent crackdown. We had our convention ID tags on, and various buttons, either McGovern or McCarthy or both, and so were recognized as friendly to their cause. We stood next to some of the protesters at the back of the room. They spoke freely with us about what they had seen and heard. Cardboard buckets that would ordinarily contain take-out fried chicken were passed around for donations to help pay bail for those arrested. Not much money was going in, only a few coins—perhaps the demonstrators were worried they might need whatever they had to get themselves through the next few days. We made a contribution, and Keith and Charlie Porter, a lawyer and Democrat from Lane County who was known for his political activism, went to the police station to offer their legal services. They were told that they couldn't practice law without an Illinois license, but many Chicago lawyers were offering their services.

On Thursday came the nomination for presidential candidate. Oregon delegates voted for McCarthy on the first ballot, as we were required to do, but, as expected, Humphrey was overwhelmingly nominated on the first ballot. The nomination the next day of Senator Edmund Muskie from Maine for vice president was anticlimactic. The convention hall was still in turmoil.

We returned to Oregon with newspapers already predicting Nixon's election in November, and we resigned ourselves to that outcome. We would not be able to work for Humphrey because of his stand on the war and because of our bad memories of the controlled and manipulated convention.

❧ ❦

My campaign for the general election was easy because of the large Democratic registration in my county-wide district. Keith's was difficult. Fred Meek had represented the East Central District for many sessions and operated a well-known drugstore in the area. Keith had to run an aggressive campaign, with many people working to cover precincts for him every weekend. He and I were out campaigning every evening as long as there was daylight. Then we went home to eat dinner and work on remodeling tasks. We often cleaned our paintbrushes well after midnight.

Ten days before the election a Democratic poll showed that, while Keith was making inroads into Meek's support, he was still behind. Son-in-law Glen, applying his mathematical skills, determined that, if Keith continued to gain on Meek at the same rate, he would overtake him at precisely three o'clock in the afternoon on the Sunday before the election. While we all treated that analysis with humor and skepticism, it gave us encouragement. We worked even harder during those last ten days.

In the evening on election day we went to the television stations where the results were posted, to get the early returns. The first results showed Keith behind Meek, but not by much. He continued to trail slightly for most of the evening. At one point during the evening, Keith and Fred met in one of the television stations. Fred told Keith he had put on a good campaign and offered condolences. When we finally went to bed, Fred was still a few votes ahead of Keith.

A good politician never gives up until all the votes are counted. The next morning, on the way to his eight o'clock class, Keith heard a radio broadcast that said he had overtaken Meek and was seventeen votes ahead. But all the votes had not been counted, and there were absentee ballots still out. He called me from a pay phone to ask me to try to get more information while he was in class. It began to look better with each report. Finally, when all the votes were in, Keith had won by 406 votes, thanks to Dian, who, during two summers working at the Elections Division, had learned that no candidate at the time sent brochure material to absentee voters. She did that for Keith and it helped seal his victory.

There was not much on the national political scene to be happy about. Nixon had narrowly beaten Humphrey and, most surprising to Oregonians, Wayne Morse had lost his U.S. Senate seat to Republican State Representative Bob Packwood. Packwood had applied the campaign techniques he so liked to talk about, and he had been successful again.

We moved into the newly remodeled house on Mount Tabor in November. I served Thanksgiving dinner on a table made from sawhorses and a piece of plywood, covered with my best tablecloth, silverware, and candles. The floors were still plywood with a few area rugs here and there, and the walls were bare studs with foil-coated insulation batts glowing between them.

Christmas in the new house was even merrier. On Christmas Eve, Apollo 8 was circling the moon, reporting back to us on the bright loveliness of the earth.

1968 was history. No other year would match it for the political upheavals caused by the Vietnam War and the long-overdue outcry for civil rights for African Americans. Perhaps no other year would match it as a turning point for our country. Perhaps the only way to view the events of 1968 was to take the long view of Apollo 8 and hope for a brighter future for our country.

For me, no other year would ever match 1968 for the intense growth experience it had provided. I had become an experienced politician and a skillful campaigner, and I looked forward to enjoying more clout in the next legislative session as a senator. My list of legal clients was growing so fast I'd soon need a regular office. I was in a new marriage in a new home, and as our children were achieving the stature and responsibility of adulthood, I had a new freedom from the day-to-day responsibilities of parenthood. The investments I'd made in my education and my political experience in the last twelve years were now reaping vast returns in the form of security, a sense of achievement and a happiness I'd never known before.

If *Time* magazine's symbolic 1968 knife had severed our country's past from its future, it surely had done the same for me.

Chapter 10

Breaking the Silence: The 1969 Session

My first conversation with the President of the Senate was about toilets. Not exactly how I'd expected my first day to start.

As Beverly, my secretary, and I unpacked and turned my desk on the floor of the Senate into an office space—the only one I'd have for the time being—a page came up and said President Potts wanted to see me. I had heard that one of Debbs's best qualities as president in 1967 had been his attempt to make serving in the Senate comfortable for everyone. I wondered how he felt about making the Senate comfortable for a woman.

He got straight to the point. "Betty, I need to talk to you about something that is embarrassing, and I need your help." This was not an auspicious beginning. "You know there was no woman serving last session," he said, "so I turned the ladies' room just off the Senate floor into the office for the nurse. It's really more convenient to have the nurse close to the floor in case one of us old guys has a heart attack. I'm really sorry, but you will have to go up to the second floor for the closest public ladies' room."

"Debbs," I said, "I appreciate your explanation, but there are a lot of things more important to me than what restroom I use."

I knew that, like the men's room, the nurse's office had a speaker system so that anyone in there could hear the proceedings on the floor. I decided the nurse's office would continue to be my ladies' room, never mind what President Potts said. I figure when men, especially men in power, make dumb decisions on inconsequential matters, it's best to ignore them. If I'd balked at Debbs's decision, he would have had to ask all the male senators about moving the nurse, and it would have become a major issue, with me as the villain. Right off the bat, I would have been seen as wanting special treatment or being insensitive to the needs of the men.

It was no surprise that "potty politics" would become an issue everywhere as more women were elected to legislative bodies. Anna Quindlen, a nationally syndicated columnist, would report in 1992 that the few women then in the U.S. Senate had to use a restroom a floor down from the Senate chambers. But when Carol Moseley Braun, Diane Feinstein, Barbara Boxer, and Patty Murray joined Barbara Mikulski and Nancy Kassebaum in 1993, the so-called "Year of the Woman," they gained their own restroom just off the Senate floor. Quindlen concluded that "plumbing is power."

In my first "power" struggle in the Senate, Debbs and I both won. He thought I'd use the second-floor restroom, but I knew I'd use the nurse's office.

Acceptance by my colleagues in the Senate was a concern, but choosing to view it as the men's problem, I adopted an attitude of *Get used to it, guys. I could be here a long time.* My credibility was already established with my reputation as a no-nonsense, hard-working legislator who'd beaten a long-entrenched Democrat. Getting to know the Republicans and the coalition Democrats who would control the Senate again in the 1969 session, as they had for the last twelve years, would require time and patience. Breaking the coalition had been one of my main objectives in running against Tom Mahoney, but the defeat of just one of their members would not tilt power to the "real" Democrats for the '69 session. The regular Democrats had to accept the coalition again; I would have to learn to work with them.

⋟　⋞

The governor's address was, as always, the highlight of the opening ceremonies. This one was a Tom McCall masterpiece. McCall's towering presence, his Boston accent, and his clearly articulated vision for Oregon's future made his speech theatrical in its impact. It was in this speech that Governor McCall, a liberal Republican, issued his famous challenge: "The time to promulgate statewide land use planning and zoning is now." He proposed "the protection of our beaches, scenic riverbanks and recreation lands" to go hand in hand with economic development. Turning to social issues, the governor singled out citizens who had faced discrimination, including women who had been caused to suffer "by abortion laws that are callous tools of shame," and "young men in Vietnam who die or go to prison, and either way are cursed by their fellow Americans."

Governor Tom McCall—a dynamic personality and an eloquent speaker. (Photograph by Gerry Lewin. Used with permission)

Finally Governor McCall wound down to his eloquent conclusion: "So to the work of the session, each of us hopefully realizing that youth, nor resources, nor time are given us in unlimited quantities. There is just so much of each allotted to us to use as we may. Then the contract is dissolved." He concluded, "We reap together, for better or for worse, in sickness and in health, so help us God."

The governor's reference to abortion was welcome support from the highest level for those of us committed to changing Oregon's archaic law. As I passed Senator Ted Hallock's desk, I said, "Ted, I assume you are going to introduce your abortion bill again."

"No, you are," was his rapid-fire response. "I have to run for reelection next year, and that bill could be a real problem for me." I was delighted to take on the task.

Hallock's 1967 bill would have legalized abortions with no regulation other than a requirement that a doctor perform the procedure. The bill had not received a hearing. Following Colorado's liberalized law in 1967, New York, Alaska, and Hawaii had either changed their laws or were moving rapidly to do so. Newspapers and television were reporting regularly on the issue. Women from all parts of the country were aggressively addressing the issue of access to abortion. That first day, I went to Legislative Counsel's office to ask them to draft a similar bill for me to introduce.

I tried not to let the abortion proposal become all-consuming. Yet it was alarming to read about the history of abortion and the hideous experiences of women who had attempted self-induced abortions or who had gone underground in the United States or to Mexico to obtain abortions illegally. The fear, the danger, the aloneness, the pain, and the humiliation that so many women had endured in miserable silence was powerfully moving.

I'd started out thinking that the abortion issue had no significance to me personally. But then I recalled certain incidents in my own life that the abortion issue placed into a new light. I remembered the time I came home on a break from Texas Wesleyan College, and my mother told me she thought a close friend of mine was pregnant. She said that if that was true she'd try to help her. At the time I didn't know what sort of help Mother meant. I hated to pry, but given Mother's strong feeling that my friend might need help, I got up the courage to ask her. She vehemently denied being pregnant, saying she was "just putting on weight." That summer I went to see my friend again, but she was gone. Her mother told me she had moved to Amarillo to live with her sister. I never saw her again.

I remembered my sister's story from our childhood, about Mother mowing the lawn hard for several hours and then going to the hospital and having a miscarriage. Now that story took on new meaning. My brother had been born without a left hand, a heartbreaking experience for my mother. As Bob grew and achieved—becoming an Eagle Scout, a Sea Scout, and later, a successful architect and avid sailor—he and others rarely gave his so-called disability a second thought. But Mother hadn't known that would be his future, and there she was facing a difficult pregnancy after having three children. Now that I was working on abortion legislation, I concluded, she knew what she was doing when she mowed that great expanse of ground.

I myself hadn't planned to have four children, but I never would have considered an abortion even if it had been available. We had a secure family, and each child was a welcome new addition. Yet if I had become pregnant during my marriage to Frank, I would have arranged an abortion with no regrets, even if it had to be illegal. I'd tried the new birth control pills, but they hadn't worked for me—they gave me day-long nausea similar to morning sickness. By this time I was the major supporter of my children, teaching had become a vitally important part of my life and professional growth, and I was in law school. A pregnancy then would have jeopardized my ability to continue providing for my children and for myself, both financially and emotionally. Fortunately I'd never had to act. But as I worked on the abortion bill in 1969, I often thought, "What if?"

I concluded that the abortion issue *was* about me. And it was about every other woman in the world, for if women could not take charge of their own bodies, could not make their own decisions about having children, then they could not take charge of their own lives. This epiphany would profoundly change how I viewed my past life, and it would thrust me early on into what would come to be known as the second wave of the feminist movement. Happenstance—or was it grace?—had put me in a position of political power at just the right time.

Jessalee Fosterling, Executive Director of Portland Planned Parenthood, and Claudia Webster, of the Oregon Health Department, came to the Legislature in support of changing the law. They provided legislators with statistical information on the numbers of women who sought out their services, and they reported facts of actual cases they'd seen in their many years of experience working with pregnant women. Their knowledge was vital to the success of any proposal on abortion. We all needed to be educated on the issue.

Medical doctors, reporting only anecdotally (because abortion was illegal and statistics unavailable), explained to legislators that the procedure was safe when performed by physicians under clinical conditions. They reported instances in which women had become pregnant while suffering from debilitating conditions that a pregnancy would worsen. They told about times when very ill or dying women had come to them after botched abortions.

Psychiatrists discussed the mental impact of unplanned pregnancy on women, especially young women, who were ostracized from their families, friends, and communities, labeled "unwed mothers" or "wayward girls," and placed in facilities to wait out the birth of babies that would be taken from them and placed in adoptive families.

Senator C. R. (Dick) Hoyt, a Republican from Corvallis, also introduced an abortion bill, one that was different from mine. His goal was to end the confusion in the law, since criminal law permitted an abortion only if the woman's life was in danger, while physicians, under the Medical Practices Act, would face penalties unless the woman's health was in danger; and they could also be prosecuted under the criminal statute. His bill would allow abortions in cases of rape or incest, when the child would be born with a serious physical or mental handicap, or whenever necessary for the physical and mental health of the woman. His proposal would require written consent of a parent or guardian of an unmarried minor, or of a husband if he were living with the woman, along with other requirements surrounding the procedure itself.

Senator Hoyt was a kind and thoughtful man, but I had to tell him that I could not support his bill because of its restrictions. Allowing women who were physically or mentally ill to have abortions but denying them to healthy women was unacceptable. And the conditions in the bill that required a woman to jump through a continuing series of bureaucratic hoops—consent of another person, a doctor's certification, a second doctor's opinion and a hospital committee's approval—were outrageous, I thought, in their denigration of women. This was more than paternalism. It was a battle for male control of a uniquely female medical procedure. Senator Hoyt said he understood my concerns, but said that his bill was the most we could realistically get through the Legislature. Ultimately he was right, but I had to try to get my bill passed.

❧ ❧

Not abortion, however, but a proposed sales tax would be the first major item of Senate debate in 1969. Oregon was one of only a few states without a sales tax, although the debate had gone on at the Legislature for years. The way the sales-tax issue was used as a bargaining chip for legislation in the 1967 session, when Tom Mahoney had tried to strong-arm it through, had influenced my decision to run for the Senate. Now, although personally opposing the sales tax, I would vote for it to get the issue out of the Legislature and onto the ballot for a popular vote, certain that the voters would defeat it.

The measure was swiftly passed in the House and arrived in the Senate less than a month into the session. The Republican-Democratic coalition controlling the Senate could deliver only fourteen votes, from eleven Republicans and three Democrats. It would take sixteen votes to pass. The regular Democrats, as we called ourselves, met in caucus to determine how to proceed. It turned out to be a bitter battle that ended with the bill's passage, sixteen to fourteen. Al Flegel, a Democrat from Roseburg, provided the fifteenth vote, and I provided the deciding vote.

I asked permission to explain my vote for the Senate's official record. I said I was frustrated with the Legislature's obsession with the sales-tax issue, and that my vote was necessary to put the question to the voters and let the Legislature return to a responsible consideration of other important issues. I said I knew I would be castigated by my own party, criticized by my friends, and misunderstood by voters, but I would actively campaign against the sales tax in the coming election.

I expected criticism, but the anger of some Democrats took me off guard. At a political event that evening, Senator Vern Cook, with a drink in his hand, walked up to me and began berating me for my vote. He had been a vociferous opponent of the sales tax. His remarks drew the attention of Senator Ross Morgan, who had served with Cook and me in the House of Representatives, all of us representing east Multnomah County. Morgan had never liked Cook's confrontational style. Suddenly, instead of being face-to-face with me, Cook was face-to-face with Morgan, who was telling him exactly what he thought of his behavior. Morgan added that Cook knew my vote had been tacitly approved by the caucus, to which Cook gave some rejoinder I couldn't hear. The next thing I knew, Cook was sprawled on the floor and Morgan was walking away. Morgan had decked Cook right there, not in defense of me or my vote, but because of Cook's attitude about what had been thoroughly discussed in caucus.

I took some lumps myself, though none as physical as those Vern Cook had taken. At the next meeting of the Multnomah County Democratic Central Committee, a resolution was introduced and passed to censure me for my vote on the sales tax. While it's more fun to be congratulated, being criticized is a part of being a politician and legislator. The lumps contributed to my toughening process. The sales-tax incident was instructive to me about the resilience needed for other matters. Successful politicians have strong egos— they have to in order to survive the inevitable personal attacks with any degree of confidence and self-esteem. It helped that *The Oregonian* commended Senator Flegel and me for providing the votes as "practical," and added that the responsibility for the sales tax was "squarely ... with the Republicans."

The day after the sales-tax vote, the Senate Judiciary Committee scheduled its first hearing on the two abortion bills. I had been working hard in anticipation of this important day. Twenty-five witnesses, including psychiatrists, obstetricians, and representatives of mainstream religious groups, appeared before the committee to testify, nineteen of them proponents of my bill or Senator Hoyt's bill. The six opponents were four official spokespersons for the Catholic Church, an obstetrician, and a woman who defined herself as a housewife. Senator Hoyt led the testimony with an explanation of his bill, and I followed.

Most of the testimony was simply for or against easing the law against abortions in general. But a major issue in the debate was the effect any change would have on poor women. Some witnesses pointed out that safe, legal abortions were readily obtained by women who had the money to travel to Japan. According to advertisements presented to the committee, an abortion there could be obtained for $1,300, including round-trip travel from Oregon. Women who could afford to leave the country could obtain safe and legal abortions, while women who could scrape together only a few hundred dollars, or who had no resources at all, faced such appalling choices as unlicensed "doctors," coat hangers, or potions of laxatives and herbs.

What is most striking about the debate from this historical distance is the lack of a distinct feminist perspective or analysis. The only groups at the hearing that could be called "women's groups" were the American Association of University Women, the YWCA, and the National Council of Jewish Women, all in favor of easing restrictions, and the Council of Catholic Women, which was opposed to any changes. None of the groups favoring abortion spoke to the principle of choice, to the idea that a woman should be free to make decisions about her own body. These ideas were developing in my own mind and the minds of many other women, but they were not yet fully formed. Those of us in Oregon who wished to reform the abortion laws argued from the economic and emotional aspects, and whether medical procedures were safe, rather than from any principle of women's rights.

My own statement to the committee reflects this. I emphasized that my bill was "by no means a woman's bill." It was important to appeal to the men because the fate of the bill was in the hands of the nine-member, all-male committee and a Senate with twenty-nine male members. In my presentation I emphasized the humanitarian character of the proposal, in testimony that today seems based on repugnant, centuries-old property laws (which were, to a large degree, still in place in 1969):

Any man who knows that if his wife or daughter is raped and becomes pregnant as a result, and that she is compelled to carry the pregnancy to term, knows this bill is for him. Any man who worries that he and his wife may create another child and she is physically or mentally unable to take care of another child, knows this bill is for him. Any man who knows his child will be severely deformed when born, knows this bill is for him. The point is that probably no man in this room would subject the woman he cares about to a compulsory pregnancy because every man in this room has the money to obtain for her a legal abortion, and is smart enough to know where to get the information.

In closing, I reported on a poll conducted by Senator Gordon McKay from the central Oregon town of Bend, which was predominantly populated by ranchers and people in the timber industry. Citizens there were no-nonsense, practical, and independent, and they lived close to the realities of nature. Among constituents responding to McKay's questions, 36 favored keeping the existing law, 119 favored Senator Hoyt's bill, and 123 favored repeal of all abortion laws. I mentioned the poll to rebut one opponent's statement that "a vocal minority was causing today's hearing." It was clear to me, and it was to become clear to the male legislators as well, that people who wanted an easing of the restrictions on abortion were a majority—and a large one.

The abortion debate in Oregon was calm compared to what was going on in other parts of the country. In New York, women representing the newly formed National Organization for Women, the October Seventeenth Movement, and a group called Women's Liberation, staged a protest at a legislative committee meeting in which only "experts"—all of them men—were scheduled to speak on proposed changes to New York's abortion law. The women, asserting that they were the true experts, demanded to be heard, but they were barred from the committee room when they shouted their objections at being called "girls" and "dear" by the male committee members.

In the hallway outside, a writer for the *New Yorker* learned that some of the women had had illegal abortions. Seven hours later, three of the women were allowed into the hearing room, where they talked about their experiences and asked for a hearing devoted entirely to the testimony of women. Later they told the *New Yorker*, "We're probably the first women ever to talk about our abortions in public." That was a major breakthrough. The fact that women would dare to talk about their abortion experiences, and to a group of men at that, forever broke the ugly silence surrounding the society-imposed degradation of women at a time when they most needed help.

I made it a point to send a copy of the *New Yorker* article to Senator Tony Yturri, the Republican chairman of the Oregon Senate's Judiciary Committee, who opposed any change in the abortion laws. I attached a note: "Tony, thought you'd appreciate more the hearing your committee had after reading this article!" The women in New York were right to question the all-male testimony. I was proud of those noisy women for demanding to be heard and for speaking about their own experiences. Women all over the country would be encouraged to be bolder. Surely that would help change the laws.

❦ ❧

Within the same week as the sales-tax vote and abortion hearing, a bill I had introduced that would prohibit discrimination in employment on the basis of sex had been assigned to the State and Federal Affairs Committee. This committee was often called the "burying ground" for proposed legislation. I concluded I could forget that bill, but Representative Connie McCready had introduced a similar one in the House prohibiting discrimination in employment on the basis of race. When I explained the fate of my proposal, she added the word "sex" to her bill, and that's the way it came to the Senate.

I went to see President Potts to tell him McCready's bill had passed the House almost unanimously, and asked him to give it a fair chance on its merits in the Senate. He said, "I don't like the bill and I won't vote for it, but I won't send it to State and Federal." I think he liked the idea that I had asked him for a favor, which acknowledged his power and put me in his debt.

At the Senate committee hearing, Representative McCready explained her part of the bill on race discrimination and I explained my part on sex discrimination. We appealed to the members' sense of fair play and argued our belief that in our free-enterprise system everyone ought to have an equal chance for a job. The issue turned out to be relatively non-controversial, but not without the jostling between us two women and the all-male committee. One asked if the bill would require him to hire women in his hay fields as he speculated about how that would change the old hayloft jokes. I had little patience for these kinds of remarks from the men, but Connie saved the day by bantering with the senator about who knew the best hayloft jokes. I told myself I needed to lighten up on these kinds of exchanges, but the issues were too serious for joking.

That bill and the abortion bill were the first legislation specifically for women, and I took the lead in both. It was a heady new experience to work with women legislators and lobbyists on issues of great importance to women. I was proud when the Senate passed the anti-discrimination bill, even though committee amendments had removed retirement, pensions, and insurance plans from the scope of the bill, and I was surprised when President Potts voted for it after saying he wouldn't. In 1969, we took what we could get. We were not yet aware of the magnitude of the task of securing true equality for women. But we were on the precipice and preparing ourselves to make the leap.

Surprisingly, it was my abortion bill rather than Dick Hoyt's that came to the floor of the Senate from the Judiciary Committee, thanks to the work Senator Bud Lent did behind the scenes. I was not happy with the amendments that had been made to get the votes. One required written consent of the husband if the woman were married and required the woman to have lived in the state for six months prior to the abortion. Another allowed private hospitals to adopt a policy against performing abortions, and a third required doctors to report abortions performed in the case of pregnancy resulting from rape or incest. Yet I accepted the amendments, which were not nearly as restrictive as those in the Hoyt bill.

When the bill got to the Senate floor for a vote on May 1, it was defeated in a fifteen-fifteen tie, lacking only one vote to pass. Close, but oh, so far. In the next twenty-four hours I tried desperately to line up a sixteenth vote for reconsideration, but I was unsuccessful. Then, with the session drawing rapidly to a close, and signaling a clear intent to do something to loosen access to abortion, the Senate Judiciary Committee passed Senator Hoyt's abortion bill to the full Senate, where it was approved with nineteen votes. The bill subsequently passed the House with an overwhelming fifty out of sixty votes. Senator Hoyt had been right. The men were willing to decriminalize the abortion procedure, but they wanted all the conditions that were in his bill.

Nevertheless, the accomplishment was monumental. I was proud of my role in putting compelling testimony before the committees, and of how hard I had worked. But there was much work ahead.

❧ ❧

I had my last run-in with the coalition late in the afternoon on May 23, 1969, the day the session was to adjourn. I was alerted by a lobbyist that, while a bill requiring pollution-control devices on motor vehicles had passed, the bill for funding enforcement of the law in the metropolitan area had not come out of the Ways and Means Committee. Neither bill was in a committee I served on, but the lobbyist spoke to me because I was from Portland and because he knew I favored pollution control. I watched for the funding bill as the remaining few from Ways and Means came to the floor. As adjournment drew near, I became alarmed. The Senate was in recess and most members were milling around on the floor.

I went to President Potts and said, "Debbs, the bill for funding the enforcement of the motor vehicle air-pollution control devices hasn't hit the floor yet. We can't adjourn without it."

"It's not going to be here," he said matter-of-factly.

"It's got to be here or we don't get motor vehicle inspection in the metro area. Why isn't it going to be here?" My impatience made Debbs want to escape, from the look on his face.

"Because Newbry doesn't want it."

I heard a voice behind me say, "That's right." I turned to face Lynn Newbry, Ways and Means Chairman.

"Lynn," I said, "we need that bill in the metro area. It doesn't mean anything to you in Medford."

"Maybe, maybe not. If you folks get it up there, next thing you know we'll be havin' those requirements in southern Oregon. It's not comin' out."

Looking him straight in the eye, I said with precision, "You son of a bitch." I was both surprised and gratified to have said those words so forcefully. I was angry that one person could single-handedly deny the metropolitan area a way to clean up its air pollution. Lynn ignored me, but I saw a slight smirk at the corner of his mouth. I concluded he took it as a compliment.

This incident dramatically defined how the coalition worked. The President of the Senate, a Democrat, had been elected by the Republicans, and he did their bidding. This was not a politically responsible way to run a Legislature. Someday we would have to regain a true two-party system in the Senate.

After that it was time to pack up our belongings and tally our victories and defeats. The Legislature had passed some of Governor McCall's proposals, creating a new Department of Human Resources and a Department of Environmental Quality—the latter a major piece of the governor's plan to protect Oregon's environment. We had approved a new Oregon Constitution, a major revision of the original, century-old one and the culmination of at least ten years of work by dedicated citizens. The proposed Constitution would be put to a statewide vote in 1970, along with a constitutional amendment to lower the voting age to nineteen, an issue supported by many of us who were concerned about our young men going to war in Vietnam without the privilege of voting.

❧ ❧

My thoughts turned to home and my law practice. Keith and I would soon celebrate our first wedding anniversary. We'd both had a good legislative session, accomplishing many of our goals and demonstrating our independent political styles, as evidenced by Keith's remark to a lobbyist who asked him to speak to me about a particular bill. Keith said, "Look, you're the lobbyist. You talk to her yourself." While we were different in our working styles and sometimes in our voting records, we were at each other's side at social events, secure in our public personalities and our personal relationship.

It seemed to me that I had lived through the hardest part of life—the growing-up years during the Depression, the conscientious efforts to become a mature young woman and then a good mother and housewife, and finally the not-so-gentle mental nudge to go back to school. These experiences were far away in time and yet still so much a part of me. They had led to my full participation in life during the turbulent decade now ending. In the past ten years I had become a teacher; received two more academic degrees; divorced, married and divorced again, and then married again; become a lawyer; lost one election and won three; served in three legislative sessions. Through all this I had raised four children who had become self-sufficient adults, and I had acquired four stepchildren. There had been a lot of grit—determination, resolve, toughness, and perseverance—in all of that. I understood grit.

My mother, still living on her own in Chicago, never let me think that I had been alone in those accomplishments. Every time I sent her pictures of graduations or news of my campaigns or serving in the Legislature, she would write back, "Betty, dear, you are so blessed, and I am so proud of you." That word of hers, "blessed," made me think about her unfailing belief in grace. I wasn't sure what grace was all about then. I thought it had to do with believing in oneself, willing oneself to succeed, and working hard toward distant goals. As I've become older, my understanding of grace has become clearer. It's less about personal willpower and more about trust.

My Unitarian minister, Dr. Marilyn Sewell, explains it well: "The nature of grace, then, is that we can't earn it or plot and plan to get it. Willpower is useless. We can't buy it. We have to humble ourselves and be willing to step out of the place that has always held us, however awkwardly."

As the 1960s ended I thought I'd probably used up my share of opportunities—my allotment of grace, if you will. I'd stepped—sometimes awkwardly—out of many places that had held me. But grace, I would learn, was following me still.

My life looked more settled than it had in a long time. I planned to continue to teach at Mt. Hood Community College until my law practice was more productive. I'd continue in the Legislature for as long as I could work on issues important to me. And Keith and I would continue to enjoy our big family.

I thought the future looked completely predictable. How wrong I was!

Chapter 11

Changing Times

By 1970 we'd left a decade of violence, assassinations, and war only to enter a new one that, at first, showed little promise of improvement. But change was everywhere. We could see it in the way our sons and daughters dressed in their tie-dyed T-shirts and blouses—the girls often braless—and let their hair grow long. We could hear it in the music mania of the Beatles and all the "garage bands" that were forming. We could smell it in the unique aroma of marijuana. Young people had turned to "flower power" with the same idealism and passion they exhibited at the National Democratic Convention in 1968. At the same time, they were moving from being the marginalized in a society that still, in many respects, favored conformity, to being the catalyst for change. They continued to protest against the war in Vietnam.

In late May newspapers reported that President Nixon would speak at an American Legion convention in Portland in September. That was sure to bring thousands of protesters to Portland for a demonstration—not a good thing for our incumbent governor, who was running for reelection against State Treasurer Bob Straub. McCall's staff and campaign committee began to search for ways to defuse the anticipated confrontation between protestors and the Legionnaires, where the police and National Guard would be involved. In August, McCall announced his plan to stage a rock festival similar to the Woodstock Festival in rural New York the summer before, to draw young people away from the demonstrations. This one would be called Vortex, located at McIver State Park near Estacada, a few miles southeast of Portland. The governor appealed to responsible adults, particularly elected officials, to join any of the young people who chose to march in demonstrations outside the convention. It was thought that our presence would inhibit both demonstrators bent on being rebellious and police who would want to retaliate.

Keith and I took part in one demonstration. I asked John if he wanted to go with us, but he declined in favor of Vortex. We marched with a few hundred other people. The only rudeness we observed were derogatory signs about Vice President Spiro Agnew, who had been substituted for Nixon as the speaker. We saw only a few police officers standing on the sidelines. The anticipated riots either were dissipated by Vortex or just plain flopped.

Ed Westerdahl, the governor's chief of staff, visited Vortex to see how things were going and reported that it was doing a good job of pulling attention away from those who wanted to urge the young people to go downtown to demonstrate. At one point a few young men tried to take the stage to make an appeal, but as they got close to the bottom of the stage, all of a sudden, young women all around them dropped their clothes, saying "Peace, brother, love, brother." Westerdahl said it was the most effective technique in nonviolence he'd ever seen.

⊱ ⊰

I wasn't on the ballot that year, but I couldn't escape political controversy. Representative Connie McCready was running for a position on the Portland City Council. She called to tell me that a sign posted in the newsroom of *The Oregonian* stated that henceforth reporters would refer to her as Mrs. Constance McCready and to me as Mrs. Elizabeth Skelton. I'd had a regular running battle with reporters over the use of "Mrs." All during the 1969 session my male colleagues would be referred to in newspaper articles as "Sen." and I would be "Mrs." When requesting that I be called "Sen.," I'd say, "It's the same number of letters. If you're trying to save space, you could use Ms." The reporters' answer was, "When our style manual changes, we'll change." Now it seemed that *The Oregonian* had completely and unilaterally renamed me. What made it even more galling was that my name is not Elizabeth—it is Betty.

I asked to meet with Richard Nokes, the editor. I showed him the Legislative Counsel's opinion that approved my use of the name Roberts for political purposes, and the Oregon State Bar's opinion saying I could use it for practicing law. I tried to explain to him that the name Betty Roberts was as much a property right as the name of any business or any person in the entertainment world. He protested a bit, so I decided I needed to be a little more persuasive. As I got up to leave I said, "Mr. Nokes, if you run any reference to me other than as Betty Roberts you'll have a lawsuit on your hands."

More than thirty years later I learned from a former reporter that, according to newsroom rumors, Mr. Nokes did consult the paper's attorney. After reviewing the documents the lawyer said, "I have to tell you that if you use any name other than Betty Roberts, she'll own *The Oregonian.*"

⊱ ⊰

Three doctors' wives from Medford had visited my law office in January and asked if I would take a case challenging the abortion statute passed in the 1969 session. The women told me their husbands didn't accept abortion patients because the law had so many restrictions and conditions that they feared they would be charged with a criminal act if they didn't meet all of them, even if inadvertently. Obviously this was preventing women from having needed abortions. Even the Oregon Medical Association didn't know how to advise its members.

We talked about the difficulty of finding a plaintiff who would have standing; that is, would be accepted by the court as having a legitimate cause to complain. The women offered to give me a list of doctors willing to be plaintiffs, and they knew of others. Keith and I agreed to take the case on a *pro bono* basis (that is, for no charge). Keith would handle all the preliminary motions, and I would do the necessary legwork in talking with the plaintiff doctors and getting their affidavits signed and notarized. I would also carry the responsibility for the substantive argument when the case finally got before the court.

The main legal issues were three: whether the law was vague and indefinite, which would make it unenforceable and therefore unconstitutional; whether it violated the right of privacy between physician and patient; and whether it made it impossible for doctors to treat their patients according to the highest standard of medical practice.

We filed the complaint, *Ralph C. Benson, M.D., et al. v. The Honorable Lee Johnson, Attorney General of Oregon, et al.*, in Federal District Court in April, 1970. Our plaintiffs were fifteen doctors, both medical doctors and psychiatrists. Later, a married couple would be added as intervenor plaintiffs. They had three children and could not have another child because of the threat to the wife's health. Their participation would allow us to argue the issue of the right to privacy of the woman and of the husband-wife relationship.

After the complaint was filed, an interesting young man, Michael "Mick" Gillette, came to my office. He was representing the Attorney General and all other defendants in the case. Mick settled into my big, comfortable client's chair, and said he hoped we could have an amicable and professional relationship as the case went forward. I agreed we should. As he headed for the door, he turned and said, "Betty, you're going to win this one. All I ask is that you help me look good." I knew what he meant: that the law was probably on the side of my plaintiffs, but he was intending to do his job in representing the state to the utmost of his ability, which was, and is, considerable.

Within a month of the filing of the complaint, the Oregon Medical Association voted to liberalize Oregon's 1969 abortion law by striking some of the conditions. This gave good publicity to the need to change the law, and it gave professional support to the plaintiff doctors in our case. The court rejected a defense motion to dismiss and certified the case to a three-judge panel. It would be two years before I'd have the opportunity to argue its merits. In the meantime, we met with a panel of volunteer lawyers to encourage the American Civil Liberties Union to join the case as *amicus curiae* ("friend of the court"), lending a respected and well-recognized voice of professional credibility and support to the case. The ACLU would file its brief in April 1971.

✣ ✤

The 1970 election gave the State Senate sixteen Democrats and fourteen Republicans. Two of the coalition Democrats from the 1969 session remained, Harry Boivin and Debbs Potts. Surprising to many was the return of Tom Mahoney. He had been a coalition Democrat; as the number of Republicans in the Senate increased, the coalition became less useful to them, but they were not yet in the majority.

And, glory be, there would be another woman in the Senate. Democrat Betty Browne had given up her seat in the House to run for the Senate and won. With our similar backgrounds as lawyers, and each of us a mother of four children, surely we would have much in common on issues.

In the House, Grace Peck and Fritzi Chuinard remained as incumbents. Three new women were elected: Republican Norma Paulus, a Salem lawyer with a lawyer husband and two small children; Republican Mary Rieke, wife of a Portland doctor, mother of three grown children, and member of the Portland School Board; and Democrat Nancie Fadeley, wife of Senator Ed Fadeley and a journalist from Eugene with two children.

Nancie had worked for Ed in the Legislature, and I knew Mary from my school-board work. Norma made an impression on me quickly when she said one of the reasons she ran for the Legislature was my proposal to fund kindergartens. She was there to help. The new women were all community activists, which meant they were well informed and energetic. They would be good liaisons in the House.

As the 1971 session opened, the only thing on the minds of all senators was who would be elected Senate president. The outcome would determine whether the coalition had finally been defeated. The convoluted process that year gives an idea of the political maneuvering that can occur as the parties jostle for power in the Legislature.

Two of the coalition Democrats, Harry Boivin and Tom Mahoney, joined the regular Democrats, as we called ourselves, but one, Debbs Potts, stayed with the fourteen Republicans. This meant that any vote for president would tie fifteen-fifteen.

We fifteen Democrats had named Bud Lent as our choice for president at a caucus held just after the November election. The fourteen Republicans and their one Democrat selected Lynn Newbry, from Medford, as their nominee. By the time the Legislature convened, negotiations had produced no progress in either direction. On that first day, the Senate reconvened after the ceremony and lunch. Nominations for president were made and votes were taken over and over, with breaks every once in a while for a caucus. Everyone was holding firm. Lent had fifteen and Newbry had fifteen, and the standoff held through thirty-seven ballots taken through the next several mornings and afternoons, including Saturday and Sunday.

The balloting went on into the second week of the session. Then the Republicans tried a new strategy: adding various other names to their candidate list, trying to see if anyone from our caucus would vote for any of their nominees and thereby break the tie. Their strategy was clear and clever, but it didn't work. The fruitless balloting continued until Thursday, when a fourth name was added.

On Friday morning our caucus was still holding in there for Lent, but when the Senate convened two new names were added to the mix. John Burns, from our caucus, was nominated by a Republican senator. Ah! A change of strategy. Then Mahoney, from our caucus, nominated Debbs Potts, the lone Democrat in the Republican caucus. Mahoney, I assumed, with his political wily ways, wanted Debbs' name in to see if the Republicans would split between him and John Burns. Surprise! Burns got all fifteen Republican caucus votes, but Burns himself voted for Lent, making it still a fifteen-fifteen tie.

The Senate adjourned until 1:00 p.m., and we headed for our caucus room. Lent told us we needed to hold firm until Monday, because talks were still taking place, and he thought Potts might be convinced to join the Democrats by Monday. Then John Burns walked in, tossed copies of his press release on the table and said, "You'd better read this before you proceed with the caucus. I am going to be president of the Senate."

Stunned, we all grabbed a copy of the press release. It said he had decided to vote for himself and break the tie so the Senate could get on with its business for the good of the state and the people of Oregon. We were all shocked, especially Lent, who had negotiated night and day.

When we convened again after lunch John Burns joined with the Republicans and the lone hold-out Democrat, Debbs Potts, by voting for himself. That broke the two-week standoff, and he was elected president. His presidency came at a high price. Burns was seen as a Judas by many who thought the coalition was very near the breaking point for the first time in fourteen years. To have two former coalition members join the regular Democrats, only to have a new one join the coalition, was a major political setback for the Democrats.

What I didn't know then, but do now from reading John Burns' oral history, was that he had been approached by members of the coalition as early as three days into the deadlock, but he had stuck with Lent until it became clear that we would put up no other nominee. I've wondered since that time what other Democrat we could have nominated. John was seen by most in our caucus as too conservative, but there was no one else who could have drawn a single vote from the other side.

Another thing I didn't know then is that John had grown up in eastern Oregon, where he and members of his extended family had had long business associations with various senators and their families in eastern and southern Oregon. Debbs Potts had even herded sheep for John's sister's husband's family in Klamath Falls in the 1920s. The Republicans were comfortable making a Democrat president of the Senate if they felt he was one of them, even if he had been elected from Multnomah County. Another instructive example of the who-knows-whom influence in politics, which can persist, clearly, over generations.

Late in the session, Bud Lent was appointed to the circuit court. Celebrating with him are members of the Senate Democratic caucus. From left: Keith Burbidge, Bill Holmstrom, Tom Mahoney, Vern Cook, Berkeley (Bud) Lent, Betty Roberts, Dick Groener, Rep. Harl Hass (who replaced Lent in the Senate), Harry Boivin, Ted Hallock. Caucus members not shown are Betty Browne, Jack Bain, Jason Boe, Ed Fadeley, Don Willner. (Photograph by Joseph Tompkins)

Some said the controversy was a waste of two weeks. I felt the battle had to be fought if the coalition was ever to die. We had come close. The Republicans had had to reach into our caucus to maintain some semblance of the coalition. How John would get anything done in the Senate because of the animosity of the Democrats wasn't clear. He had a lot of making up to do.

President Burns made his committee appointments on the Monday after the battle was over. I would be a member of Ways and Means for the first time—a coup for me. In addition, I would be Chairman of the new Consumer Affairs Committee and a member of the Education Committee. From a personal standpoint it could not have been better. It appeared John had, to his credit, attempted to balance the assignments with no hint of favoritism to either side. He was working hard to put Democrats in committee positions where they could be most effective. We could finally get to work.

‹ ›

The near-defeat of the coalition in the Senate, the hard-fought battle to elect a president, and all the new faces appearing before committees in support of citizen-proposed legislation were signs that the 1971 session would be different from previous ones. Legislation that would protect consumers, protect the environment, and make government workings more accessible to the people— the so-called "sunshine bills"—began pouring in.

Some of the bills on consumer protection, migrant farm-worker housing, and gun control were spearheaded by activists in a young Democrats' group called DemoForum.Other new citizen-activist groups were 1000 Friends of Oregon, the Oregon Environmental Council, and Sensible Transportation Options for People (STOP). These and other groups and individuals converged on the Legislature, where committee meeting rooms and the hallways in the Capitol took on new vigor and excitement.

I heard a long-time lobbyist for business complain one day about how "everybody and their dogs" had taken over the State Capitol. He asked rhetorically and without irony, "Do they think they own this place?" Clearly, the Legislature was changing with the same dynamic urgency we were witnessing in our everyday lives. The young people we'd seen publicly protesting or becoming "peaceniks" were now turning to politics to influence the future they rightly claimed. That year there were more women lobbyists than ever before. Individually they represented nurses, libraries, dentists, wheat growers, the movie industry, mental-health organizations, and others. Some were independent lobbyists, and others were volunteer lobbyists for the newly formed activist groups. There were two women reporters, a welcome change in the formerly all-male press gallery.

As for me, seniority was paying off. As a committee chairman I hired a clerk and had an assigned committee room and an office just across the hall. And I'd finally made it to that all-powerful Ways and Means Committee—and as the vice-chairman—where just three sessions before I'd been admonished to become a member if I wanted to get a bill passed there and had decided that was good advice.

Serving on the Education Committee again, I introduced my kindergarten bill with a new twist. The bill said nothing about kindergartens, but instead lowered the mandatory school attendance ages from six to eighteen (or graduation) to five to seventeen. I made no bones about the bill's purpose; kindergartens were more important than the senior year in high school. When I had taught in high school, many of the seniors in my classes had dropped out, or were dismissed for half a day to do part-time work if they had enough credits to graduate. Any senior could go to high school for only a half-day and go to a community college or some other school during the other half. For those seniors who remained in school for a full day, much of their time was spent working on the yearbook and planning senior graduation activities— picnic day, senior prom, the all-night party after graduation—and arguing over what their senior colors and motto should be.

Surprisingly, the state superintendent of schools, Dale Parnell, testifying in committee, agreed with my premise. So did a majority of the Senate Education Committee. They voted the bill out of committee and onto the Senate floor. I intended to argue that the proposal would not require any new funding and would give the seniors in high school an earlier opportunity to get started on college or other vocational training.

On a Friday in April the bill came up for a floor vote. After extensive debate, the vote was thirteen to twelve, with sixteen (a majority) needed for passage. Five senators were absent. I changed my vote in order to move for reconsideration. That would give me time to lobby the senators who had not been present, as well as some of those who had voted against it. On Tuesday, when I walked onto the floor of the Senate, a few senators who had voted for the bill told me that they had been contacted by their alarmed school superintendents, and that they would now have to vote "Nay." Over my objection, the bill was re-referred to committee. Many senators did not want to go on record voting for or against the bill. *Someday kindergartens will come to the State of Oregon,* I assured myself. For now, there were plenty of other issues to work on.

The Ways and Means Human Resources Subcommittee, among its other responsibilities, considered budgets for the state mental institution, the state hospital, schools for the deaf and blind, and other facilities that housed and cared for people who required specialized care. In one hearing we were considering the small budgets of various boards that operated as a part of the State Board of Health. I noticed one called the Board of Eugenics. I was curious about the purpose of that board and was told that it decided who in the mental institutions should be sterilized.

Sterilized? Why should anyone be sterilized? Answer: the women were sterilized because there could be situations where they might become pregnant, and that just couldn't happen. I suggested that maybe the men who caused the pregnancies ought to be sterilized. Then there were clumsy attempts to explain that it was the women who had, you know, periods, and that could be taken care of through sterilization as well, because some women in the institutions couldn't take care of themselves, and sterilization avoided all the mess.

I sat silent in shock and disbelief, wondering what could possibly be done to change that practice. It was in that legislative session and later that the idea of community mental health facilities, such as group homes, began to form. The old notions about sterilization would also change, but not until a decade later, when an emergency-room doctor from Roseburg named John Kitzhaber would be elected to the Senate and would sit on the same Ways and Means Subcommittee. In 1983 Kitzhaber would spearhead the abolition of the Eugenics Board.

Serving on Ways and Means gave me valuable education in how state government functions. It's an axiom that no legislator really knows how state government works until he or she has served on either the Revenue Committee or the Ways and Means Committee. One needs to know about the money coming in and the money going out.

The Education Subcommittee was easier. I understood basic school support as well as community colleges because I was continuing to teach part-time at Mt. Hood Community College. My relatively recent contacts with Portland State University and the University of Oregon were helpful in interpreting the overall budget for higher education.

The Chancellor of Higher Education and his staff often appeared before our committee. One day I couldn't resist asking Chancellor Roy Lieuallen if the U of O political science department had yet begun to admit women to its doctoral program. An odd question, of course, but I explained that I had been denied admission and it still troubled me. He would get an answer, he replied, but he was hopeful that there was no discrimination against women students in any of the institutions. It was the best political answer he could give, but I thought, *Garbage, Mr. Chancellor.* This was a time when news stories were surfacing on the conditions women athletes endured while all the money in athletic departments went to men's activities. Maybe Chancellor Lieuallen was telling the truth as he saw it, but at that time many discriminatory practices in higher education were not yet being recognized.

Under my chairmanship, the Consumer Affairs Committee passed an important bill prohibiting deceptive trade practices such as false advertising and the so-called "bait and switch" tactic of dishonest salesmen. Another bill prohibited the common practice of deficiency judgments against debtors: under a deficiency judgment, a major consumer item, usually a car, could be repossessed and then resold for less than was owed, and the debtor was responsible for the difference. We also considered legislation that regulated door-to-door sales by requiring that the customer be given three days to cancel a sale. Not exactly the hot-button issues most legislators wanted to work on, but of great significance to average citizens.

One bill, introduced by Senator Dick Groener at the request of the Oregon State Barbers Association, was hard to take seriously, although the proponents warned of an enormous social catastrophe if the committee didn't pass it. This bill would prevent women hairdressers from cutting men's hair. Yes, indeed. I was amused, but I could see their problem—with boys and men letting their hair grow, barbers were hurting economically. They didn't say this, of course, in their proposal. They said women weren't trained to cut men's hair properly, and, well, men just wouldn't be men if women cut their hair. The hairdressers, both women and men, reacted as expected. They raised the specter of sex discrimination, but primarily they focused on the differences in training for the two vocations and made the point that anyone could train for both. I listened to all this courteously while other committee members drifted in and out of the room waiting for the hearing to conclude and to get on to other things. In March we tabled the bill. But that wasn't the end of it.

The sponsoring senator put pressure on me, because he was getting pressure from the barbers, to take it off the table and hold another hearing. As a courtesy to the senator, I did. Senator Sam Dement and I sat for almost two hours hearing arguments both for and against. This time it was all about the horrors of throwing men and women together in a beauty salon, where a man might chance to see a woman getting her legs shaved (which would completely unman him, no doubt) or the fear that men might create a "disturbance" in a hairdresser's shop—exactly what kind of disturbance was delicately left to the imagination. If women can cut men's hair without the training to be a barber, we were asked, then can a plumber be an electrician? Can a doctor be a lawyer? Earth-shaking questions all. You understand I was being very patient and making no comments. After lectures by two college students who, confessing they had no pecuniary interest in the bill, warned of impending discrimination and violations of civil rights if it should become law, another witness wondered what ingenious device the Legislature would come up with that would enable beauticians to determine whether a person was male or female. The time to adjourn the meeting finally came. I decided the committee would not table the bill again; we'd just let it hang in limbo for the rest of the session.

All my amusement about this bill aside, I always tried to look at a proposal from the standpoint of the proponents, because the Legislature is truly the people's forum. It is a place where anyone can exercise the old saying, "There ought to be a law." To the individual, group or organization that brings it forward, the proposal is always serious. I tried to respect their intentions even if I couldn't agree with their remedy.

ఠ ఴ

As the chairman of the Consumer Affairs Committee I had to work with the Attorney General, Lee Johnson, on issues that would require enforcement by his office. Johnson had been in the House when I was there, and now, as Attorney General, he was at the Legislature a lot. One incident involving him and Keith that session could have put a cloud over any continuing work we'd have to cooperate on.

Keith and I were at a cocktail party—there were many cocktail parties back then—when Lee Johnson came in. He walked up to Keith, extended his hand and said, "Good evening, Mr. Roberts." It was a jibe about the fact that I'd retained my former name when I married Keith, and just a sample of some of the flak Keith took for that decision.

I held my breath waiting for Keith's reaction. He casually dumped his entire drink into Johnson's hand, then turned and walked to the bar to get another one. About a half dozen people had seen the exchange, and there was the drink all over the floor for everyone to see. Johnson, in his typical nonplussed manner, laughed his funny laugh—some called him "Porky" for his crazy laugh—dried his hand, and meandered on over to harass someone else. I was proud of Keith for not taking a verbal jab back, for it certainly could have escalated. Because of Johnson's reaction I assumed he was happy to have made the belittling remark to Keith and the drink dumping hadn't bothered him. It's always good politics not to hold grudges. There is a time for letting your colleagues know about unseemly or distracting tactics, and a time to put it aside and work together.

It was good we could do that, because I had to rely on the testimony of the Attorney General in considering the most famous bill to come before my

Consumer Affairs Committee—Oregon's celebrated bottle bill. In the previous session Paul Hanneman, a Republican from the coastal town of Tillamook, had introduced a bill that would require refundable deposits on certain bottles and cans. The bill failed, and few took the proposal seriously—certainly not the governor.

Hanneman's 1971 version was essentially a repeat of his 1969 version. The bill would require purchasers to pay a deposit on bottles and cans containing malt beverages and carbonated beverages. The deposit would be reimbursed when the container was returned. This time, Governor McCall immediately took proprietorship, recognizing the great public popularity of the proposal. The bill passed the House by fifty-four votes, a major victory and testimony to both its simplicity and its attractiveness to legislators and citizens from all over the state.

When the bill came to the Senate, President Burns assigned it to Consumer Affairs. We had already held hearings on a Senate version, and extensive hearings had been held in the House on the bill now before our committee. I favored the bill, and given the large vote of approval in the House and our previous hearings, I thought it would be an easy pass. I did not anticipate the intense lobbying from the container industry. Unable to stop its passage in the House, opponents were now aiming their guns at my committee and on me, its chairman, in particular. At the start, I knew I had three votes in my five-member committee—Don Willner, Hector Macpherson, and myself. I worried that one of them might be influenced by the heavy lobbying.

In late April our committee held a three-hour hearing on the bill. The proponents emphasized their concerns about littering and the accumulation of solid waste in our society. The opponents, including an official from the American Can Company, warned of the bill's dire effect on can and bottle manufacturers and tried to show that deposits were ineffective in motivating people to return containers. Attorney General Lee Johnson rebutted this testimony by showing that the American Can Company had no manufacturing plant in Oregon, and that the problems encountered in British Columbia arose because the two-cent deposit was too small to motivate people to return the container. All in all, it was an orderly and informative hearing that swayed not a single member of my committee one way or the other. I was ready to put the bill on for a work session and take the vote to send it to the floor of the Senate.

One day about this time Governor McCall spied me in the hallway outside his office. He walked toward me, turned and walked with me, then leaned his tall frame down to look me in the eye and said, "How's our bottle bill doing? Is it safe?"

"It's safe, Tom, so long as my two committee votes hold." I knew he made a mental note to check up on Senators Willner and Macpherson to be sure they were still strong "yes" votes.

                ❧   ❦

The lobbyists opposing the bill were getting nervous. They persuaded me to have one more evening hearing so executives of the manufacturing industry from the East Coast could testify. I agreed. That hearing was held in the largest hearing room in the Capitol Building, and the room was overflowing. Executives of National Can Company, American Can Company, and Continental Can Company flew in their company-owned jets to Oregon to testify. I resigned myself to a long evening of listening to the same testimony we had already heard, but some of it was new and disturbing. We heard belittling and disdainful remarks regarding the intelligence of Oregonians and our inability to understand the irreversible harm to the economy that would occur if the bill should pass. In my mind that tactless, demeaning testimony was bound to backfire. After the hearing ended, our guests from the east departed immediately, and everyone else milled around, feeling something between disbelief and anger.

I went by my office to pick up my coat. It had been a very long day. On my desk I found an unsigned note. It said, "Senator Roberts, you must think you're pretty smart for a little ole' Texas gal."

Who in the world? I wondered. Not many people around the Legislature knew about my Texas background. I didn't fret about the note for long, taking it only as another bit of belittling that had been going on all evening. But I did say to myself, *You're damned right I think I'm smart.* I never found out who left the note, and I didn't care. That bill would be out of my committee in no time.

But the opponents were not done working their mischief. At the meeting of the committee to vote the bill out to the floor, one of the bill's opponents asked to amend the definition of "beverage" by simplifying it and making it less specific. That should have raised a red flag in my head. But the Attorney General believed that the proposed new definition was not so vague as to make the law unenforceable, so the committee made the amendment. We thought it would be a goodwill gesture that would remove some of the opposition to the bill. We were wrong.

On voting day I walked onto the floor of the Senate and saw containers lined up on senators' desks. Every kind of beverage was there, from canned milk to squeeze-bottle lemon juice to canned baby formula to cooking oil and more. I knew the trap had been set. When I spoke on the bill, the senators began asking if the items they displayed would be covered. I realized this was a ploy to create confusion and thereby defeat the bill. Then one of the opponents moved to re-refer the bill to my committee. The opponents assumed that the Legislature would adjourn before the bill could be considered again by the Senate. But I knew that if the committee acted fast enough we could yet save it.

I told Hector Macpherson and Don Willner, my other two "yes" votes, to meet in our committee room immediately after adjournment, and I told my committee clerk to have amendments ready to restore the old language on the definition. All committee meetings had to be announced publicly, so I announced the meeting at the end of that session as we prepared to adjourn for lunch. The lobby had all left the gallery after the bill was re-referred, thinking they'd defeated it by sending it back to committee. The two "Nay" votes in my committee wandered off for lunch, apparently thinking the same thing, or they weren't paying attention when I announced the meeting.

We three members met and, by voice vote, restored the old, descriptive language. We intended to make it crystal-clear what constituted a "beverage." Then we re-passed the bill. I instructed our clerk to get the bill back to the Senate desk where it could begin to be processed for another floor vote. Then we adjourned. As we were leaving the room the two other members and a few lobbyists were trickling in, asking what had happened. I said only, "You'll see."

The lobbying on the bottle bill had been so intense that there were rumors of bribes. It was said that one lobbyist took the job on the basis of payment only if the bill was defeated—a major ethical violation. Near midnight on the night before the bill was to come to the floor for a final vote, I got a phone call. A male voice said that if I could keep that bill in committee until adjournment, there would be plenty of money for Democratic candidates in the next election. I said I wasn't interested and hung up.

The next day, I reported that phone call and said that it was verification of the type of pressure that was being placed on legislators to defeat the bottle bill. I said I wasn't interested in electing Democrats under those circumstances, and I hoped any Republicans who'd been approached with a similar offer felt the same way. I added, "We may not be able to keep the environment and politics of Boston, Washington, D.C., and New York clean, but I'd prefer to keep Oregon's environment and politics clean."

When the bill came up on the floor of the Senate, not much had to be said. There was an attempt to re-refer it to committee; that failed, and then the bill passed with a good majority. The next day there was an attempt to reconsider the bill, and that also failed. Oregon's landmark bottle bill had finally cleared the Legislature and was on its way to the governor for his signature.

Chapter 12

Turning Points

During the 1971 legislative session I had many opportunities to view the changing times from a woman's perspective. Along with young people, we women were looking for ways to make society fairer, more aware of injustices, more equal in opportunities.

In 1969 we'd passed the law that prohibited discrimination in employment on the basis of sex, and we'd decriminalized abortions. This session Betty Browne and I sponsored a bill that would prohibit sex discrimination in public accommodations. I asked Grace Peck to be the major sponsor in the House. The need for such a bill had become clear when women began complaining that some restaurants in Portland refused to serve them during the lunch hour, saying that women, who were assumed to be shoppers, could eat at other times.

At the first hearing before the five-member all-male Senate State and Federal Affairs Committee, I explained the reason for the bill. Nine women then testified in favor. The first woman said she'd been with a party that had made reservations at the Perkins Pub in Lipman Wolfe, a popular department store. When the party arrived, they were refused service because women were part of the group. As the bill passed through the Senate, someone raised the question of whether, if the restaurant could no longer refuse to admit women, could women use the men's restroom? That was such a silly and irrational question, but it had to be answered. I tried patiently to explain that the restrooms were not the accommodation under discussion. The bill passed the Senate with only four "Nays" in late May as the Legislature was working toward adjournment, but it died in the House State and Federal Affairs Committee because it was too late for the committee to consider it properly. There'd been no time to line up the witnesses and organize a lobbying effort. With the good support we'd had in the Senate, I thought it might get out of the House committee without any special lobbying, but no. Eliminating discrimination against women in public accommodations would have to wait for the next session.

During the 1971 session a few young women House employees came to me about a situation in the Legislature that they felt amounted to discrimination.

They told me the Speaker had forbidden them to wear slacks, and they didn't think that was fair when some of the women legislators were wearing them. It was still a new thing for women to wear pants in a professional setting, and women themselves were divided on this question. Some thought wearing pants meant emulating men, and we shouldn't want to be like men. Others thought pants gave women more freedom of movement, and furthermore, that in the business world looking more like men was not a bad idea. It was generally agreed that darker-colored tailored suits with matching jacket and pants were acceptable business attire.

I told the young women I would see what I could do. I went to see Representative Grace Peck. Grace had her own distinct taste for brightly colored clothes, jewelry, and make-up, though she herself had not yet begun to wear pants. After hearing me out, Grace said, "Let me take care of it." It didn't take her long.

A few days later Grace appeared on the floor of the Senate. She sashayed up the center aisle to the desk of a senator at the front of the chamber. We all gawked in disbelief. Grace had on the loudest purple pants and the most colorful flower-patterned blouse I'd ever seen. On her way back down the aisle she came to my desk, sat down beside me, and whispered, "How do you like my outfit?" I assured her it was memorable. Then she added, "I talked with the Speaker this morning, and I think everything will be just fine for those young women." I'm sure the Speaker, in giving in to the younger women employees, knew they would be more discreet in their choice of pants to wear at the Legislature.

⋇ ⋇

Archaic attitudes about women's roles surfaced in many ways. One telling incident occurred on the floor of the Senate when we were debating a bill introduced at the request of the League of Women Voters that would require candidates to provide more biographical information and a recent picture for the voter's pamphlet. Jack Bain, probably the oldest member of the Senate, took the floor to oppose the bill. He had been using an old photo of himself for the Voter's Pamphlet for years, one that showed him more youthful and handsome than he now was. He had just one thing to say to League of Women Voter members observing from the gallery: they had no business getting involved in political issues, and they should be home in the kitchen where they belonged.

I sprang to my microphone to interrupt by raising a point of personal privilege. The president asked, "What is your point, Senator Roberts?"

Betty Roberts and Keith Skelton with their children on the steps of the Oregon Capitol, 1971. (Photograph by Joseph Tompkins)

"Because I am a member of the League of Women Voters, I assume the remark just made applies to me, too," I said.

Senator Bain replied only that that was not the intent of his statement. He came to my desk issuing apologies all over the place, and then said, "I wasn't talking about you, because you're okay. It's all those other women."

That put him out of the frying pan and into the fire, as far as I was concerned. *He should have quit while he was behind.* The bill passed and became law.

❧ ❧

On Tuesday, March 30, 1971, a strange sight greeted everyone as we arrived at the Capitol. To the right of the entrance, the white marble wall was spray-painted in large letters, "Lt. Calley is getting fucked by the Army, Calley died for your sins." The day before, Lieutenant William L. Calley, Jr. had been convicted of murder for his part in the infamous My Lai massacre of an entire village in Vietnam in 1968.

There were "tish, tishes" all over the Capitol at the vandalism, and outright concern for the defacement of the building. Assurances were given that a maintenance crew would get it cleaned up, but the most they could do immediately was paint over the word "fucked" until sandblasting could take care of it all.

On Wednesday the newspapers were full of stories reacting to Calley's conviction. There were angry speeches in Congress about the Army abandoning its fighting men. Draft-board members were resigning their positions, saying they could not send young men to fight if that was the way they were going to be treated. People petitioned President Nixon to pardon Calley.

I was struggling with my own reaction, thinking of my son who went to Vietnam promising me that he wouldn't kill anyone. I remembered what I'd said to him: "Do what you have to do to come back." I needed to express my concern, too. A news article speaks for me here:

> Each day in the Oregon Senate members and visitors stand for the posting of the colors and opening prayer.
>
> Normally, this is the only period of complete and respectful silence in the chamber.
>
> Wednesday there was another period of such silence, but the circumstances were different. On this occasion the speaker was a woman, the mother of a Vietnam veteran and a member of the Senate and her voice could well have been the voice of the conscience of America.
>
> The speaker was Sen. Betty Roberts, D-Portland, and she rose to speak in the period devoted to "remonstrances."
>
> She spoke in a low voice and one never completely under control but in the total silence of galleries and on the floor, a whisper would have sufficed.
>
> Sen. Roberts said she rose to speak of the defacement of the front of the Capitol Building—a defacement of red paint daubings spelling out in crude letters, "Lt. Calley is getting … by the Army," and "Lt. Calley died for your sins." This occurred after the conviction but prior to the sentencing of Calley.
>
> She said she did not approve of the obscenities. She did not approve of the defacement of the Capitol Building, but …
>
> She said she does not know how many members have or have had sons in Vietnam, but she told of the night of the departure of her son for Vietnam.
>
> His parting words were, "Don't worry Mom, I won't kill anyone."
>
> Within her struggled the satisfaction at this response to his lifetime of instruction in the sanctity of human life and the sudden and pressing need for self preservation.
>
> "I told him," she said, "'don't say that—you don't know what you may have to do.'"
>
> On the following Memorial Day, while the Legislature was conducting the usual ceremonies for those who died in previous wars, Sen. Roberts said she walked in the Capitol grounds thinking of those involved in war who were still living.

During the Tet offensive, she sent an anguished letter to her son and eventually received an "all is well" reply.

"I had conflicts within myself," she said, "as a result of my teachings—not to be brutal, nor to be destructive and to be morally right.

"But I said to him, kill, if that is what you have to do in order to come back."

Her son is back now, Sen. Roberts told the Senate members, but he and many of his Vietnam companions are confused and troubled as to what their standard of values should be.

"Perhaps," she said, "Lt. Calley on departure for Vietnam said, 'Don't worry, I won't kill.'"

Sen. Roberts repeated that she could not condone defacement of the Capitol.

"This was not the proper place," she said, "but thank God somebody said it."

It was the war in Vietnam that gave impetus to ratifying an amendment to the U.S. Constitution that would lower the voting age to eighteen. Governor McCall had his heart set on Oregon's being among the thirty-eight states needed for ratification. The amendment was supported by many of us who were concerned about our young men being sent to war without the privilege of voting. In the previous session the Legislature had referred a constitutional amendment to the voters to lower the Oregon voting age to nineteen; Oregon voters had defeated the measure and, as a result, some legislators opposed the federal amendment.

Senate President John Burns sent the bill to the Elections Committee, of which he had named himself chairman. While he had no personal opposition to it, his strategy was obvious—in deference to members who opposed it, he would not allow the bill to get out of his committee.

Politics can sometimes create strange sequences of events. In late May Governor McCall had to go out of state for a few days. That meant the President of the Senate—Burns—acted as the governor, and that in turn meant the Senate president *pro tempore*, Harry Boivin, became the president. As acting president, Boivin appointed two additional members to the Elections Committee, claiming that he needed to do so to keep a quorum. Boivin, Ted Hallock, and the two new members voted the ratification bill out of committee and sent it to the floor of the Senate, where in due course it would be processed and voted on.

Burns knew immediately what had happened, and he was outraged. He ordered the chief clerk of the Senate not to process the bill. This was a questionable act, since he was acting governor, not president of the Senate. He couldn't be both at the same time. It was all very befuddling. The Democrats caucused and decided drastic action was needed.

On Monday, May 31, John Burns, back as president, opened the session. After one or two items of business, the Senate recessed until after lunch. The Democrats failed to show up for the afternoon session. The Senate could not proceed without a quorum, and because we were nearing adjournment, bills yet to be voted on, many from Ways and Means, were stacking up waiting for action. The Senate reconvened and recessed all afternoon and then recessed until ten o'clock the next morning. All this time, we boycotting Democrats were hanging out in the Democratic caucus room talking strategy on how to get the eighteen-year-old voting bill to the floor for a vote. We delegated staff members to sit on the side aisle to observe what happened on the Senate floor and relay messages back to us.

The following day, about mid-morning, Burns and the sergeant-at-arms knocked on the door of the caucus room, where we Democrats were still holed up. They were not allowed in. Soon after being rebuffed, President Burns announced from the podium of the Senate that he had "requested the Oregon State Police to bring in four members of the Oregon State Senate to provide a quorum in order to conduct the business of the Senate." He didn't need all the Democrats; four would make a quorum and the Senate could continue its business.

We learned of this plan when our designated lookout burst into the caucus room in a panic and reported the president's words. As we all fled out the east door of the Capitol, Jason Boe and Harry Boivin told me to come with them, and we went to Harry's apartment. We set up telephone contact with the caucus room, where Beth Wilson, our loyal secretary, acted as our eyes and ears in the Senate and kept other caucus members informed when they called in from their various hideouts. Then Harry and Jason placed a call to President Burns' office. Burns, knowing that the work of the Senate must proceed and having no personal opposition to eighteen-year-olds voting, agreed to reconstitute the Elections Committee and get the bill out if the Democrats would end their boycott. Jason, Harry, and I walked back to the Capitol Building and strolled up the front steps as though nothing had happened. Legislative staff members and lobbyists were all standing around, dumbfounded at the developments of the last few days and the drastic action the Democrats had taken.

When the Senate convened in the afternoon, all senators were present. Two days later the resolution was on the calendar for a floor vote. After various parliamentary maneuvers by the opposition were defeated, and after debate on the bill itself, the vote was sixteen to fourteen. Not one vote to spare. One week later the Legislature adjourned *sine die.*

We'd had a hard time getting started that session, taking two weeks to elect a Senate president in an attempt to make our two-party system more responsible. We'd had an equally hard time adjourning, with the Democrats' determination to get the eighteen-year-old voting amendment ratified. In my mind, both actions were necessary. No one has ever said democracy is easy or that our representative form of government is efficient. It's not supposed to be easy or efficient, but it is supposed to act in behalf of fairness for all its citizens.

⋈ ⋈

While the 1971 Oregon Legislature went about its work, the U.S. Congress was preparing to send an Equal Rights Amendment to the states for ratification. Such an amendment had been regularly introduced in Congress ever since women got the right to vote in 1920. There had been a flurry of proposals during the 1950s, but it was not until 1970 that one actually passed the House of Representatives and went to the Senate. The Senate failed to act on it that session. In 1971 a proposal was introduced in both the U.S. House of Representatives and the U.S. Senate, and it was finally referred to the states for ratification in 1972.

Beyond its necessary practical requirements, the Equal Rights Amendment was highly symbolic. Its passage demonstrated that our highest legislative body, still with few women members, had finally recognized the need for equality for women in all aspects of life. The ERA was the rallying point around which women coalesced and organized—exactly what was needed to give women a purpose and the courage and strength to accomplish it. The goal was to get the ERA ratified in thirty-eight states, the two-thirds majority required for a constitutional amendment.

The National Women's Political Caucus was founded in 1971 by, among others, New York's Representative Bella Abzug, the first woman to run for office on a women's rights platform. Her slogan was, "This woman's place is in the House—the House of Representatives." Bella was fondly known for her big hats. On her first day, the sergeant-at-arms told her hats were not permitted in the House. Her response, in characteristic style, was, "Is that so? Well, go fuck yourself."

In Portland a group of young politically active women had begun meeting once a week. They'd worked on the presidential campaigns of Eugene McCarthy and Robert Kennedy and the city council campaigns of Neil Goldschmidt and Tom Walsh. They called themselves the "Wednesday Winos." According to Gretchen Kafoury, "We gossiped and yakked, chased children and drank cheap wine. The consensus was ... that the women's liberation movement didn't really have much to do with us—we were, after all, college graduates who had chosen to stay home with our children. I was already a member of NOW ..., and even those who had read Betty Friedan weren't sure about all the Lib stuff."

The all-male City Club was a civic organization that studied issues, made recommendations, and invited speakers to its regular Friday luncheons at the Benson Hotel in downtown Portland. Some of the Wednesday Winos' husbands and friends belonged. The club's motto was "Conscience of the City."

The women learned that the club had scheduled a vote on the question of admitting women at a January 1971 meeting. They expected it to pass. It didn't. They learned that one member had said, in the midst of the debate, "This club has too much cleavage already," to great hilarity. Another: "They'd all get here early, since they don't have jobs. They'd take all the best seats in the front." One man argued, "Has momism grown so great? Frankly, gentlemen, do we really need Mother with us all the time? Are we unable to make effective, valid decisions without mom around? I think not."

The women were dumbfounded. They had never experienced outright discrimination before. According to Gretchen, "It wasn't until after that first vote that we got kind of active. ... When the second vote failed [in October 1971] we went on the warpath." The women changed their name to Politically Oriented Women (POW). After that second vote, in the words of one of the women, "The POWs were pissed."

Women picketing the City Club of Portland after the club voted to deny membership to women. Gretchen Kafoury in the foreground with the rolling pin leads the group.

Thereafter every Friday, the POWs marched around in a circle in front of the Benson Hotel carrying signs and cornering the members. I was asked to join them. My job was to buttonhole the club's speakers as they approached the hotel, especially nationally known women who were usually there to discuss issues of concern to women, such as women's health care, family planning, and the welfare of children. The women speakers always took time to talk with me, were always cordial and sympathetic to the marchers and the issue, and always agreed to speak to it in their remarks to the club. None refused to enter.

In January 1972, I was asked to fill out a City Club questionnaire relating to campaign funds and election procedures. The request said, "You have been suggested as one of a number of influential people concerned about politics and political campaigns. Your opinions and thoughts on campaign financing, expenditures and reporting practices would greatly assist our efforts. Won't you share your thoughts and opinions with us?"

Wait a minute, I thought. *I'm not good enough to be a member, but you're asking for my expert opinion? You're asking for Mom's advice?* The controversy cost the club hundreds of members who resigned in protest. Others remained but supported the women and worked to get the necessary two-thirds vote from inside the organization, but that didn't happen until October 1973.

❧ ❧

The abortion case finally went to trial in mid-summer of 1972, before a three-judge court. I was recognized to present plaintiffs' side of the case. "Your Honors, if it please the court …" I knew my arguments backward and forward. I knew the persuasive examples of how the laws infringed on the doctors' right to practice medicine without fear of prosecution. I'd argued all those provisions of the law in 1969 to legislators, and I'd spoken to groups all over the state about the law and its problems. And I argued the rights of our intervenors, a married couple in which the wife could have no more children because of her health. All of that came very easily. It was hard to stay within the time limit, there was so much to say.

Then Mick Gillette presented his case, arguing that the statutes were not so vague as to prevent the plaintiffs from conducting their medical practices unhindered by the fear of prosecution, and that a woman's right to privacy was not violated by any of the provisions of the law. It was a good defense by a good lawyer. While we waited for the judges' decision, Keith and I went back to work on our general election campaigns, our law practices, and more politics.

Keith and I were again delegates to the Democratic National Convention, held in Miami in July. U.S. Senator George McGovern led the numerous Democratic candidates. Keith and I had supported him from the beginning.

We left Oregon early to fly to Miami by way of Texas. I wanted to see Wichita Falls and Goree again after leaving there so many years before. Keith had had his basic training at Sheppard Field. It would be a nostalgic stop-over for both of us, and a detour worth taking. It greatly reinforced my gratitude for those formative influences, but when I tried to imagine what my life would have been like if I'd never left, I felt stifled, repressed, even smothered. It would have been no life at all. A knot formed in my stomach until I thought of my beautiful, abundantly nurturing state of Oregon, and the life I would continue to have, all because I'd said, "Keep walking," on the way down that long church aisle to marry a soldier from Oregon.

As in Chicago four years before, young people gathered in Miami from all over the country, and there was a police presence. This time, however, there were few rabble-rousers and few demonstrations. I remember walking alone through an almost-deserted hotel lobby one night after attending a late McGovern strategy meeting, looking for something to eat and enjoying the Miami night. The humidity had tapered off and the cool breeze from the ocean flowed in. I saw a man walking toward me. I recognized him as Abbie Hoffman, one of the most radical of the leaders in Chicago. He had been one of the Chicago Seven, who were prosecuted after the 1968 convention for conspiracy to incite riots, and ultimately acquitted. I recalled that the writer Norman Mailer, testifying for the defense at the trial, had said, "Left-wingers are incapable of conspiracy because they're all egomaniacs." But Abbie Hoffman said it better: "Conspiracy? Hell, we couldn't agree on lunch." Apparently they couldn't agree to go to Florida, either. I spoke to him, told him I was a delegate and had been a delegate in Chicago. He nodded his head, then said, "Where is everyone? This place is too fucking quiet." With that he wandered on down the empty hallway.

How things had changed since Chicago! But the young people, including our young delegation members, were still saying, "Never again. No more old-time politics where decisions are made by a few behind closed doors." When George McGovern, who won the nomination, selected Senator Thomas Eagleton from Missouri as his candidate for vice president, this angered many of our first-time delegates—it looked to them as if the "old pols" were selecting the running mate without consulting them or the other delegates.

I had the responsibility for leading our unusually diverse thirty-four-member delegation. The Democratic National Committee had requested that all states choose a delegation that represented the population of the state. Oregon's delegation had thirteen members under thirty years old. Half of our delegates were women, and two were African American. Some of these young, enthusiastic delegates, mostly women, wanted to support Frances "Sissy" Farenthold from Texas as the vice-presidential nominee. But tradition calls for the presidential nominee to name his own running mate, to ensure that the ticket reflects a balance in geography and political philosophy, and, more practically, to make it more likely that the candidates can truly run as a team. I could see the sense in that, even as I was torn between a desire to cast a symbolic vote for feminist Farenthold and an obligation as delegation leader to support McGovern. Twenty years later Floyd McKay wrote in *The Oregonian*, "With the practicality of an elected legislator, Roberts voted for Eagleton." But inside me it hurt, not being able to vote for a woman, and a liberal Texas woman at that.

A McGovern presidency was not to be. Nixon won by a landslide; McGovern carried only Massachusetts and the District of Columbia. I had been his Oregon campaign co-chairman with Jim Redden. The campaign went as well as could be expected, but the Democrats were still too divided for him to win or even make a good showing against an incumbent president, even in Oregon.

The 1972 election saw me and Betty Browne back in the Senate and sent more women to the House than ever before. My new district (by then Oregon's legislative districts had been reconstituted as single-member districts) had three Catholic parishes within its boundaries. I worried about how my support of abortion would affect my constituents' votes. As always, I campaigned hard, and I took the issue on straightforwardly whenever it was raised. I won my race after covering every precinct in my district that could be walked, losing only five precincts out of more than a hundred. My opponent never raised the abortion issue, but I was told by others that it had been the subject of sermons at Sunday mass. Many Catholics had told me not to worry about it, that they would all vote their own convictions on the issue.

In the House races, Vera Katz had taken on Fritzi Chuinard on the west side of Portland and beaten her, and Mary Roberts, Frank's daughter, had won a seat in east Multnomah County. Mary Burrows was elected from Lane County, along with Margaret (Peg) Dereli from the Salem area and Pat Whiting from Tigard in Washington County. With the women who had been reelected—Nancie Fadeley, Norma Paulus, Mary Rieke, and Grace Peck—there would be nine women in the House, which made eleven total in the Legislature. The most ever!

Many important issues and events had propelled us there. But it was the Equal Rights Amendment that was, as we would say today, the "tipping point." The proposed amendment was brief and to the point: "Equality of rights under the law shall not be denied or abridged by the United States or by any State on account of sex." After the resolution was passed by Congress in 1972, states that had annual sessions of their legislatures began ratifying the proposed amendment, one by one, for a total of twenty-two by the time the amendment would come before the Oregon Legislature in the 1973 session.

Women's groups pushed into high gear, including the Oregon chapters of the National Organization for Women and the Oregon Women's Political Caucus. The Oregon Council for Women's Equality was formed, naming as its first president Eleanor Davis, well known for her organizational skills and her diplomacy. Gretchen Kafoury remembers Eleanor: "I never heard her swear or speak ill of anyone, except some of the Neanderthal legislators ... When things got dicey, and they often did, Eleanor could usually be counted on to call us back to reality and civility. It was hard to argue with her or go against her."

Eleanor Davis pulled together the Equal Rights Alliance—its acronym, of course, "ERA"—for the sole purpose of working for the ratification of the Equal Rights Amendment in Oregon; its members were the Oregon Women's Political Caucus, the American Civil Liberties Union, the Governor's Committee on Status of Women, NOW, and the Council for Women's Equality. The Alliance hired Gretchen Kafoury to be the lobbyist, with Eleanor helping Gretchen as a volunteer.

The women's revolution had not come about by magic, nor did it emerge suddenly with the ERA proposal. It had been brewing for a very long time. The united effort behind the ERA made this a heady time, and the future looked promising. There was a long, hard road ahead, but the women, especially the younger ones, were confident that everything was possible. For them, many the age of my own children, Helen Reddy's song "I Am Woman" became their anthem: "I am woman, hear me roar/ In numbers too big to ignore/ ... ."

For the past ten or fifteen years I'd done my roaring mostly alone—certainly without a chorus backing me up. My maturity and years of experience in the Legislature now made me useful to the women who surged to the front in the battle for equal rights, and this gave me great satisfaction. I could sing right along with them: "If I have to I can face anything/ I am strong/ I am invincible/ I am woman."

Chapter 13

When Everything Was Possible

There were many reasons to anticipate a vigorous and productive 1973 legislative session. First of all, the Democrats had an honest-to-goodness, legitimate majority in both houses. In the Senate, Democrats numbered eighteen of the thirty members, and for the first time in eighteen years—nine legislative sessions—the Democrats named the president of the Senate, Jason Boe from Reedsport. The Democrats had also gained control of the House thirty-three to twenty-seven. With both houses under Democratic leadership, a second-term Republican governor who worked well with Democrats, more Republican moderates, and a new crop of younger legislators, I expected the session to be more energetic and unpredictable than usual. Maybe my kindergarten bill would have a chance this time.

At the opening-day ceremonies on Monday, January 8, 1973, Governor McCall, noting that this would be his last such address, expressed once again his love for Oregon: "Oregon is an inspiration. Whether you come to it or are born to it, you become entranced by our State's beauty, the opportunities she affords, and the independent spirit of her citizens." McCall went on to celebrate the cleanup of the Willamette River—"our ecological Easter"—and to commend the Legislature for supporting the bottle bill in the face of intense pressure from lobbyists. He urged his listeners to continue their efforts "to keep Oregon lovable, and make it more livable."

Of all McCall's exhortations, most welcome to my ears was this: "But you will need no special message from me to act upon the Women's Rights Amendment to the Federal Constitution. I urge you to ratify this Amendment as your first order of business in this session—and as a continuation of our mutual respect for human rights."

With the pomp and circumstance completed, the Senate convened at two o'clock that afternoon. I contemplated my overflowing plate of committee assignments. Again I would serve on the Joint Ways and Means Committee as its Senate vice-chairman, and again I would be chairman of the Consumer and Business Affairs Committee and a member of the Education Committee. A new assignment was co-chairman, with Representative Bill McCoy, on a new joint committee on aging. In an unusual break with tradition of scattering the women members around among the various committees, Speaker Eymann appointed five women to the eleven-member House Environment and Land Use Committee and named Nancie Fadeley the chairman. An appointment that puzzled me was the naming of Mary Roberts, a freshman legislator, to the Ways and Means Committee, ordinarily composed of senior legislators. Some assumed my relationship with Mary was chilled because of my divorce from her father. But that wasn't the case at all. I didn't know her, even though she had been, legally speaking, my stepdaughter during the few years Frank and I were married. We met for the first time at a DemoForum conference at Kah-Nee-Ta, a resort on the Warm Springs Indian Reservation in central Oregon, following the primary election that year. Between meetings, everyone congregated around the pool to soak up the sun.

Doug Yokom, a reporter from the *Oregon Journal,* said to me, "Mary Roberts is over on the other side of the pool," in a voice that indicated that that was something I'd like to know. Because she had refused to ever see me while Frank and I were married, I told Doug I'd never met Mary—a big surprise to him. He said, "Would you like to meet her?"

I answered that our meeting would be up to her, since she'd had plenty of opportunities in the past and refused. Apparently, that word spread rapidly around to Mary, and she came over and introduced herself. I congratulated her on her primary win, and we said nothing more.

An article in the society section of *The Oregonian*—just below a recipe for Greek broiled leg of lamb—stated succinctly and accurately, "Sen. Betty Roberts and Rep. Mary Roberts agree that their closest tie is membership in the Democratic Party."

❧ ❧

Soon after opening day Norma Paulus came to my desk on the Senate floor and said, "Betty, we women in the House think we need to form a women's caucus to talk about getting the ERA passed. Since you're the senior woman in the Senate I think you should call and chair the meeting." I hadn't thought of that, but it made sense. I wouldn't presume to organize the women in the House, although there was no question in my mind that most of them would work for the ERA, as Betty Browne and I would in the Senate. But Norma's proposal gave me permission to reach out to them. I called the meeting for late one afternoon in my third-floor committee room.

What a gathering! The incumbent House members, Norma Paulus, Mary Reike, Nancie Fadeley, and Grace Peck, along with Senators Betty Browne and myself, had already proven ourselves effective legislators. Freshmen Representatives Vera Katz and Mary Burrows were quickly making their mark.

Representatives Mary Roberts, Peg Dereli, and Pat Whiting rounded out our caucus. We were a diverse group of Republicans and Democrats ranging in age from thirty to seventy-five, lawyers and housewives, office workers, social workers and union workers, most married but some not, with children from pre-school age to grown and out on their own. The convergence of these women in my committee room was no accident. Every one of us had spirit and a common purpose. We were all warriors. For me, it seemed the cavalry had finally arrived.

The Equal Rights Amendment was our first order of business. We wanted Oregon to be an early supporter. Because our Legislature meets only every two years, we'd lost the opportunity to be among the first, but we wanted to hurry to be the first in this new year of 1973.

Three ratification bills were introduced in the Legislature, two in the House and one in the Senate, all within a few days of one another. Our women's caucus decided to work with the Senate bill, Senate Joint Resolution 4, which was sponsored by nine of the women legislators. Because of committee schedules, however, the first hearing on an ERA proposal was held by the House State and Federal Affairs Committee, chaired by Representative Les AuCoin, on January 17, 1973. People were packed into the largest hearing room in the Capitol Building and overflowed into the hallway.

The major witness was Carol Hewitt, an attorney and the ACLU's representative to the Equal Rights Alliance. She spoke on behalf of the Alliance and gave the first in-depth testimony advocating ratification. Then I addressed the "right to privacy" issues, primarily because we knew the issue of integrated restrooms had been raised in other states.

Representatives Roger Martin and Nancie Fadeley testified in favor of the bill, as did Norman Nilsen, Labor Commissioner, and Kathleen Nachtigal, attorney and Chairperson of the State Wage and Hour Commission. Others speaking in favor were representatives of various women's organizations— Business and Professional Women's Association, the Oregon Home Economics Association, the American Association of University Women, and a representative from the Governor's Committee on the Status of Women.

Opposing the ratification were a number of women representing themselves, as well as people speaking for the Preservation of Womanhood (whose state chairman was a man), the Movement to Restore Decency, and Parents for the Preservation of the Family. One woman stated, "We women have so much to lose if we are granted equality." Other opponents said women would be subject to the draft as soon as it passed and would have to report to induction centers,

Women in the 1973 legislature: Senators Betty Browne, Betty Roberts; Representatives Mary Burrows, Peg Dereli, Nancie Fadeley, Vera Katz, Norma Paulus, Grace Peck, Mary Rieke, Mary Roberts, Pat Whiting. (Photographs from *Oregon Blue Book, 1975-1976*)

that school children would have to share restrooms and shower facilities, that the ERA would destroy the American family, because wives would no longer be obligated to take their husbands' names when they married and that husbands would no longer be obligated to support their families.

The committee hearing went well. Our witnesses were well prepared, and we learned what to expect from the opponents. But how sad to hear women say they didn't want equality. That meant they didn't support the basic tenets of our democracy; they didn't want to be responsible for themselves or their government. Of greater concern to me was their selfishness in not wanting other women to have equal opportunities to live their lives as they chose without enduring discrimination. Those women could not see how demeaning it was to them to reject liberty and justice.

Having heard the opposition, the women legislators' caucus made an even greater effort to prepare ourselves for the hearing on the Senate bill, scheduled for the Judiciary Committee just five days later, on January 22, 1973.

That morning began for me like every morning of that session, with an eight-o'clock subcommittee meeting in Ways and Means. About an hour into the meeting I was called to the telephone. It was Mick Gillette, the opposing attorney from the Attorney General's office against whom I'd argued the abortion case. His message was straight to the point. "Betty, the U.S. Supreme Court released its opinion in the abortion cases this morning. You won."

"Wow, Mick, that's great," I said. The Supreme Court had finally rendered its decision in the famous *Roe v. Wade* case. The decision in *Roe v. Wade*, which essentially made all statutes limiting access to abortion unconstitutional, would decide our Oregon case.

"I thought you'd like to know that, and I wanted to be the first to tell you," was his good-loser response.

"But how much did we win?" That was an important question, because there were so many issues wrapped up in the case.

His response was beautiful. "You won it all."

I was so elated, I had to tell everyone I saw. I told the committee members and whoever was in the hearing room that day. Then I left the meeting and went in search of Gretchen and Eleanor, the women legislators and lobbyists and, of course, Keith. Eleanor says she still remembers seeing me running toward her with the good news.

Then it was back to business in a hurry, to prepare for the afternoon Judiciary Committee hearing on the ERA. The House committee hearing had given us an idea of what we were up against. We knew advocates in other states had been running into last-minute, mostly irrational opposition. In California, state senators favoring the ERA were sent dead mice—the message apparently being that if they supported the ERA they were mice, not men. In another state, legislators received bullets for their wives.

As the debate picked up steam, the name Phyllis Schlafly was heard more and more. Schlafly was becoming well known as an opponent of the ERA. The ERA, Schlafly stated, would upset "a tradition of special respect for women which dates from the Christian age of chivalry, (and) the honor and respect paid to Mary, the mother of Christ." What she and her followers didn't seem to understand was that this so-called chivalry consigns women to permanent second-class citizenship. We ERA supporters not only had to give logical, compelling reasons for ratification, but we had to counteract dozens of such frivolous arguments.

The first ERA proponent to speak at the Senate Judiciary Committee hearing was Labor Commissioner Norman Nilsen, who advocated the ERA as a way to give equality to women in working conditions and in other areas. Next was Sidney Lezak, the U.S. Attorney for Oregon, who told the committee he had resigned as president of the Portland City Club when the question of admitting women was voted down.

I testified next. After congratulating Sid Lezak for resigning as president of the City Club, I said I had been given only one issue to address—the old question of whether men and women would use the same restrooms if the ERA became a part of the Constitution. My arguments were well rehearsed. First, I explained the right of privacy under the Ninth Amendment to the U.S. Constitution. Then I tackled the subject of custom and convenience, suggesting that the committee members and opponents who might raise this issue had, in fact, experienced so-called unisex bathrooms when riding on airplanes, trains, and buses, as well as in small restaurants, gas stations, or similar businesses. *And the sky didn't fall, did it?* I wanted to say, but I didn't. Finally, I urged the committee to be aware that this was not a serious argument, but only a tactical diversion. The committee should not be deterred—the members needed to concentrate on the seriousness of the ERA in achieving the ideals of equality that we all sought.

Then the focus shifted to the women who had worked to prepare and organize testimony. Carol Hewitt, representing the Equal Rights Alliance, testified again as compellingly as she had at the House hearing. She explained in lay terms, plainly and clearly, the need for the ERA: because the United States Supreme Court had refused to use the Fourteenth Amendment to the U.S. Constitution in sex-discrimination cases as it had in race-discrimination cases.

Then Representative Grace Peck began her testimony. We held our breath. Grace, a devout Catholic, was celebrating her seventy-fifth birthday. She had been reelected repeatedly because she had an innate ability to keep up with the times, even as she agonized publicly about her stand on issues. A number of Catholic women, she said, had tried to talk her into voting against the ERA. But she'd talked to the archbishop just that morning, and he had told her that some Catholics favored the ERA and some were opposed. He saw it as a personal matter for each individual. Therefore, she said, she would rely on the fact that Oregon's Congresswoman, Edith Green, had worked diligently for the approval in Congress of the proposed amendment, and because she had such great respect for Mrs. Green, Grace had signed the bill and she would vote for it.

Whew! We could breathe again.

After more testimony from proponents, the opponents had their turn. Some represented only themselves, while others listed the American Independent Party, Voice of Liberty, Committee for Preservation of Women, and another group with a similar name, Committee for Preservation of Womanhood, an organization called "Motorede" (which was never explained), Parents for the Preservation of the Family, Women for Constitutional Government and Citizens for Constitutional Government. Their testimony rehashed the same old arguments.

There was, I had to admit, a splattering of creative rhetoric. One witness stated flatly that there would never be complete equality because "men cannot have babies." Then she said, "If the Equal Rights Amendment is ratified, then in the eyes of the law there will no longer be men and women, only persons." And further, "… a husband (would) no longer be a husband, but an anonymous spouse." Her written testimony went on in that vein for three typewritten pages.

One woman spoke compellingly for anti-discrimination protection in our state laws, rather than a federal amendment. Her argument had merit from a states' rights point of view, but this was not the time to engage in the age-old debate of federalism versus states' rights. The Congress had acted, and it was an amendment to the U.S. Constitution that was before us.

The bill reached the Senate floor on February 1, 1973. With only two women in the Senate, it was up to the men to carry the burden of the argument for the ERA. As he opened the debate, Senator John Burns observed that Oregon had "a very, very progressive state civil rights act … there is very little discrimination in our laws … based on sex." But other states, he said, do have discriminatory laws, and as a lawyer he thought it important that there be a uniform standard for the courts to follow. Burns then listed what the ERA would *not* do. It would not override the constitutional right to privacy, it would not suspend legal obligations such as child-support laws, and it would not abrogate criminal laws such as those against rape and prostitution. It would allow women to be drafted, but Congress could establish criteria for the kinds of duties they would perform. He concluded by stating that Presidents Eisenhower, Kennedy, Johnson and then-President Nixon all supported the ERA, and that Oregon should join the other states that had already ratified it.

I observed the ensuing debate among my male colleagues with admiration, for they had not been taken in by the scare tactics of the opposition, but were truly interested in the need for the ERA. Finally I stood and had my say once again. First, on the issue of women being drafted into military service: Congress presently had the power to draft women. Whether a woman would actually be in combat would depend on her training and physical capability. The committee had heard from women who had served in the military and had benefited from the experience.

Next, the question of whether we really needed the ERA, when we could change our state laws to prohibit discrimination, was an opening to talk about the benefits of an ERA for men. For example, when a man retired and started drawing Social Security, his wife could choose to take her own Social Security benefits or one-half of her husband's, whichever was larger. Without the ERA there was no comparable provision for men.

On work protections for women, I noted that men regularly made claims for injuries resulting from jobs that were too stressful either physically or mentally, and that there were protections already in the law that were applicable regardless of gender. "It is time," I said, "that we get out of our minds that there are certain kinds of work that only men can do and that only women can do." Finally, I read a passage from Professor Leo Kanowitz's book *Women and the Law*:

> Delegating women to special tasks by perpetuating the ancient myths about the alleged physical and psychological limitations of women, we American men have subjected ourselves to an awesome burden. For the doubtful joys of feeling superior to women, we have paid a terrible price. ... our insistence that men and only men are entitled to be society's doers and shapers, has led to our dying from eight to ten years earlier—on the average than women of our country. Perhaps, even more important is that because of arbitrary social and legal distinctions, both men and women are prevented from relating to one another as people—as fellow members of the human race.

Appealing to the men again—as I had in the abortion debate—I concluded with a heartfelt belief that both "men and women will be better protected by ratification of this amendment."

The resolution passed the Senate with a good majority: twenty-three "Ayes" and only six "Nays," with one member absent. One of the "Nays" was Tom Mahoney—no surprise—who went so far as to request that the following explanation be inserted in the Senate Journal: "God created all men equal, but he put women on a higher plane than men. Because of my high regard for womankind I voted 'No.'" Thanks, but no thanks, Senator. I'd never known any woman who felt elevated to that higher plane of which he spoke, wherever or whatever that may be.

When the Senate recessed at noon, I went to the lunchroom in the hallway behind the Senate chambers. As I passed the men's restroom, there on the door was a hastily hand-printed sign tacked under the always-present word "Men." It said, "and Women (please knock)." I could only hope it was a joke.

☙ ☙

A few days later, on my fiftieth birthday, four young women who were working for various legislators or committees in the House approached me. One said, "Could we talk to you for just a second?"

"Sure, of course, find some chairs."

The boldest of them, Ann Aiken, introduced herself and the others. Ann said they had a present for me for my birthday. With some diffidence, she handed me a small, flat red-and-white box tied with a paper ribbon. Thanking them profusely, I opened the box. Inside was a white bra that had been partially burned. It was, let's say, a full-size bra, with black burn marks around the generous cups and up into the wide straps. I joined in their giggles and grins, and, looking around to be sure no one was standing nearby, I took it out and held it up to my chest to get a better look. We laughed and blushed and fumbled around with the darn thing to get it back in its box before anyone saw what was going on.

These four young women were roommates. Ever since the Senate debate on the ERA they'd planned to surprise me with a birthday present. When they told me about the hard time they'd had deciding which of the three could most afford to give up a bra, both on a financial and physical-needs basis, we had another good laugh. And then they handed me my real birthday present: a Helen Reddy album with "I Am Woman" on it and all the other great songs she sang. What a wonderful gesture between generations! "I Am Woman, Hear Me Roar," I sang to them as they departed.

☙ ☙

The final hurdle for the ERA was passage in the House. The House floor debate took place on February 8, 1973, only a week after the Senate vote.

Representative Nancie Fadeley spoke first. She painted a compelling picture of what the ERA would mean to ordinary human beings, black and white, male and female, on a day-to-day basis. She spoke of women in poverty who had children to raise, who had to do lower-status work because they lacked opportunities, who had to settle for lower pay than men.

Representative Bernard Byers, a Democrat from Lebanon, a small town south of Salem, opposed ratification because he believed it wasn't needed. Women already had laws on equal pay for equal work and other laws could be passed if they were necessary. So there! Short, but not so sweet.

Representative Norma Paulus made a forceful plea:

> I believe I can separate the Equal Rights Amendment from the Women's Movement for those of you who feel uncomfortable about certain aspects of the Women's Movement. ... The Women's Movement purports to change attitudes—I support that movement, wholeheartedly. It seeks to change the attitudes, social attitudes between men and women. But that's not what the Equal Rights Amendment does. The Equal Rights Amendment seeks to change the *government's* attitude toward women. Today, I don't care what you men really think of me or what your attitude toward me is, but I do care what the government thinks of me and what *its* attitude is toward me.

Norma went on in her own unique style to point out that the U.S. Supreme Court had always recognized white males as persons—picking out a good-looking male representative to illustrate her point—but that it had only recently recognized race as a protected status under the law. Here she mentioned Bill McCoy, the only African American representative to have served in the Oregon Legislature; the Court had finally recognized him as a person, but only after "it smelled smoke from the courthouse burning." The Court, she said, had yet to recognize women as persons. "I know I am a person," she said. "You know I am a person. And it is about time the United States Supreme Court knew it."

Vera Katz then had her say. She gave examples of sex discrimination in the "progressive State of Oregon," pointing out that, because of their sex, women may be barred from renting apartments, buying homes, or receiving loans. They may be denied entrance to vocational or training schools and prohibited from entering public accommodations. There has been an extraordinary change in America, Vera continued, marked by a new surge of idealism and a new insistence on reality in our democratic order. But more must be done, because women are demanding it, and "because, by any moral standard, it is right."

Opposition then came from Paul Hanneman, a Republican from the coastal town of Cloverdale, where he said he saw men and women working "side by side on the farms, women working in the barns carrying almost as heavy milking machines as the men." That didn't seem unfair to him.

Majority Leader Les AuCoin, a Democrat from Forest Grove just south of Portland, was the first man to speak in favor:

> [T]he question before us is simply this: Do we have the will to guarantee the full rights of citizenship to both men and women? …
>
> … In ratifying this amendment, we are not saying that one role in life is superior or inferior to another. Instead we are insuring that each individual has the full opportunity to be what he or she wants to be and then leaving it up to the person's ability, *not the happenstance of one's sex,* to determine if his or her aspirations will be met.

Yay, Les! He was followed by Representative Roger Martin, a Republican from Lake Oswego, a suburb of Portland, also a proponent. Roger had drawn latrine duty, so I could sympathize with him. To fulfill his obligation, he'd informally surveyed four of the major oil companies that did business in Oregon. Did they plan to change the restrooms in their service stations should the ERA become a part of the Constitution? After he convinced them he was serious, they replied that the service stations were there to serve the public, and that the public would continue to want separate facilities. However, Roger continued, one of the managers pointed out that some of the rural communities have only one restroom. "When I stopped to think about it," Roger said, "I realized that he was right. This has been historical; usually they have not been differentiated between men and women, but between one-holers or two-holers."

Good argument, Roger. I wished I'd thought of that.

The speeches were getting shorter as the noon hour approached. Representative Gordon Macpherson, a Republican from the Newport area, didn't exactly endear himself to the women when he said he would join the "girls" in voting for the resolution, and that he had just heard "the two finest speeches made on the floor of this house *by women.*" But it was easy to forgive his *faux pas* in exchange for his vote.

Other legislators, all favoring the ERA, spoke in quick succession—Keith Skelton, Mary Rieke, Wally Priestley and Howard Willits, who pointed out that Oregon hadn't even ratified the Fourteenth Amendment yet, and that we should do that and ratify the ERA, too.

Finally, Nancie Fadeley made her brief closing remarks. She spoke of the Oregon pioneer suffragist Abigail Scott Duniway, who was turned away when she tried to vote in 1870. Duniway then worked diligently to get the vote for women and was finally successful in 1912, almost a decade before women nationally could vote.

The roll was called. The vote was fifty "Ayes," nine "Nays," with one person excused. An overwhelming victory.

While we had wanted to be the first state to ratify in 1973, two other western states beat us to the punch—Wyoming and South Dakota. Oregon was number twenty-five to ratify the ERA. We'd done it. There would be similar battles in other legislatures. In Oregon it was a sweet victory.

Chapter 14

Give Me Liberty, or Get out of the Way

With the ERA passed only a month into the 1973 legislative session, our attention turned to bills that would bring Oregon laws into conformity with the new constitutional amendment. It may be hard to imagine today that women couldn't keep their birth names when they got married, couldn't get credit in their own names, couldn't stay at a motel alone, couldn't eat at certain restaurants at lunchtime, couldn't get insurance unless they had a husband, couldn't be admitted to some trade schools. It was shocking how fast the bills piled up. It was too big a task for one session, but we were determined to make a good start.

Top priority, our women's caucus decided, were the bills that would affect the largest number of women. Those were the proposals prohibiting discrimination in public accommodation, allowing a woman to choose whether to keep her name upon marriage or to return to a former name if divorcing, and prohibiting discrimination in educational institutions and in insurance matters.

Civil rights as a theory, as in the ERA, is one thing, but applying that theory to specific practices can sometimes stomp on people's hidden prejudices. When that happens, there is sure to be opposition, because it makes people uncomfortable to have their beliefs and attitudes stirred up and publicly exposed. I counted ten men in the Senate who would consistently support the women's legislation. With Betty Browne and myself, that was only twelve votes, and sixteen were required for passage. That meant we'd have to rely on senators who might see one proposal as reasonable but vote against another that triggered one of their personal feelings.

Prospects in the House looked better. There were nine women out of the sixty members. I estimated about twenty men in the House who could be counted on to support the ERA-based legislation consistently. The women in the House would still have to work to pick up a few more votes on each bill, but we thought it would be easier to get our bills passed there first.

Being in the minority in both houses, we women legislators were constantly mindful that women made up more than 50 percent of the population, while men controlled 90 to 100 percent of everything—government positions, management positions in business, labor unions, school administration, the medical and legal professions, architecture and engineering, and nonprofit and religious organizations.

More urgently, women's wages were only a little over one-half those of men. *Earning power, that's what it's all about,* I told myself. *When women make what men make, there will be equality.* I'd known that for a long time. As the women's bills flowed in and my frustration level rose with the realization of how much work we had to do, my inner urge was to join women protesters into the streets chanting, "Equality Now."

Well, get a grip, Betty, I scolded that inner self. I was right here in the Oregon Legislature, the best place I could possibly be. I was in a position of power, and now I could use that power to help women gain equality under the law. It had been a long climb since that 1965 session, when I had been confronted with my powerlessness in the Ways and Means Committee over whether a kindergarten bill would be funded. Now I'd learned what it means to have unilateral power. I'd learned that power also comes from being informed and from building alliances—collaborative power. To achieve our goals, we women had to work together just as workers did in the early part of the twentieth century, when solidarity led to labor unions and, eventually, to better working conditions.

Nevertheless, as important as women's rights were, I didn't want to be viewed as a single-issue legislator, even for that one session. There would be important bills coming out of the Ways and Means Committee, my Consumer and Business Affairs Committee, and the new Joint Committee on Aging. And other major issues needed attention that session—the most controversial and far-reaching of which was a statewide land use planning bill, Senate Bill 100, under consideration in the Senate Environment and Land Use Committee.

I intended to work hard to pass some of these proposals, and I knew I'd need the votes of men who did not vote favorably on the equality bills. I did not want to alienate male legislators to the point that I could not work effectively with them on other legislation. It was a tightrope on which I had to find a constant balance.

❧ ❧

Our bill to prohibit discrimination in public accommodations started out as a replay of the bill I had tried to get through in the last session. This time, we'd work with House Bill 2116, expanding it to prohibit discrimination in housing and in getting credit and insurance. Also added to the bill was a provision prohibiting discrimination on the basis of sex in admission to vocational and trade schools.

The bill had its first hearing in the House State and Federal Affairs Committee, chaired by Les AuCoin, who had spoken eloquently on the ERA and who was counted among our for-sure supporters. Some of the women who testified at the hearings cited problems they'd had in obtaining credit in their own names. Some reported that they had withheld information about divorces or deaths of husbands for fear that their credit or insurance would be cancelled. With its multiple provisions, the bill was met on the floor of the House with many of the same arguments, both pro and con, that had arisen in the debate about the Equal Rights Amendment, including the unisex bathrooms. *When, oh when, will that issue ever be put to rest?*

The bill passed the House with a good vote of forty-four "Ayes," paralleling closely the vote on the ERA. When it reached the Senate, the president referred it to my Consumer and Business Affairs Committee, where Betty Browne was my vice chairman. We ran into problems when Hector Macpherson opposed the addition of "marital status" to the housing anti-discrimination portion of the bill. He thought a hotel or motel ought to be able to choose not to rent to an unmarried person. On the first committee vote, the bill failed four to three. Women lobbyists were subsequently able to convince Debbs Potts and Bob Smith to vote "Aye." The day of the second vote, Senator Macpherson was absent and only Tom Mahoney voted against the bill. A few days later it passed the Senate with twenty-eight "Aye" votes—including Senator Macpherson's. The almost unanimous vote—only one senator voted against the bill and one was excused—is an important example of the women lobbyists at work.

Another priority bill was House Bill 2925, which would allow a woman to keep a prior name when she married and would require a judge to allow a woman to change her name when she was granted a divorce. The bill was introduced early in the session and referred to the House Judiciary Committee, where both Norma Paulus and Vera Katz served. The other committee members were not particularly friendly toward the bill, and it didn't get to the floor of the House until mid-June, close to the end of the session. It passed there with only two votes to spare.

In the meantime we worked on other bills, all priorities in our women's caucus. One, introduced by Senator Ed Fadeley, funded the Bureau of Labor's affirmative-action program. A related bill, sponsored by Senator Fadeley and Representative Bill Gwinn at the request of the Public Employees Association, directed the Personnel Division to review all state job classifications for discrimination on the basis of race, religion, sex, and national origin. Both passed, giving good examples of men working individually and together to help bring about more opportunities both for women and for minorities.

Senator Keith Burbidge, a Democrat from Salem and one of our outspoken supporters, introduced two bills that our caucus adopted. One would extend workers' compensation benefits to a married man with children if his wife died in a work-related accident. That one had no trouble passing. We women supported it on the basis of fairness to men and as necessary for the children. The other, which didn't pass, would have required the Public Employees Retirement System to cease using sex as the only criterion for computing annuity rates. That issue would be revisited again in another session.

Of all my good experiences of the 1973 session, the one that remains warmest in my memory is watching men and women working together on proposals on which we women tended to claim ownership. That and the satisfaction that came from working with a community of goal-oriented women who never spoke ill of each other, never showed signs of jealousy or envy, and bonded together as if our lives depended on it. And so they did—at least the future opportunities of all women in Oregon depended on it.

In a more playful mood (but still along the lines of helping working women), Representative Vera Katz introduced a bill to repeal the law that prohibited women from engaging in professional wrestling and boxing matches. Seeing that there could be some fun in arguing that women ought to be able to work at whatever appealed to them, Norma Paulus quickly gave the bill her public support. The Equal Rights Alliance, by this time working hard on other bills, noted solemnly that this was a proposal that would affect very few women and that, therefore, they would not spend their valuable time and political effort on getting it passed. The bill never saw the light of day except to be referred from the House State and Federal Affairs Committee, where it had been tabled, to the House Rules Committee, where it was tabled again. So much for having women wrestlers and boxers any time soon in Oregon.

A significant bill for low-income working women, Senate Bill 74, was a comprehensive act that created a Children's Commission in the Department of Human Resources. I was the sole sponsor. SB 74 recognized the need for government involvement to the tune of $4.2 million from the state general fund. That money would produce $5.4 million in federal funds and $2.4 million in private funds, all to be administered by the new Children's Commission. The bill passed both chambers handily and made a significant policy statement about working mothers' need for adequate child care.

The *Roe v. Wade* case, so recently out of the U.S. Supreme Court, prompted all sorts of proposals on abortion. The *Roe* case had decided the case that Keith and I had initiated in the United States District Court of Oregon, *Benson et al. v. Johnson et al.* The Oregon Attorney General's interpretation held that the state had no laws regulating abortion. That conclusion energized some legislators to fill the vacuum one way or another. Some wanted to write something into the statute affirming what *Roe v. Wade* had already said. Others who'd disagreed with the ruling wanted to add consent provisions and exempt some medical facilities from performing abortions. Still others would strip the tax-exempt status from a medical facility that refused to perform the procedure. The Equal Rights Alliance took the position that the best legislation was no legislation at all. And we women legislators agreed with that.

Other bills on family planning show how much we were still living in the world of "the birds and the bees" in 1973. One bill would make it possible to buy condoms outside of pharmacies, including from vending machines and other outlets, as long as they were licensed by the Board of Health. The representative from the Board of Health spoke of the dire consequences of putting vending machines in restrooms, especially women's restrooms. Oh, my goodness, how scandalous for a woman to buy a condom.

We'd had a similar issue in the 1971 session; then the question had been whether condoms could be put on public display, like other products in drugstores. The practice at that time was for the pharmacist to keep them behind the counter, so that a customer had to ask for them. Of course this inhibited the use of condoms, particularly by young, unmarried males in smaller communities. An attempt to keep the kids virgins a little longer—I guess that was the idea. But it must also have had an inhibiting effect on adults, since they probably didn't want their friend the pharmacist to know that much about their personal affairs, at home or otherwise. Given all this feigned prudishness, I had no idea how this new bill in the 1973 session would fare, even though the 1971 bill had become the law.

The condom bill made it through both chambers, along with one that would permit a person to be voluntarily sterilized without consent of a spouse and one that would require all county health departments to provide family-planning information. None of these was earth-shaking in itself, but the bills sent a signal that it was becoming more acceptable to talk about prevention of pregnancy.

While we're on the subject of sex, a bill came before my Consumer and Business Affairs Committee that would make it a crime to buy the services of a prostitute. At that time, it was illegal to practice prostitution, but not to buy sexual services. The bill was sponsored by every woman in the Legislature including Gracie Peck, who considered herself a friend of prostitutes. She'd introduced a bill in the 1969 session to increase the penalty for pimps. Her bill had been enacted into law, but it hadn't helped "those unfortunate girls"— Gracie's term—all that much.

This session the idea had come from Shirley Field, who had been my divorce lawyer and who, as a legislator in my first term, had taken it upon herself to teach me about the Legislature in often unkind and ineffective ways. But that was then. Now she was a judge; she called me about introducing this bill, explaining that she regularly saw prostitutes in her courtroom and had concluded that it took two to tango. She had taken to asking the police officer where the other party was. After the officer answered that he had not been charged, Judge Field would explain that she saw the buying and selling of sexual favors as a contract, and that she would not sentence a prostitute for her half of the crime until the male client was charged with his half. Judge Field wasn't the only one who saw the act as a business deal. When President Boe assigned it to my committee he told me he thought Consumer and Business Affairs was exactly where the bill should be.

When committee member Senator Tom Mahoney began asking questions at the hearing on the bill, I knew it could be in trouble. Senator Mahoney was a scrawny, sharp-featured man nearing his eighties. When he questioned witnesses, he half-closed one eye, cocked his head, and looked piercingly at his prey with the other, open eye. I had never trusted him, and I didn't trust him now. Mahoney's prey at this hearing was Don Paillette, a lawyer and former prosecutor who had advised the Legislature on a major revision of the Oregon

Criminal Code in the previous session. Mahoney explained—primarily for the benefit of the audience—that it still was a matter of a plainclothes police officer, or "stool pigeon" (his words) saying, "This is a bust," after the woman has accepted his money and has started to disrobe. His big concern was that the police officer could be convicted of a crime. "Not so," said Paillette, and explained that what the officer did came under the "justification" section of the Criminal Code.

Senator Mahoney pushed on. He asked if Paillette thought jurors would actually convict persons accused under this provision if it became law—implying that in his opinion

Senator Roberts presiding over the Senate, as various senators did from time to time. (Source unknown)

juries would see the law as unfair for the male. On this, too, Paillette differed: he didn't think such a law would be unfair, and he didn't think most members of a jury would think so, either. On the vote to send the bill to the Senate, only Senator Mahoney voted "Nay."

Debate in the Senate also centered around how the law would be enforced. Of particular concern was the use of female police officers whose assignment was to pretend to be a prostitute in order to bust the "john." Some expressed worry that the officer would be beaten when she revealed her identity and made the arrest. But if women police officers could not be used for that reason, then the law would be difficult to enforce. Senator Betty Browne, who took the lead in debate for the committee, said: "If we didn't pass laws because they would be difficult to prosecute or enforce, we wouldn't pass many laws. We pass laws with regard to what is best for society." She chided the senators by saying, "What I see is that there is some hypocrisy going on here that doesn't happen with ... other kinds of laws. Senator Burns noted that women police officers who pose as decoys under this bill might be beaten up. Well, I suggest to you that the police are people who are capable of arranging the situation where women are not beaten up. But I would also say that if we are worried about police women ... why are we not concerned with the sixteen- or seventeen-year-old girl who is beaten up every day in this profession." She added that there was no connection between this bill and women's liberation.

That was a good retort, but I disagreed with Betty's conclusion that this was not a woman's bill. Yes, it was primarily intended to reduce prostitution by making it harder on the customers. But it was a fairness bill, too, just as Judge Field had pointed out. And maybe, just maybe, there wouldn't be as much opportunity for pimps or young women to find their way into that business with this law on the books.

The bill passed with a good majority in both the Senate and the House, where Representative Norma Paulus said, during a committee hearing: "If it is against the law to sell it, then it should be against the law to buy it." So simple. End of debate.

⋟　⋞

As could be expected, there were any number of bills our caucus advocated that failed to pass. Among them was a bill that would prohibit the state from using facilities for governmental meetings that discriminated on the basis of sex, and another that would have suspended an organization's liquor license if it discriminated. That last one didn't go over so well with the Elks Clubs or the Lions Clubs—all those "animal clubs," as Vera Katz, the sponsor of the bill, called them. Another unsuccessful bill would have prohibited any tax exemptions to organizations that discriminated. That was a Katz bill, too. We all admired Vera's passion and courage in filing those bills, along with the first bill ever introduced in the Legislature that would have added sexual orientation to the civil rights protected under the laws of Oregon. It would be 2007—thirty-four years later—before the Legislature would act favorably on this issue.

I introduced a bill myself that I should have known would go nowhere: it would have repealed the law that made it possible to bring a civil action for alienation of affection. The idea came from an experience I'd had while representing a client in a divorce. Her soon-to-be ex-husband had brought an alienation of affection suit against the man she planned to marry as soon as her divorce was final. She believed her husband was using the civil action to help him get custody of their children and to inflict as much pain as possible on both her and her fiancé by getting a money judgment. She didn't understand that to inflict pain was the intent of the statute.

While working on that case I realized that, while women were making progress publicly, in private matters the law still treated them as property. Alienation of affection cases were always brought by a man suing another man over a woman. The law was also used for harassment and blackmail; cases were usually initiated only if the defendant had money. It was an archaic law that allowed a man a great measure of vindictiveness, and it was not in keeping with other reforms the Legislature had made in domestic-relations law, particularly the landmark no-fault divorce law passed in the 1971 session.

My nemesis again was Senator Tom Mahoney. All these bills about prostitution, adultery, and alienation of affection seemed to titillate the old man. He said he opposed repealing this law because it would encourage "homewreckers"—as though anyone deliberately sets out to wreck a home. He blatantly stated, "What this law does, as it exists, is to warn others don't encroach on a man's preserve." And then he added, "There are plenty of single people that a person can engage with without breaking up the family."

I was fairly certain that my colleagues would see Senator Mahoney's opposition for what it was—a silly game on a subject that he found amusing for some reason or other. Surely he would be the only one to oppose the bill, or so I thought. When Ed Fadeley took the floor to oppose the bill I was surprised. I knew Ed was not always consistent in his views, but he had worked with us on some other women's issues. I expected he would go into some legal reasons for retaining the law. But Ed didn't talk about the law. He talked about the Bible and how it advocated co-equal partners in a marriage, saying, "So, I think we can put aside the question of women's rights in any way when trying to decide this issue." This was nonsense, but I had to consider the source. Then he went into society's desire to protect the family, and concluded with, "I would not want to be a part of further deterioration in the position of the family in our society and feel that this bill would be an additional deterioration of the family."

How could Ed reconcile his support of equality in the workplace with his position that equality before the law doesn't apply in personal matters? When the vote was taken there were only eight "Aye" votes. Well, I'd taken a hit, but it wasn't anything to bleed about. Maybe they all owed Tom Mahoney or Ed Fadeley a vote on something. On the other hand, I had not done any lobbying on the bill, and some opponents had. Time to shove that one out of my mind and get on to other matters that needed my attention.

꙾ ꙾

Before the session began Keith had given some thought to seeking the position of Speaker of the House. He never became a candidate, but it put him to thinking about his long tenure in the Legislature. Toward the end of the session he announced that he would not run for reelection. I would miss him and so would many other people. He told me he wasn't comfortable working with "these new, young upstarts who are not respectful of either the process or the decorum we've always had in the past." Keith had complained about some of the younger legislators not wearing ties or otherwise dressing improperly— according to his standards—and "acting out" in challenging other legislators or the speaker instead of using parliamentary procedure to make a point. He was shocked one day, he told me, when one of the new legislators from Portland, Earl Blumenauer, came on the floor right after lunch wearing his running shorts to cast a vote. Never mind that a call of the House was on and every legislator had to be present or excused, no matter what they were wearing, and Earl hadn't had time to change his clothes after his regular noon run.

Governor Tom McCall was winding up his last term, too, and could not run again. By March, the press began to speculate about who might be interested in becoming the next governor. Already a few people had begun to tell me that I should consider running. To a query from Harry Bodine, a reporter for *The Oregonian*, I replied that I was "thinking about" it. To say anything else would not have been true. I was thinking about it because some people were talking to me about it, and that was exactly all there was to it.

One of my earliest supporters from outside Multnomah County was Nancy Hayward, a Lane County commissioner from Eugene. She offered to do everything she could in Lane County to help with a campaign. As an elected official herself, Nancy knew that there would be other serious candidates, and the political battles on issues would be tough. She would not stand back and watch; she would help me in the fight.

About that time a message came in the mail on a note-sized piece of paper "From the desk of Forrest Amsden," that said simply, "Betty, Do It!" Forrest was the manager of Portland television station KATU-TV, an affiliate of the King Broadcasting network in Seattle. I'd known Forrest ever since entering politics and had great respect for him.

All this encouragement was flattering, of course, but what I could see shaping up was the press trying to promote interest in the next governor's campaign. Reporters always wanted something different to write about. A serious woman in the race would be different, all right. When I talked to Keith about it, I could see him brighten—old political warhorse that he was. He and I would have a lot to talk about before decision time came. This wasn't an election year for my Senate seat, so I knew I could run for governor and still have my seat if I lost. The hardest part of the campaign wouldn't begin until early 1974; in the meantime, I could continue teaching part-time and work on my law practice. As I pondered my circumstances, the idea that there might be another opportunity just over the horizon was tantalizing.

My legislative work had placed me consistently within Oregon's tradition of progressive thinking on urgent social and environmental issues. My new committee assignment as co-chairman of the new Committee on Aging convinced me that the Legislature was on the cutting edge of a relatively new public issue and an urgent social problem. We heard about the growing numbers of older citizens whose needs were not being met. Many privately owned care facilities were inadequately staffed; some had reputations for abuse and neglect of patients. There was a need for facilities offering different levels of care. Regulations and enforcement procedures needed to be established. There was a great need for in-home services for the elderly. So many older people needed just the basics—housekeeping, transportation to the doctor, the pharmacist, or the grocery store, help with cooking. Looming over all this were the costs involved and the inability of many senior citizens to pay for the care they needed. Oregon was recognizing these problems and it was time to take action.

Another indication of Oregon's progressive spirit was Senate Bill 100, setting forth a comprehensive statewide land-use planning system that affected many generations to come. This was, to my mind, the most significant single piece of legislation to come out of the 1973 session. Even then I knew it would require a long, ever-evolving balancing process to protect our land and plan for economic growth at the same time, and so it has proven to be. But it was another sign that Oregonians were ready and willing to confront complex, long-range problems in a comprehensive, nonpartisan way

There is no question in my mind that the combination of the popular, dynamic Governor McCall, a Legislature that worked across party lines, and well-informed citizen lobbyists put Oregon on the political landscape as forward-looking, intelligent, and fearless in protecting our environment, opening up governmental processes, and making life better for all our citizens. How Oregon could maintain that reputation would depend upon strong and courageous leadership in the future.

❧   ❧

A few days before the Legislature adjourned, the women's-name bill arrived on the floor of the Senate. It came too late to help me, and in any event I had helped myself. But it was still needed for other women. Nevertheless, I chose not to participate actively in the debate because I had been assured there would be no problem in getting the bill passed, in spite of the trouble it had encountered in the House, where it had passed with only a two-vote margin.

In the Senate debate only one person, Keith Burbidge, spoke on the proposal, and he favored it. It passed, and with a good majority vote. But then Senator Lynn Newbry, who had voted against the bill, changed his vote, which is permitted under the rules of parliamentary procedure, so he could move for its reconsideration the next day. This was not a good sign.

After we convened on Saturday morning—not unusual when the Legislature is nearing adjournment—Senator Newbry moved to reconsider the vote on the bill and spoke in opposition, arguing that the proposal would make it difficult to trace people's genealogy. Senator Vern Cook spoke against reconsideration, but it was allowed by an eighteen to nine vote. Clearly the opposition was up to something.

How quickly things can change! I had thought the bill was sure to pass, but now I had to speak because we were about to lose it. My instincts told me not to talk about my personal problems, so I kept my comments brief and factual. I explained that Oregon law was silent on what name a woman had to use, whether married, single, or divorced. I pointed out that some domestic relations judges were refusing to let women reclaim a former name following a divorce, particularly if there were children, because the judges thought the mother should have the same name as the children. That was shortsighted and illogical, of course, because if a woman remarried she was expected to take her new husband's name, while the children's name remained the same. As a lawyer I frequently went "judge-shopping" for one who would not object to my client's request, because I thought it should be the woman's choice. Finally, I stated that both women and men had always had a hard time tracing their family lineage on the maternal side, and that this bill might, in fact, help correct that for future generations.

Then Senator Mike Thorne spoke. He said he had noticed that there had been some "little things" passed this session "that tend to continue to get at the real jugular of the heart or the real essence of a family life." It was obvious he was referring to proposals that would put women on an equal footing with men, whether in the home, at work, at school, or in society in general. We had no time, he said, to be considering measures of this nature, and we ought to get on to more significant things. That last, off-handed comment was gut-wrenching. He was dismissing the importance of the legislation many women's groups and the women legislators had been pushing.

The vote was taken. Senators Newbry and Thorne had lobbied well. We lost an astonishing eight votes from the day before, and the bill failed. I was furious.

When the Senate recessed for lunch a few minutes later, I saw a woman staff member stop Mike and berate him for speaking against the bill and killing it. Margot told him he was "a goddamn son of a bitch" and that he knew how important that bill was. Mike's reply was dismissive. "Look, now, it's not that important, and besides, everything is getting pretty tense around here this late in the session. We need a little fun." With that comment Margot, a good campaign worker and prone to blunt language, went into an even greater rage and began to cry. I walked out with her and tried to comfort her, but I was angry too.

At lunch a senator told me there would be a bill in the one o'clock Ways and Means Committee meeting to fund a park project on Catherine Creek, in Mike Thorne's eastern Oregon district. He had decided to vote against it to protest Mike's killing the women's-name bill. That sounded like a good idea to me. Before the committee meeting began I told Keith, who was the House vice chairman of the committee, what had happened and what I planned to do.

Mike was a young, tall, lean, tanned rancher, courteous and personable. He reminded me of boys I had grown up with in Texas. I liked him and enjoyed working with him in the Democratic caucus. But even though he was a freshman legislator, he should have known by now that every piece of legislation is important to someone. If he wanted to oppose it, fine, but not because "we need a little fun."

After Mike testified on his proposal for the park, a vote was taken. The "No" votes swelled as the members' names were called. The proposal failed. Mike was clearly stunned. So were the co-chairmen. I was surprised that the bill was defeated, but gratified, too. It was mighty comforting to know that there were men in the Legislature who supported women's efforts to gain self-identity and independence and who would take that retaliatory action on our behalf.

How disappointing to end the best session ever for women, and for me personally, on a sour note. But the women's organizations were ecstatic about the bills that had been passed. These new laws showed for the first time what can be accomplished when we were united in a common goal. Even the ones that failed had introduced the broader concerns of women and stirred important dialogue and debate. And they would be there next session.

❧ ❧

Adjournment finally came on July 6, 1973. The summer, with days spent at home and my law office, beckoned as a welcome respite. The family was expanding rapidly, with our eight now-adult children marrying and having children, and the younger ones dating seriously or into shared-living arrangements with a special person. Sunday night dinners were always catch-up time, and with so many of us, there was usually a birthday, anniversary, promotion, new job, or graduation to celebrate.

The best description of those dinners comes from an article in the spring 1973 issue of *Dome*, a student publication at Mt. Hood Community College. The author, Paula Bentley, had picked up on the press stories about my possible campaign for governor and asked for an interview. Her story ran as "Madam Governor?"

> The only time Ms. Roberts had free [for the interview] was Sunday afternoon, if the interviewer didn't mind her preparing a family birthday dinner for husband Keith at the same time.
>
> Grown children drifted in and out, the family German Shepherd—banished outside—peered in through the window, a black mama cat took time out from her new litter in the basement to check on the proceedings, Newton—a stray puppy who's just joined the household—scampered about chewing on available shoe laces and forgetting his paper training lessons.

Preparing dinner was a family affair, with one daughter preparing the mashed potatoes, Ms. Roberts basting the turkey, Mr. Skelton fixing the salad, a son raiding the freezer for frozen peas, and Newton getting underfoot.

The arrival of more sons and daughters and granddaughters brought the noise level even higher, as greetings were exchanged and family news brought up to date.

"We all have busy lives, so we try to make the most of these special family occasions," said Ms. Roberts.

How does life look at fifty?

The eyes twinkle and she laughs, "I don't feel fifty, at least not the way someone younger looks at it.

"Fifty is only halfway through my life, and I expect the next half to be as productive as the last."

Chapter 15

Running for Governor

By late summer, talk about my possible campaign for governor had swollen from a trial balloon into a big blimp. I'd already determined there were no personal hindrances. Now it was time to turn to the political analysis. If I took the next step there'd be no turning back; I'd follow Forrest Amsden's advice—"Do It."

Keith and I decided that the most prudent thing was to have a professional survey done. The survey concluded that "the race is a blank sheet at this time." Not surprising, considering the primary election was more than eleven months away. At this point, name familiarity was the only thing that mattered. Given a list of six names—Congresswoman Edith Green, former State Treasurer Bob Straub, State Treasurer Jim Redden, Senators Jason Boe and Betty Roberts, and Multnomah County District Attorney Harl Haas—the surveyed voters recognized them about equally. More respondents were able to offer an opinion about Straub than about the rest of us. That was to be expected for someone who had been on a statewide ballot nine times and who'd been state treasurer for eight years.

Of course, it matters whether a person's opinion is favorable or unfavorable. One-third of those who gave an opinion of Straub had an unfavorable opinion. When Straub's and Edith Green's names were removed from the list of potential Democratic candidates for governor, Jim Redden led with 15 percent. It was clear that voters had a hard time picking out any one of us lesser-known hopefuls. The message I took from this was that if Bob Straub did not run, a primary race would be wide-open and ripe for the candidate who could put on the best campaign. The big question was whether Straub would run, and on that question he was totally silent.

The survey also revealed that "a significant fraction of Democrats is still skeptical of putting a woman in the top administrative job." Respondents gave various reasons: "Men are stronger." "Politics is no place for a woman." "If a qualified man is available, why vote for a woman?" "A woman would be too emotional." "Men do a better job above a certain level of job difficulty." "It takes a strong person." "They would run all over a woman." "Too dirty a business for a woman up there." "[Women] break down under pressure, it's their nature." Interestingly, the survey also said, "Those with a sexual bias tend

to be less interested in politics, less well-informed, and less likely [to vote]… "
On the other hand, 45 percent of Democratic voters would have no hesitation
at all in voting for a woman for governor, and 20 percent had only some
hesitation. Fifteen percent would vote only for a very experienced woman, and
20 percent would not vote for any woman.

The report told me what I already knew: "Bluntly, a woman must be prepared
to spend more time than a man in laying a groundwork of acceptance. … In
this situation, the capacity to organize a campaign is by far the most important
resource for any candidate." The report offered suggestions on how such a
campaign should proceed.

I felt the best course for me was to talk to Bob Straub and ask him point-
blank if he planned to run, and if he wasn't, whether he'd consider supporting
me. I called him in late July. We agreed to meet at my Battle Creek condo
in Salem. I wasn't sure where our conversation would go, but it was worth
exploring. I took the lead. "Bob, I'm moving beyond just thinking about the
governor's race. I plan to have an analysis done but I need to know if you are
running. If so, it's not worth it to continue to put a campaign together."

His response was evasive: "Well, you do whatever you have to do." I asked
him bluntly what his intentions were. He said he honestly didn't know yet.

Whatever the reason for Straub's indecision, it was decision time for me. As
he left our meeting, I said, "Bob, if you decide not to run, I'd sure like your
support." That surprised him, but he mumbled something like, "I'll think
about it."

Len Bergstein, a Legal Aid lobbyist who had urged me to run, made no
bones about wanting to be my campaign coordinator. He certainly had the
needed energy, enthusiasm, and smarts. I had come to know him as one who
fit George Bernard Shaw's description of those "… who get up and look for
the circumstances they want, and, if they can't find them, make them." Len
was a happy person with a ready laugh that put everyone at ease. He proved to
be the driving force we needed, and his loyalty and confidence in me was an
added asset that permeated the entire campaign. I had to do my very best for
those who believed this was a winnable race.

To start organizing we had to raise money—at least a hundred thousand
dollars, my survey had suggested. To raise money we had to look like a
campaign, even though I had not formally announced. On a late-summer
Sunday afternoon, a few of us sat in my living room strategizing on how to
get the voters to start thinking about next year's governor's race now. With
us were George and Gay Carver, who had lent their considerable talents in
photography and graphic arts to develop campaign materials in my legislative

races. I was glad to have them back for this larger, more significant campaign. We brainstormed the details of how to get an image and my name into the minds of voters, so that George and Gay could start working with a theme that would give recognition and visibility to the coming campaign. We talked about words that conveyed special messages to voters. All kinds of descriptive words and phrases were suggested—"hardworking," "independent," "decisive"—you get the picture here. After a few suggestions someone would intersperse, "What we need is a great idea."

Well, we all knew that. When that ridiculously obvious statement had been repeated a half dozen times, someone said, "Hey, guys, that's it!"

"What's it?"

"A great idea for governor—Betty Roberts." So was born a phrase that would get our campaign off the ground. George and Gay went to work immediately, developing buttons, signs, letterhead, and all the necessary paraphernalia. The "great idea" slogan stayed with us all during the campaign.

After that start, I never looked back. Not at the negative things people said about a woman running for governor, not at the numbers of voters who would never vote for a woman, not at whether Bob Straub or anyone else might get into the race. Everything was on forward motion.

Jewel Lansing, a CPA, had offered to be our campaign treasurer back in May 1973, when she wrote, "I would urge you to run even if the polls show resistance to the image of a woman governor. I believe that part of any such resistance would be simply a lack of prior images on which to focus." Bonnie McKnight, who'd worked on my 1972 Senate campaign, became my all-around go-to person, willing to drive the candidate and change a flat tire if necessary, pound in lawn signs, and make phone calls into the evening hours. Every campaign needs a Bonnie on its team.

Co-chairman Nancy Hayward, a Lane County commissioner, would bring needed credibility to the campaign in the Willamette Valley communities and perhaps statewide. The other co-chairman, Don Marmaduke from Portland, would help me reach the many voters in the urban area. I knew Don through

Democratic Party politics, and I knew of his reputation as a fine lawyer and his ardent support of civil rights and other progressive causes.

An event that would influence my campaign in a not-too-subtle way was a sports contest billed as "The Battle of the Sexes." The "battle" was a tennis match between Billie Jean King, a slim, dark-haired, bespectacled twenty-nine-year-old tennis professional, and Bobby Riggs, a fifty-five-year-old man who was also a tennis professional. Riggs had previously challenged the top-ranking Margaret Court and beaten her. Then he challenged King.

Billie Jean King reported that Riggs had asked her many times to play the

The Oregonian, November 1, 1973

(Artist: Art Bimrose. From *The Oregonian*, November 1, 1983)

match and she'd said, "No." Then when he beat Margaret Court, she said, "I just had to play," because she didn't feel women were accepted as athletes yet.

Watching King beat Riggs 6-4, 6-3, 6-3 in Houston before a huge national television audience was the thrill of a lifetime for women all over the country. We knew King's victory would send a crucial message about women's abilities and the importance of equal opportunity.

❧   ❧

On October 29, 1973, I stood on the steps of our beautiful Capitol and announced my candidacy for governor. I said I was announcing early to end the hinting and speculation; that I chose the Capitol to make the first of four announcements that day because of my ten years of service there; that "I want to run a 'no-nonsense' campaign;" and that "in the face of Watergate I want to reassure Oregonians of the honesty, integrity, and competence of public officials." Then I spoke briefly about Oregon's bountiful natural resources and the balance necessary between the protection of those resources and economic development. I spoke of the need for better planning to avoid another energy crisis. I ended by saying, "I believe I have the toughness of mind, coupled with the mercy and patience that comes with maturity and wide experience, to lead the way."

There was polite applause. A reporter asked whether Oregon was ready for a woman governor. That let me use my favorite answer: "The question should not be, is Oregon ready for a woman governor, but is this person ready? Is this person qualified to become governor? I hope that is what the voters will look for in my candidacy."

≻ ≺

In October the campaign hired a media consultant, Roger Bachman. He and his wife, Eve, also offered to help with fund-raising to buy print and television advertising. They developed a plan that included a series of lunches where I would meet potential major contributors. After Roger observed me at a couple of the lunches and at one particularly important evening meeting, he wrote a memo on the subject, "How you are coming across to people." He critiqued my performance, suggesting, as an example, a better answer to "Why are you running for governor?" as well as advising me to avoid specific words like "politician" because they tend to leave a negative image. His comments were well taken, I thought.

I shared Roger's memo with Bonnie McKnight on one of our drives to a campaign function. Bonnie thereupon wrote an indignant memo defending me and criticizing Roger's remarks, sending a copy to campaign coordinator Len Bergstein. What got Bonnie riled was that Roger had begun by suggesting I be more like Neil Goldschmidt and Tom McCall in making speeches; that is, more spontaneous and less reliant on notes. That was a fair comment, in my opinion, but the comparison with two prominent male politicians was the tipping point for Bonnie: "It is TRUE," she wrote to me, "that you do not project the hard-driving authority of Neil Goldschmidt. That is HIS style. It is TRUE that you do not project the glib phrase-maker quality of Tom McCall. That is HIS style." And then she laid out what she thought was my style. All good stuff, of course. She closed by saying, "I suggest we stop trying to remake Betty Roberts and just spend our time and energies presenting the one we have to the public."

In the scheme of the campaign this memo exchange was a relatively minor event, but it revealed the stark truth that there was literally no one else to compare me to. There were no women politicians in executive positions who might have served as role models for me. Comparison to men was the only game in town.

Yet here I was, at a point in my life when I could be a serious candidate for governor. Nationwide, six women were running for governors' offices in 1974: Ella Grasso of Connecticut, Louise Gore of Maryland, Nancy Brown of Ohio,

Patricia Scherr of Pennsylvania, Frances "Sissy" Farenthold of Texas, and me. A Philadelphia *Daily News* reporter concluded that of the six, three—Grasso, Farenthold and I—had a fifty-fifty chance of winning. The opportunity was there, and I was prepared to take advantage of it. Here was that darned chicken wandering across my path again.

I didn't agree that being a woman was necessarily a disadvantage. Yet there was always that nagging statistic: 20 percent of voters said flatly that they would not vote for a woman for governor. I saw three ways to deal with this: convince them otherwise, recognize that many of those people won't vote, and work harder to get more votes to compensate for that prejudice.

It was important to tackle the issue head-on, talk about it and get it out of the way. I invited Ben Padrow, forensics coach from my days at Portland State University, to work with me on presentations and especially on answering questions well. George Carver, head of the media and communications department at Mt. Hood Community College, offered the school's television studio for an evening of virtual reality: I would be on camera, and Ben, George, and my husband, Keith, would play members of an audience asking me questions about my candidacy.

The questions were tough, both those related to issues and the more personal ones: "What does your husband think about you running for governor?" "Why don't you use your husband's name?" "Who takes care of your house and who buys the groceries?" "Why do you want to be governor?" "Are you a women's libber?" "Do you really think you can be elected?" All those questions had to be answered sincerely. I often found humor effective. When someone asked me how I found time to do the grocery shopping, I said, "It happens when the dog and cat run out of food. And then it's two or three carts piled high, and you don't want to get behind me in the checkout line."

જ ઝ

Fund-raising was by far the most tedious and difficult thing for me. Most candidates feel the same way. It's hard to contact people, one after another, and ask them for money. We needed a large outlay of money for television ads, and we needed to get commitments for these funds early so we could reserve the air time in advance.

We had a good team of women working on fund-raising, led by the indomitable Betty Schedeen, an ardent Democrat from Gresham. She was a wonderful hostess, good at throwing receptions and cocktail parties for Democrats she supported. One story I've heard about Betty says she once invited John F. Kennedy, then in the early stages of running for president, to her home for a gala fund-raiser. She asked all her women friends to come and clean the house beforehand. There was one problem: she had brought a flock of baby chicks in from the wet, cold winter weather and let them take up residence in the basement. Those chicks had raised a big stink in the house. The women asked her to put them somewhere else, and at first Betty resisted. She finally agreed the chicks could go, but only for John F. Kennedy.

Betty and her team put together all sorts of fund-raisers: theater parties, a cookbook of Oregon chefs' recipes, an art auction, a style show. Margot Perry came up with an idea for a silver charm in the shape of the symbol for women and printed with the words "A Great Idea." We sold a lot of those.

But you can't run a campaign on cookbooks, theater parties, and silver charms. Our team made lists of potential contributors whom I had to call personally, and the list kept growing. By January the allocation of my time had become a serious issue. Should I be out making speeches to groups and getting press coverage, or should I be telephoning possible contributors?

To complicate matters, Governor McCall announced the convening of two special sessions of the Legislature in January and February. February was a crucial month for fund-raising, and these special sessions would severely get in the way. Our media consultant thought I should skip the Legislature and devote that month to raising money. It is putting it mildly to say that I was repelled at the idea of shirking my duty as a legislator. More to the point, if I failed to show up, my opponents could turn it into an unpleasant issue. I could just see the television ad showing my empty seat at the Senate—"If she doesn't care about her job as a legislator, why should she care about her job as governor?" I took my list of names with me to Salem and made calls when I was not in a committee meeting or on the Senate floor.

The formal opening of our downtown office on my birthday, February 5, 1974, was another successful news event that received television coverage. Just having an office gave the campaign more visibility and greatly boosted the morale of the staff and volunteer workers, some of whom walked in right off the street.

❧ ❧

The stakes in the political guessing game of who was running for what got suddenly higher in February, when Congresswoman Edith Green, a Democrat, and Congressman Wendell Wyatt, a Republican, both decided to step down from their congressional seats, a surprise to everybody. The first question on my mind was whether either of them was interested in the governor's race. The second question was who would run for their seats in Congress. Would

Tom McCall run for the Wyatt position? And would any Republicans take on the incumbent Bob Packwood for the U.S. Senate in the primary? Packwood had been in the Senate since 1968, when he defeated the long-entrenched Senator Wayne Morse. Heating up the game of political chair-swapping was the question of who among those of us running for governor would find one of these new openings more appealing.

All of this had to come to a head on March 19, the final day for filing for both the Republican and Democratic primaries. Calls started flooding my campaign office: Was I going to run for Edith Green's U.S. House seat? My answer was "no." I was committed to the governor's race and that's where I would stay. To convince everyone where I stood, I'd formally filed for governor on February 21, ahead of the deadline, as is any candidate's prerogative.

In the midst of all of this speculation came Bob Straub's announcement—finally—that he would indeed run for governor. That was not a surprise to me or anyone else, just another political fact of life. Also, Jason Boe announced that he would run against Wayne Morse in the Democratic primary for Bob Packwood's Senate seat.

So Boe was out of my race and Straub was in. Redden was still in, but Haas had also announced his exit. Again not a surprise, since he was relatively new in his position as Multnomah County District Attorney, and I'd felt all along that that was where he would stay. We had a three-way race for Democratic candidate for governor—Roberts, Redden, and Straub.

Not that any of this made any difference in how my campaign would be conducted. No matter who else was in the race, we had a plan and we'd stick to it. A poll in March showed that our be-everywhere, do-everything campaign was paying off in name recognition and positive responses. Straub was still in the lead, but I was in second place, with numbers ten percentage points below his. The poll also showed that with Straub in the race I lost votes to him in greater numbers than Redden did. Clearly the "but she's a woman" factor was still present.

With filing day out of the way, I took my campaign everywhere I could reach voters on their own turf. One morning I was standing outside the doorway of a manufacturing company as men were leaving the graveyard shift. I handed a brochure to as many as I could catch and introduced myself. Seeing me there at that early hour was surprising, but most seemed pleased.

As two men approached me one said, "Hey, are your dishes done?" As I handed him my material I said, "You bet! And dinner's in the oven. How are things at your house?" The other man poked him in the ribs and said, "She gotcha," as they both walked away chuckling, but I doubt if I got that man's vote. On the "but she's a woman issue" the least I could do was not let those kinds of remarks affect the campaign and humor was the best way to deal with it.

⤜ ⤛

In late March we did an in-depth poll that showed Straub still scoring high on name familiarity, but when voters were asked how certain they were to vote for a particular candidate, his numbers fell significantly. The numbers still showed me ahead of Redden. Among committed voters—those most likely to vote in the primary—Straub got 36 percent, I got 29 percent, and Redden got 21 percent. Fourteen percent were undecided. Strangely, perhaps, I was not disappointed in those results. The poll showed that our campaign was getting through to voters, and we'd keep working on them. And gaining seven percentage points didn't seem like an impossible obstacle.

As the campaign went into high gear, Len and Bonnie showed up at my house one evening as I was making a gigantic batch of meat loaf—some for the freezer—to talk about a dispute between the two of them. It seems that Bonnie, as my scheduler, thought Len was asking me to make too many out-of-town appearances. This was another instance when Bonnie was looking out for what she perceived to be my best interest. She'd seen me napping in the car, working on speeches in the car, giving interviews and speeches all day long, getting to bed after midnight and rising before dawn for a 6 a.m. breakfast. She maintained it was wearing me out, and she was resisting Len's scheduling decisions.

Len took the position that Bonnie had to schedule according to our plan. We'd already laid out how much time I was to spend in various parts of the state, based on population and voter turnout. As I listened to them argue and cajole, I continued with the meat loaf. I took some eggs out of the refrigerator and put them on the counter to add to the mixture. When I turned my head, one of them rolled off the counter onto the floor. Len and Bonnie went silent. I grabbed a big spatula and paper towel and scooped Mr. Humpty Dumpty into the sink. Len, in exasperation, said, "Betty, you shouldn't be doing that. You may be the next governor of Oregon." His exasperation was at Bonnie, not me, but he directed his anger at me. I was upset with both of them. I looked at Len and thought, *And who do you think cleans up the messes in state government?* I looked at Bonnie and thought, *Right now I'll clean up the mess the two of you are making.* They remained silent, perhaps chastened by my thoughts and what Keith called my "teacher look."

In the end we agreed that we'd follow the schedule. Being bone-tired at the end of the day was just a part of the campaign. If I didn't go to bed every

night with sore feet and an aching body, a head full of names and faces to try
to remember, and a full schedule for the following day, I wasn't doing my part.
In fact, I harbored a little resentment that anyone in the campaign would try
to protect me, even Bonnie. I could take care of myself, thank you.

⋟ ⋞

We were monitoring Redden's and Straub's campaigns, which were also
going full-bore. All through April they were getting good press coverage, but
so was I. We were all talking about the issues of the day—the energy crisis,
development of geothermal power through leases, state loans to veterans,
opposition to nuclear power, the need for national health care. There were
not many differences between us. We were all Democrats, and one of us
would be running against a Republican candidate in the fall. My campaign,
however, was covering precincts with hundreds of volunteers, talking to
voters. We saw no evidence that either the Redden or the Straub campaign
was doing that.

Organizations were starting to make their endorsements, and the press
would soon begin to make theirs. I'd approached the Teamsters back in
March, and they came through for me in late April. I was grateful for their
support, and not just for the money. Here was an organization known for its
tough-guy image supporting a woman in an important political campaign.
The psychological effect was good for me, and the endorsement would make a
heck of an impact in the campaign literature.

I was dismayed, however, when Oregon Education Association decided
not to endorse any candidate in the primary. I was a teacher and a supporter
of public education, and I'd expected them to support me. I asked them to
reconsider, but the organization remained neutral—a major disappointment
after all the years of being the primary sponsor for their legislation. My take
was that, on the advice of their lobbyist, John Danielson, they were hedging
their bets because they didn't want to back a loser. The Portland Teachers
Association independently endorsed my candidacy; that was good news and
good for votes, but didn't bring as much money.

As the May 8 primary date approached, I reaped rewards from another
phenomenon that comes toward the end of campaigns, when lobbyists make
their final decisions about contributions. Because I'd still be in the Senate
if I lost the governor's race, the lobbying contingent apparently thought it
would be a good idea to be listed among my contributors. Even the Oregon
Education Association sent a check in the last week, though they probably did

the same for Redden and Straub. The amounts of money were not large, and they came too late to buy more television time. But we could use the money to repay the loans that had bought what television time we had.

With three of us in the race, the newspaper endorsements were bound to be split. All the papers, regardless of their final choices, said good things about all of us. The larger newspapers were pretty well divided between Redden and Straub, but I was usually included somewhere in the editorial with a few good words, too. My endorsements came from the smaller newspapers scattered around the state—The Dalles *Chronicle,* the Gresham *Outlook,* the Woodburn *Independent,* the Albany *Democrat-Herald,* and Salem's *Capital Journal,* as well as the student newspapers at the University of Oregon and Portland State University.

As a finale to the campaign, we aired a thirty-minute television program produced by our public relations firm that portrayed our neighborhood coffee gatherings on the night before the election, where citizens asked questions and I answered. It was well produced and had a good audience.

◈ ◈

On election day we waited tensely with the campaign staff, fortifying ourselves with wine, beer, sodas, coffee, and various kinds of fast food for what could be a long night. Three television sets were placed strategically around the office so we could get the returns simultaneously from the three major television stations. Keith and I went out for a quiet dinner to talk about possible eventualities and what my message should be to reporters, depending on the outcome.

When we got back to the office Straub was leading. I was second and within striking distance, close enough to give us reason for optimism. The crowd of supporters erupted with shouts of joy and enthusiasm. Keith and I began to tour the television studios. As long as there were many votes left to be counted, my response to reporters' inquiries was a simple "wait and see." The usual question was, "Aren't you surprised to be ahead of Redden and so close to Straub?" Answer: "No, not at all. We've always been in this campaign to win. It's been a good campaign and now it's paying off."

And that's the way it was all evening. Straub led, I was behind—and still behind with fewer and fewer ballots left to count. Finally, near midnight, Keith and I went home. If Straub and I had been see-sawing back and forth it would have been different, and I would have waited up all night for the results. But the consistency of the vote told me that that was probably the way it would stay.

The morning paper verified that Bob Straub had won. I was a close second. By the time all the ballots were counted, Straub had 105,128 votes, or 33.5 percent; I had 97,323 votes, or 31.0 percent; and Redden had 87,529 votes, or 27.9 percent. The remaining 7.6 percent of the votes were divided among seven minor candidates.

I was disappointed, of course. But the big surprise was that a woman in her first bid for statewide office had almost beaten a well-known candidate and officeholder. I heard through the grapevine that Straub himself was the most surprised of all. I looked at the results and thought about the poll we'd had in late March. Since then I had come up 2 percent, while Straub had dropped 2.5 percent, leaving a spread of only 2.5 percent.

Perhaps even more surprising, I had won in some traditionally conservative strongholds. In fact, I had led in eleven eastern Oregon counties, including the rough-and-tough, cowboy-centered Lake County. This was accomplished with the considerable help of my old friend Delpha Plato, a woman who could hold her own in any roomful of men.

In my opinion, the finest thing that was said in all the articles and editorials following the election was in an *Oregonian* story by Todd Engdahl: "And there's one final lesson that a lot of people may have learned, even though the issue never really surfaced during the campaign. A woman can run a credible campaign for governor and win or lose strictly on the issues and on the campaign." In that sense I had won a great victory. The part about wanting to show that a credible woman candidate must be taken seriously when running for statewide office—that part came true.

And the part about winning? Well, there's always another campaign, somewhere, sometime.

Chapter 16

So Soon Another Chance

The biggest challenge I'd ever had in politics was over. It was history. I knew I'd done everything possible, so I felt fine. I was proud of all the people who had worked throughout the state, and especially the staff at the campaign office.

I couldn't help them clean up and close up, however. I had a surgery appointment that had been pending since the previous December, when my doctor had told me I should have a hysterectomy, the sooner the better. When I told him it would have to wait until after the primary election, he said, "You know the risks, don't you?" At the time I nodded my head; of course I do. But, frankly, I had no idea what he was talking about, and I didn't want to know. He said, "Okay, we'll schedule it for a couple of days after the primary."

Len was the only person in the campaign who knew about the impending surgery, and I think he conveniently forgot it as soon as I told him way back in December. Now that the time was at hand, we thought it would be a good idea to put out a small press release explaining why I was not available for comments to the press on the election's outcome. I suggested the release add that, in lieu of flowers, anyone wishing to send get-well greetings should instead make a similar contribution to help pay off the debt of the campaign. Small contributions poured in, but a representative from a florists' association wrote me a letter chastising me for taking business away from them. I reviewed my contributors' list and noted that the florists were not on it.

On my first day home from the hospital Len came to see me. He was all business—he didn't even notice I hadn't yet felt like washing my hair or even getting properly dressed. We sat out on the deck in the late-spring sunshine while he told me that both Bob Straub and Les AuCoin, who had won the Democratic nomination to Congress from Oregon's First District, had asked him to run their campaigns. He wanted my advice.

I said, "Len, where are your interests? Washington, D.C., or Oregon?" He said he did not want to go back to the East Coast. "Well, you can still work for AuCoin if he assures you that you will remain in his Oregon office if he wins, but you'll be dealing with national issues instead of state issues."

We tossed that around a bit, and he finally said, "I really like Oregon. I want to work in state government. Would it bother you very much if I accept Straub's offer?"

What a devoted guy for asking! "Of course not, Len. I plan to support Bob Straub myself." With that he helped me back up the deck stairs and into the house, and then he was happily off on a new campaign trail.

❧ ❧

I started an idyllic summer, meeting with my law clients, working with the staff on my interim committee, and spending time with family, especially my three granddaughters, ages five, four, and one. This mellow time was abruptly interrupted when Wayne Morse, the former U.S. Senator who had won in the Democratic primary in an attempt to regain his seat from Senator Bob Packwood, died on July 22, 1974.

His body lay in state in the Capitol rotunda on the day before his funeral in recognition of his service to the people of Oregon. He had served as a U.S. Senator from 1944 to 1969, first as a Republican, then as an Independent, and finally as a Democrat in 1955. I joined other national and state officeholders in a civilian honor guard, standing near the casket as citizens filed through to pay their respects. Then I was asked to serve as an usher at the funeral on July 26.

During all these proceedings no one spoke openly of the political complications that were sure to follow in filling the vacancy on the Democratic ballot. The death of Wayne Morse was a shock to everyone, but politics has its own momentum. The political wheels began turning immediately, with only a brief time out to pay proper respects to a great man.

As for me, I was not exactly standing still. The thought kept coming: Was I interested in another campaign?

Until then I'd never been tempted to run for national political office. Working in Washington, D.C., had never appealed to me. I loved Oregon and could not imagine being so far away from my family. But Keith assured me that if I were elected to the U.S. Senate he would accompany me to D.C. regularly. He told me I would never feel alone there. In fact, he speculated about the possibility of practicing law in D.C. or becoming a lobbyist, or both. Keith was a versatile, talented lawyer, and I figured he could probably keep two offices going.

The children were equally reassuring. We'd keep our house in Portland, of course, and we'd always make time for our family gatherings, even if it meant regular long flights all the way across the continent.

That support meant everything in the world to me. I'd always known that I needed my family as much as they needed me, or even more. Yet there was more than family to think about—thoughts I couldn't share because no one would understand. I had to sort out some tough questions for myself.

Why did this idea seem so compelling? Why was this happening to me again? Was it an opportunity I couldn't pass up? Another chicken crossing my path?

Was it the challenge of another campaign, or the challenge of serving in the U.S. Senate? At that time there was not one woman in the Senate. Was that the driving force? Or was this only a matter of being in the right place at the right time? Just because there was an opportunity to run didn't mean I should run, or that I'd win.

What if I lost again? Would I be seen as a consistent loser, or would there be benefits, if not for me, then perhaps for other women? Yet if I didn't get in the race, would I be seen as a quitter, or even a coward? On the other hand, why not turn it over to the guys and stay out of this fight?

In all my campaigns I had set high standards for myself. I had helped open the way for more women to run for high-level offices. The governor's race had made me aware of a disturbing trend in voter attitudes about women candidates. Back in 1954, the year Edith Green was elected to the U.S. House, her polls showed that 8 percent of the voters would not vote for a woman, while another 8 percent would vote for a woman *because* she was a woman. By 1974, my polls showed that, while between 10 and 15 percent of the voters said they'd vote for me because I was a woman, 20 to 25 percent would *not* support a woman, and another 10 to 15 percent resisted a woman candidate.

Why was there less support for women in politics in 1974 than there'd been twenty years earlier? When Edith Green was running for the first time it was rare for a woman to be elected to Congress. Perhaps the voters thought a few women in high office wouldn't cause any problems. By the time I was running, the women's movement was in full bloom. I thought at the time that the progress on behalf of women would have softened some of the public's aversion to voting for a woman. But it may have had the opposite effect. Some voters, male and female, may have been disturbed to see the changes in the traditional role of women on a larger scale and were expressing their disapproval at the ballot box.

None of these reflections gave me answers for any of my questions, but I knew I had a commitment both to myself and to other women who aspired to make a difference by running for public office. I had to do the best I could, for them and for myself. So I went with my gut. If my insides were telling me to run, then I would run. *Some questions don't have answers,* I told myself, *so stop asking.* Go with faith in those who are willing and eager to pick up where we left off in the governor's race. Many had said they were ready. Go with hope that this time the result will be different. Just go!

My instinct was confirmed when Ann Aiken came to talk to me. Ann, just graduated from the University of Oregon, had done a fine job of running my Eugene campaign office. She told me she had received a scholarship to work on her master's degree in political science at Rutgers University. She'd already called to see if Rutgers would hold it for her until the fall of 1975. She wanted to know whether I'd decided to get into the race for the U.S. Senate. If I had, she wanted to stay in Oregon and work for me.

I told her, "Ann, go to school."

"No," she said. "If you run, I'm here for the campaign."

That demonstration of commitment and dedication was overwhelming. I knew there were many more people making similar decisions on my behalf, even if not as dramatic as Ann's. How could I not run?

❧ ❧

According to state law, when a statewide office on the general election ballot becomes vacant after the primary election, the state central committee of the affected political party names the replacement. The Democratic Central Committee called a meeting for Sunday, August 11 in Baker, a town in northeastern Oregon, to decide who would be on the Democratic ballot in Wayne Morse's place.

I was approached by a union leader, Walter Gray, regional director for the Committee on Political Education (COPE), the political arm of the AFL-CIO in the northwestern states. Unions were disappointed, he told me, in Bob Packwood's stand on labor issues during his six years in the Senate. The AFL-CIO saw this as an opportunity to defeat him. They wanted a candidate who could match Packwood in campaign strategy and technique. I pointed out that the Oregon AFL-CIO hadn't supported me in the governor's race. Walter assured me that this time I would get their support and their money. They knew how close I'd come to winning the recent race for governor. This time they wanted a win.

Just days before the Baker meeting, the central committees for Multnomah County and Washington County, two of the three most populous counties in the state, named me as their first choice. Other, less-populous counties also supported me. Because the votes were only advisory, however, the outcome at the state meeting was far from certain. In some of the counties supporting me, Jason Boe came in second and in others R. P. (Joe) Smith took that place. Smith, a former district attorney in Umatilla County, was a serious entry into the race. He held no political office at the time, but he had run for state

Attorney General in 1972. Boe, president of the Senate, and Richard Eymann, Speaker of the House, were both formidable candidates as well.

On the appointed day, Keith and I drove to Baker for the state meeting. Riding along were Keith's daughter Ann and husband, Bill Lefors, and my brother Bob, who had come from Boston to see what his sister was up to in Oregon. It was a long, hot drive, but one I'd always loved. Resting my eyes on the flat horizon between The Dalles and Pendleton had always put Texas in my mind. I was glad my brother was with us. He promised that if I got the nomination he'd stick around for a week or so to help however he could.

We climbed Cabbage Hill toward the Blue Mountain summit at Meacham and then dropped down into LaGrande, where we took a quick detour to go by our old house. Then we continued the last forty miles to Baker.

This process of choosing a candidate to run for a vacant seat was an unusual exercise in party politics as well as an important decision for the party. The county representatives were taking their responsibility seriously as they listened to the candidates speak. After the first ballot I was ahead, but I had not achieved a majority of the weighted votes. I picked up a few more votes on the second and third ballots.

Then, abruptly, Joe Smith pulled out. Between the third and fourth ballots, he announced that he had been told to quit the race or he was through in Oregon politics. I knew that labor was putting pressure on Joe because he was trailing the other three candidates, but I wanted no part of that. As far as I was concerned Joe could stay in to the bitter end. On the fourth ballot I received a majority and became the Democratic nominee for the United States Senate.

Election day was set for November 5, 1974. We had eighty-four days. Everything was put on fast-forward. We reopened our downtown Portland office the day after the decision, and many of our former campaign workers were running things there. We'd lost Len Bergstein and some of our staff to the Straub governor's campaign, and others had moved on, but we picked up some who'd worked for Wayne Morse.

A campaign for national office would be different from a campaign for governor. We had to raise money nationally, and I had to become informed on national issues literally overnight. By August 22 I was in Washington making the rounds. Dave Yaden conducted a survey to take with us. Everyone was cordial; they were all happy to meet me. But nice as they were, I found that Yaden's survey of Oregon voters, even though it showed me less than 10 percent behind Packwood, didn't carry much money-raising clout in Washington, D.C.

The Senate Campaign Committee offered to pay for a survey by Pat Caddell and his Cambridge Survey Research, a Democratic polling organization. Depending on its results, they would consider helping me gather contributions. Senator Lloyd Bentsen promised a small contribution, and he gave me the Democratic Fact Book for the 1974 campaigns, which would prove to be a good reference manual on issues. The Caddell survey said pretty much what the Yaden survey had. Packwood's support among voters was greater than mine, although it was "broad but thin"—"a mile wide and an inch deep" is how we characterized it later during the campaign. While the Caddell survey found that a majority of the voters said they would vote for Packwood, their support was "unenthusiastic." The survey concluded with guarded optimism: "All in all, Betty Roberts faces a difficult campaign. She is, however, well within striking distance of a vulnerable opponent. An intensive, well-directed campaign will be needed but it has the possibility of success."

My second trip to D.C. yielded significant results in money-raising, mostly from unions and organizations that traditionally support Democratic candidates. Supporters held a reception for me at a home near the Capitol late one afternoon. I asked the hostess if I might bring my mother and sister, who lived in nearby Alexandria, Virginia. Mother was not well, but she was dressed in her finest and looked every bit the proper matriarch. The number in attendance was small, but the group was impressive, especially when Senator Eugene McCarthy showed up. He greeted my mother warmly, which pleased her immensely, and I'm sure she treasured that brief moment for the rest of her life.

Senator Edward Kennedy offered to do radio spots if the air time could be worked into our media budget. And two prominent men offered to come to Oregon to help with a fund-raiser. One was Robert Strauss, the chairman of the Democratic National Committee. The other was Jimmy Carter, governor of Georgia. Our Oregon fund-raising staff chose Strauss. We didn't have time to prepare for two successful dinners, and at the time no one really knew Jimmy Carter.

Back in Oregon, we had to pack even more appearances into an even shorter time period. I knew I was up to it. The Eugene paper said it best: "If one word characterizes the Roberts campaign, it is 'energy.' There is an inner drive to the attractive candidate that won't permit pessimism. There is the toughness acquired during ten years as one of few women in a male-dominated legislature. There is the shrewdness and innate intelligence that won respect, often time begrudgingly, from other legislators. And there is her own personal thermostat that keeps the adrenalin and energy flowing."

I will never forget leaving Portland one evening after an event and heading to central Oregon in the van to be at a breakfast the following morning. Two reporters were riding along to cover the activities the following day. One of them, Tom Stimmel, a staff writer with the *Oregon Journal,* offered to drive. I relaxed in the back seat until we hit freezing rain going over Santiam Pass. To keep our spirits and energy up I passed around a can of cookies. And then I sat in the seat behind Tom to try to keep him calm despite the rain and the late hour. Tom was tired and tense but alert and careful as he eased the van down the east side of the pass, where the temperature was warmer and we had only the wet road to contend with. We arrived in Redmond at 2:30 in the morning.

In his newspaper account of the trip, Tom wrote, "Five hours later, over coffee in the 97 Café, Roberts greeted Shirley Webb, indefatigable Deschutes County Democratic chairman who had arranged a campaign day of eleven stops in three towns over the next thirteen hours." The stops included radio stations, newspapers, senior-citizens' centers, day-care facilities, Redmond High School (where I got a rousing welcome from the students), a noon Rotary luncheon in Bend, a talk at Central Oregon Community College, and finally an evening event in Prineville. In one day I talked to, and listened to, people of all ages and backgrounds: babies to teen-agers to college students to adults to old folks. It was one of the most stimulating and memorable days of the entire campaign.

⅗ ⅗

From the very beginning we'd been talking with Packwood's campaign about debates—how many, where, when, and what format. We wanted debates, but we weren't sure Packwood would agree. Usually a strong incumbent has nothing to gain and lots to lose by debating a challenger. On the other hand, if the incumbent refuses to debate, that can be criticized by the challenger as a refusal to talk about the issues. His campaign consented to the debates, and we decided on three, one each in Coos Bay, Salem, and Portland, all to be held within a two-week period in October.

They would be "debates" only in that we would each answer the same questions—we would not counter each other's answers, and we would know the questions beforehand. With this format there was not much that was spontaneous or risky to either candidate. Nonetheless, as always, I prepared well.

After the Coos Bay debate, one press account noted that Packwood and I agreed on some issues—abortion, reforestation, opposition to log exports, a

Debating Bob Packwood in
the campaign for U.S. Senate,
1974. (Photograph by Gerry
Lewin)

200-mile fishing limit—but that we disagreed on Social Security (the reporter
noted that I advocated shifting its "welfare provisions" out of the fund), and on
how a national health insurance plan should be financed. In his final statement,
Packwood raised my support for stronger gun control. I was more than pleased
when the press called the Coos Bay debate a draw, but I failed to grasp the
significance of two issues that had been inserted into the campaign—Social
Security and gun control. These would come back at the end of the campaign
in an unsettling and dramatic fashion.

By the time of our next debate at the Salem City Club both Packwood
and I had warmed up to the idea of joint appearances. We could and did
take jabs at each other in the course of answering the questions. By a flip of
the coin I spoke first in the beginning and therefore gave my opening and
closing statements first—not a good place to be in a debate, because it's always
best to have the last word. We both spoke to the issues we were asked to
address—federal assistance to mass transit, environmental issues, federal aid
to education and other revenue-sharing programs, management of national
forests in Oregon, and inflation. Then Packwood made his closing statement.
His last words were something about my having the third-worst attendance
record in the Oregon Legislature.

My mouth fell open, but the debate was over. I could not respond, and
he exited so quickly I couldn't confront him. The reporters who covered the
Legislature and knew my record were likewise surprised. What in the world
could he be talking about? No matter, the Salem debate was judged another
draw. My campaign staff and I went back and looked at my Senate attendance
record. It showed a number of excused absences "for business of the Senate,"
which meant I was working in committee at the time a vote was taken on
the floor. These were the absences Packwood was referring to, but the voters
wouldn't know that. He knew very well how the Legislature and the U.S.

Senate record those absences. They mean a person is present and available for a floor vote, but is busy with other work of the Senate.

Then we researched his "absences." We found so many that I began using those in my appearances just as he continued to use mine. The gloves were indeed off from that time forward.

The final debate was in Portland at Temple Beth Israel on October 18, nine weeks into the campaign and with little more than two weeks to election day. I knew it would be a friendly audience for Packwood because of his strong support for Israel. That was my position, too, although he had had more opportunities at the national level to proclaim it.

This appearance was reported as being more "upbeat" because we found less to disagree about. I believe Packwood wanted to be seen as "Mr. Nice Guy" because he knew he had most of the votes of this audience. But it was not an unfriendly audience for me, and I continued to give my answers and statements with bold confidence.

The press evaluated that third debate, too, as a draw. I considered that evaluation a win. Packwood had had six years to learn national issues. I'd had little more than six weeks.

❧ ❧

The election was two weeks away, and every moment counted. We bought all the media we could afford. Many volunteers put boots to the pavement in precincts again to talk with people on the doorstep and leave material. I was hanging out at factory sites at 6 a.m., as the night shift left and the early morning one came on, to introduce myself to the workers—all guys—and ask for their votes as I handed them my leaflets. They were surprised to see me, but some gave a thumbs-up or other affirmative sign. Then there were the nonstop appearances the remainder of each day and into the evening.

Again the media began making their endorsements. An overwhelming majority of them went to Packwood. Some papers gave a nod to my campaign, with a few nice words tossed my way. Often the papers gave Packwood the endorsement with little analysis except that he had just completed his first term and should be given more time to develop seniority.

A week before the election, Dave Yaden, our pollster, called to tell me he had been monitoring the Senate race while doing other survey work, and he needed to talk to me. He came to our house at the end of a busy day and told me he was finally seeing some movement in voters' position on this race. He spoke of a survey he'd taken, not a formal poll but an in-depth diagnosis of how voters were making up their minds as the election drew near. The survey responses and interview comments, he said, led him to conclude that the race was virtually even. "I would put the race at: Roberts 45 percent, Packwood 45 percent, Undecided 10 percent." As he got up to leave, he said, "Betty, you can't let up." I assured him I would not. The last week was planned, and we'd continue doing all the work we'd been doing that got us to this point.

A simple, heady message: I had a good chance to overtake Bob Packwood and beat him in this election. Dave's survey concluded, "… it will take a very finely tuned and massive ad campaign by Packwood to do anything about it in the last week."

That is exactly what Packwood did. Early Friday morning before election day, our campaign coordinator in Ontario, Oregon (where there is an hour's time-zone difference), called and excitedly asked, "Has Bob Packwood bought the radio stations over here, or what?" Negative Packwood campaign ads had started airing early in the morning and were running at regular intervals.

Throughout the campaign both of us had talked about a whole range of issues—the energy shortage, Watergate, defense spending, health care, Social Security, the economy, election reform, foreign affairs, the environment, and others. After the issue of Social Security came up in the Coos Bay debate, I raised it occasionally myself before groups where I appeared alone, and it was sometimes picked up by the press.

That was a big mistake. Social Security is complex and difficult for the average citizen to understand. Most people are familiar with its retirement payments, but there are other parts to Social Security, programs to help people who are disabled or otherwise unable to work. When I talked about "reforming" Social Security to make it more predictable and stable for senior citizens, I was advocating moving the disability program into other federal funding programs. My opponent easily turned that into an attack on Social Security.

Those negative radio ads were the first hint of things to come for the weekend. The ads presented what we now call "sound bites" on four issues: Social Security (Packwood would protect it; Roberts would eliminate the trust fund), gun control (Packwood opposes; Roberts favors), welfare (Packwood opposes any increases; Roberts supports increasing), and voting attendance (Packwood had the highest of any Northwest senator; Roberts had the third lowest in the State Senate). Because the ads were timed for the last weekend before election day, there was nothing my campaign could do in response. We had radio and TV ads running, but we couldn't change them to respond to the attacks.

The attack ads demoralized our campaign workers, and they had the intended effect on voters. On Monday before election day I went with a group of Democratic candidates on a bus tour around the Portland area, visiting places where we could stop and meet voters, including senior citizens' facilities. There, I knew Packwood's Social Security ad had hit the mark. Nice older people would tell me how much they appreciated what I had done for them in my legislative work, but now they were sorry they would have to vote against me because of my stand on Social Security. I assured them that what the ads said was not true, but the people were confused. Of all the four ads, the one about Social Security was the one that hurt the most, politically and personally.

On election day our campaign workers, still with a flicker of hope, started cleaning the office and packing up. Then we waited. It was clear from the first reporting that Packwood would win, which didn't make for a happy election night. The vote stayed consistent throughout the evening, giving Packwood a lead of 55 percent in the final tally.

On the bright side for Democrats, Bob Straub won in the governor's race over Senator Victor Atiyeh, and all four congressional districts would be represented by Democrats. These Democratic victories were attributed to the Watergate scandal, which had come to a head in the summer. Although I was not among the happy winners, the lifting of the enormous burden of carrying on a campaign was a welcome relief.

We'd had three days to anticipate this outcome, and we had already begun to wonder if any of Packwood's advertising violated Oregon's Corrupt Practices Act. After talking with an attorney who had represented a client in a similar situation before the Oregon Supreme Court, and with Jim Redden, who'd co-chaired my campaign, I held a press conference and announced that there would be no challenge. I would not be seen as a whiner or a sour-grapes loser. I would accept defeat and become State Senator Betty Roberts again.

One analysis summed up the election outcome quite well: "[I]t seemed to confirm views expressed two months ago that Roberts' late entry into the contest did not give her sufficient time, money or organization to wage a winning campaign against the well-financed, well-organized Packwood." In hindsight I also agree with the analysis that we made a strategic error in basing much of my campaign on criticism of Packwood's record. My side of the campaign might have appeared too negative to the voters, particularly coming from a woman. In post-election analysis, there is never any point in making excuses. There are, however, good reasons to reflect on what happened in order to learn and be prepared for next time.

A river of telegrams, cards, letters, and contributions flowed in and helped wash away the disappointment. Most of them came from supporters in Washington, D.C., which surprised me. Many U.S. senators conveyed their disappointment. My most prized letter came from Senator Eugene McCarthy. It expressed both sympathy and encouragement, with words that gave me great peace of mind. To this day that letter gives me strength to go forward. Senator McCarthy wrote:

> I was sorry to learn the outcome of the senatorial contest in Oregon. Might I suggest the spirit of some lines from an old English ballad:
>
> > "Fight on, my men!" says Sir Andrew Barton
> > "I am hurt, but I am not slain,
> > "I'le lay me downe and bleed a-while,
> > "And then I'le rise and fight again."

Chapter 17

Back to Basics

Two big campaigns in one year were over. I welcomed the end as a long-distance runner welcomes the end of a race. There was no victory lap I could give to all who did the cheering, but other signs said the victory was in the trying. That I'd lost both races had not diminished my reputation personally or politically. Supporters and colleagues convinced me of that. Bob Straub, then governor-elect, offered to share a fund-raiser in December with me and Jim Redden to help pay off our debts from the governor's race. This act of kindness was also a vote of confidence. I'd won the right to be a serious candidate in the future. Now it would be good to get back to the regular work of the 1975 session.

Not only would I be back in the Senate, but both Frank Roberts and Mary Roberts would also be there—a development that would confuse Oregon voters for years to come. Frank had served three terms in the House but had been defeated in the 1972 election at the same time that his daughter, Mary, was elected to the House for the first time. In 1974, they both ran for the Senate from different districts in east Multnomah County, and were both elected. Veteran legislators, lobbyists, and reporters knew that Frank and I had had a brief marriage, that I had not known Mary before she became a legislator, and that I was now married to Keith Skelton, but pity the newer people and the voters who tried to figure it all out.

During my campaigns in 1974, the Equal Rights Alliance was evolving into the Women's Rights Project of the ACLU of Oregon, and women's groups were drawing up their to-do lists for the 1975 session. The same eleven women as in the 1973 session were in the 1975 Legislature, and we were champing at the bit to make it all happen. We and the women's groups made a powerful coalition.

On the Women's Rights Project's list were: passing a "rape shield" law, which would restrict admissibility of evidence of a victim's prior sexual conduct; eliminating sex discrimination in education; guaranteeing female prisoners equal access to vocational, recreational, and educational programs; funding the Bureau of Labor to enforce laws against discrimination on the basis of marital status; providing a private right of action for employment discrimination;

and funding the Governor's Commission on the Status of Women as an independent commission.

The list for the American Association of University Women addressed discriminatory effects of inheritance tax laws on women. These laws did not recognize a wife's contribution to her husband's estate unless she was employed outside the home and had records to prove it. A widow had to pay a heavy tax on her deceased husband's estate, the burden of which could force her to sell her home quickly and at a loss.

The League of Women Voters focused on passage of an Equal Rights Amendment to the Oregon Constitution, funding for 100 percent of need in welfare payments, reforming landlord-tenant law, making low-cost housing available, and banning discrimination in education.

An ambitious agenda indeed. And then two bills defeated in the 1973 session were back by popular demand. Those were the name-change bill and the proposal that would allow a woman to have a different residence than her husband.

The name-change bill passed the House in May with a good vote of forty-three "Ayes." From there it went to the Senate Judiciary Committee, of which I was a member, and went to the floor for a full Senate vote on May 30. Betty Browne, chairperson of the Judiciary Committee, asked me to carry the bill on the floor, to be the lead speaker.

I wondered whether to talk about the problems of women in general or my own personal experiences; it occurred to me that what senators most needed to see was that women lived with this problem every day. So I started out by explaining that the choice of someone to carry the bill had been a toss-up between Senator Betty (Browne) Fort, as she was married to Judge Bill Fort, or Senator Betty (Roberts) Skelton, as she was married to Keith Skelton. There was a bit of uncomfortable chuckling. Then I talked about the problem that courts often refused to grant a woman's petition for a name change. I spoke of my own experiences with the Oregon Bar Association and the Registrar of Elections and outlined the legal opinions that held that a name was a property right. The vote was twenty-three "Ayes" and two "Nays."

❧   ❧

By this time we were using "chairperson" instead of "chairman." This welcome development came about during the interim between the 1973 and 1975 sessions, when Legislative Counsel had been directed to search through the statutes for words that should be made gender-neutral.

The words we use to speak about persons, objects, or acts are always important, but in the law words take on an even greater significance. The words legislators use to speak about the laws they are considering often have a great impact on those who are responsible for enforcing or interpreting the laws. For example, the problem of "battered wives" once was thought of as the result of lovers' quarrels, and a private issue. When we started calling it what it really was—"domestic violence"—it became a major public issue. Similarly, rape was once assumed to be an act of excessive sex drive and lust. When we started calling it "sexual assault," attitudes and laws changed. Incest or sexual activity with an unrelated minor was seen often only as immoral. It was already a crime, but when it became "sexual abuse," more prosecutions and civil suits resulted. When "alimony" became "spousal support," it helped dispel the old notion that a housewife contributed nothing of tangible value to the marriage.

These changes in concept and many more came about as the result of the women's movement. We called things what they were from the woman's perspective.

The bills on women's issues introduced in 1975 numbered at least twenty-five. The most far-reaching were a series of bills that would prohibit discrimination in education on the basis of sex. Congress had passed Title IX in 1972 as an amendment to the Civil Rights Act of 1964. It prohibited discrimination on the basis of sex in any federally funded program or activity. This law did not come about effortlessly, nor did it flow from a natural enlightenment of members of Congress. The national women's groups were becoming a powerful presence in politics in Washington, D.C. Like the women's groups in Oregon, they were making that presence felt.

At least six of these education-related bills were introduced. Four passed. One required the State Board of Education to adopt rules prohibiting public elementary and secondary schools from discriminating between the sexes in determining participation in interschool activities. Another prohibited discrimination in public educational programs on the basis of age, handicap, national origin, race, marital status, religion, or sex. Another provided grants to develop non-sexist teaching materials. The fourth bill changed the procedure for the adoption of textbooks, requiring that "[r]espect for all people, regardless of race, color, creed, national origin, age, sex, or handicap, and their contributions to our history and system of government shall be reflected in the textbooks adopted by the State Board of Education."

Representative Mary Rieke was the lead sponsor of the inheritance-tax bill, and the AAUW took responsibility for lining up witnesses. It came as a shock to many lawmakers and citizens alike that for inheritance purposes a widow was not considered a contributor to the estate of her husband. Representative Rieke explained to a reporter, "[In] court cases ... the widow was presumed to have worked solely for the love and affection of her husband. As far as the accumulation of the estate went, services were considered to have been gratuitous." The new law, which passed overwhelmingly in both chambers, provided that the surviving spouse automatically became owner of one-half of the estate, whether the property was held in joint tenancy or passed by some other means, such as a will or trust. It provided for a three-hundred-thousand-dollar exemption on the remaining half of the estate and eliminated most inheritance taxes on property of over six hundred thousand dollars if inherited from a spouse. These changes helped to shield the family home, farm, ranch, or other business that the widow needed for her own support.

Other bills are mentioned here only to show the broad range of issues in that session. Equalizing the age for marriage of both parties had been introduced in previous sessions, but there had been disagreement on what the age should be. It was back again this session. This time the Senate wanted to set it at age sixteen and the House at age eighteen. That made age seventeen an easy compromise, and the bill passed. Another success was realized when the Legislature approved a tax deduction for child-care payments, and another, spearheaded by Vera Katz, for a change in the law that allowed married people to establish and maintain separate residences to correct the old assumption that the wife's residence is that of her husband's for all legal purposes.

There were a number of bills on the subject of rape. Of the six that were introduced, only two passed, both forbidding the use of prior sexual conduct of the victim as evidence in a rape trial. However, one of them, House Bill 2241, also prohibited the use of the sexual character or reputation of the alleged victim, and it narrowly prescribed the admissibility of evidence that the alleged rapist had had prior, consensual relations with the accuser. It passed the House with fifty-eight "Aye" votes and two members excused. This bill had tremendous support from law-enforcement personnel, which was undoubtedly an important factor in the unprecedented support on the floor of the House. After going through the Judiciary Committee in the Senate, and in a rare showing of approval, it received a floor vote of twenty-nine "Ayes" with one member absent.

❧ ❧

Despite the importance of these bills, women's issues did not dominate the 1975 session. Far from it. Besides the usual tax bills and school funding, we considered field burning, medical malpractice, the banning of aerosol cans, creation of a state energy department, and many, many more. One political writer suggested that the session deserved good marks but that it was not spectacular. I thought it was pretty spectacular as far as women's issues were concerned. In its summary of the 1975 session, an article in an Oregon Women's Political Caucus publication stated, "Rep. Vera Katz and Sen. Betty Roberts no longer need to carry the entire burden of sponsoring women's bills." The article went on to recognize the work of Mary Rieke, Mary Burrows, Nancie Fadeley, Norma Paulus, Mary Roberts, and Pat Whiting, as well as Dave Frohnmayer, Ed Fadeley, Tom Marsh, Bill Wyatt, and Hardy Myers.

The comment about "no longer needing to carry the burden" validated the hope and expectation I'd had when all these women showed up in the 1973 session. I said then that it was like the cavalry arriving to take over the fight. I would add to the OWPC list Senator Betty Browne, chairperson of the Senate Judiciary Committee, who was able to get every piece of legislation on women's issues through her committee with a minimum of fanfare and conflict. The fact that Betty was intensely private and unassuming may have been misleading to some. Highly intelligent, she had a good, legally trained mind and a keen grasp of all the legislation in her committee.

In the fall, as thoughts turned to the coming election, *The Oregonian* reporter Doug Yokom wrote the first of a series of articles on the possible effects of the women's movement on women running for public office, mentioning four women who were running, or considering running, for statewide office—Norma Paulus and Betty Browne for secretary of state, Caroline Wilkins for secretary of state or state treasurer, and Jewel Lansing for state treasurer. I liked to think my two statewide races in 1974, although unsuccessful, had encouraged women to "go for it." The Women's Political Caucus commended me for this when they presented me with their Woman of the Year award at their fourth annual statewide convention in Eugene in November. Norma Paulus, in her usual good form, gave a rousing keynote address at the gathering, admonishing women not to pull "the ladder up after them," and to treat "Mary Homemaker" with respect.

☺   ☺

Sometime during that 1975 session I'd started thinking about my own political future. I was up for reelection in 1976, but I wasn't sure I wanted to stay in the Legislature. Should I step down? Or, knowing it would be an easy campaign, should I run, be reelected, and then decide what to do?

I knew I had a solid reputation and a staunch constituency. In May, while the Legislature was still in session, I was named Education Citizen of the Year by the Oregon Education Association for the work I'd done on education issues and for my teaching and local involvement as a school board member. Post-session evaluations by a number of newspapers put me among the most effective legislators. They were encouraging and gave me political security to remain in the Legislature for as long as I chose.

Nevertheless, I was feeling a desire to develop a full-time law practice. It had been hard carrying files back and forth to Salem and trying to stay in touch with clients. I'd reserved my Saturdays for office hours, but that way of practicing law was beginning to take its toll. I wanted to be a successful lawyer as well as a successful politician—more the first than the second, since the politician part had been achieved. The entire year of 1976 could give me a running start on that goal.

As I took stock of where my life was heading, I saw our family stretching out in all directions. Son Randy would marry the pretty young Spanish girl he'd met on his tour of Europe; Jo returned to her banking job after serving as my secretary for the last two legislative sessions, bought her first home, and worked hard at being a good single parent; Dian and Glen continued their professional careers with the help of excellent day care for their two daughters; and John was in Baltimore studying to become a maritime engineer.

As for Keith's children, Carol was married and lived in Connecticut with her husband and young son and another child on the way. Ann and Bill LeFors were both working at building careers. Doug and Ann Yoshiwara would marry soon, and he was looking forward to commercial photography school in California. Tom, at nineteen the youngest of our eight, was living with his mother in Eugene and working at odd jobs while trying to find some direction in his life.

I decided not to introduce anything new into this mix. I'd let the re-election go forward. I'd win with little campaigning, and I'd have another legislative session to consider whether I would miss being in politics.

❧ ❧

Anticipating a presidential election year, candidates for both parties were stepping up their campaigns in late 1975. I was leaning toward Jimmy Carter. I knew the Georgia governor had the credentials to be president, and he was not afraid to express his moral and ethical convictions about helping people in need. I volunteered to be his Oregon campaign chairperson.

Keith decided to support U.S. Senator Frank Church. The press called us "a house divided." The *Oregon Journal* ran a cartoon by Bob Bledsoe depicting "His" and "Hers" towels hanging side by side, and at the bottoms the faked signatures of Jimmy Carter and Frank Church. Keith obtained the original drawing of the cartoon and gave it to me along with a note saying that we independently shared our lives together—different in thought, but alike in love.

Jimmy Carter won the Oregon primary. On a visit to Oregon he was taken on a short cruise on the Willamette River to view the commercial shipping area. It was a cloudy day, and rain threatened. I remained on the dock with the port dignitaries and an entourage of reporters. I found myself standing next to Sam Donaldson, the political reporter for ABC. He asked me a question or two about how the campaign was going in Oregon, and then it started to rain. I put up my umbrella and Sam stepped under it with me. Just then Carter's vessel docked, and he was quickly escorted back to the waiting buses. Sam grabbed my umbrella and joined the pack of reporters in pursuit. I never saw that umbrella again, nor Sam, for that matter, except on television.

The best thing that happened in the Carter campaign was meeting the young woman lawyer who had won the *Roe v. Wade* case at the U.S. Supreme Court three years earlier. Sarah Weddington campaigned nationally for Carter and was the featured guest at a fund-raiser for Carter at our house. Keith and I were eager to congratulate her and tell her how *Roe* had influenced our case in Oregon.

Jimmy Carter was elected president of the United States, defeating the Republican incumbent, Gerald Ford. Norma Paulus was elected Oregon secretary of state, the first woman ever to be elected to a statewide office in Oregon. As expected, I won my reelection with little effort. Three new women were elected to the House: Gretchen Kafoury, the lobbyist for the Equal Rights Alliance in the 1973 session; Sandy Richards, a Democrat from Portland; and Mae Yih, a Democrat from Albany, some thirty miles south of Salem. Our net gain was only one woman, however, because we had lost Norma to higher office and Grace Peck had been defeated in the primary election. We would enter the 1977 session with the same three women in the Senate and nine in the House of Representatives.

As the session began, I felt little enthusiasm at the thought of spending the next six months in Salem. I wondered if this one would be my last. It turned out to be, but not for any reason I could possibly have predicted.

Once there, however, I entered into the process as enthusiastically as ever. The women's groups, now old hands at lobbying, were becoming more prolific at begetting legislation (if I may use that masculine metaphor). They'd been a busy bunch during the interim with the creation of the Women's Rights Coalition. They prepared for another session by drafting legislation, training their members to lobby, and hiring a lobbyist, Mary Souther, a third-year law student at Willamette University. It was no longer necessary to have a women legislators' caucus to plan strategy. The women activists were well informed, and with Gretchen Kafoury's lobbying experience, she was the "go-to" person for advice.

The House of Representatives had a mini-revolution when Phil Lang, a moderate Democrat from Portland seeking re-election as Speaker for his second session, almost lost his position on opening day: a coalition of Republicans and conservative Democrats came within one vote of preventing him from being elected. While the Democrats in the House numbered thirty-seven and the Republicans twenty-three, a group of young, feisty, and vocal conservative Democrats would make Phil's job as Speaker very difficult. I could see that they could also spoil the process of getting the women's bills through the House.

We got a little taste of what might happen when one of the conservative Democrats, Drew Davis of Portland, introduced HJR 62, a bill rescinding Oregon's ratification of the Equal Rights Amendment. When the proposal came before the House for referral to a committee, Speaker Lang referred it to the Special Committee on Equal Rights. That was a big surprise, because at that point there was no such committee. A Republican legislator, Mike Ragsdale, moved to suspend the rules to withdraw HJR 62 from the Speaker's desk and place it before the House for immediate consideration. His motion was soundly defeated.

Just before adjourning for the day, the Speaker announced the membership of the Special Committee on Equal Rights. The Speaker himself would be the chairperson and Nancie Fadeley the vice chairperson. The new committee met. Nancie Fadeley made a motion to amend HJR 62 by removing the word "rescind" and inserting the word "reaffirm." The motion passed. At that point Drew Davis, the sponsor of the original bill, who had also been named to the committee, asked to have his name removed as the sponsor. That was put to a vote, and it lost. Then the bill was voted out of committee and onto the floor of the House for a vote.

On February 23, 1977, the bill, which had been turned into a reaffirmation of ratification of the Equal Rights Amendment, passed the House with forty-eight "Aye" votes. In the Senate it was referred to the Aging and Minority

Affairs Committee, where I served with others who also approved of the House's action. The full Senate voted on the bill on March 2, 1977, and passed it with twenty-five "Aye" votes.

Oregon is probably the only state in the nation to have ratified the ERA twice. But that little exercise put legislators and lobbyists on alert. We were there to make progress, not to let past victories be revisited and repealed.

⋟ ⋞

One very important victory for women in the 1977 session was the "displaced homemaker" bill. The bill would establish a multi-service program for women who had been dependent on the income of another family member but who were no longer supported by that income because of divorce or death. All twelve women legislators signed on as sponsors of the bill.

In working on this bill, I had to confront the specter of myself in this situation, because that's where I might have been if I hadn't returned to college. My mother had been, in effect, a displaced homemaker. The memory of her taking in washing after spending fifteen years as a housewife with children and a working husband, a woman who, to all appearances, had enjoyed a comfortable lifestyle and then had it wrenched away—that gave me great empathy with the brave women who told their stories. The bill passed with large majorities in both houses, thanks to the oral and written testimony of hundreds of women who had experienced the circumstances the legislation addressed.

A related bill required the courts, when dividing assets in a divorce, to view the contribution of a homemaking spouse as having value. In effect, it required the court to presume that both spouses contributed equally to the acquisition of marital property. The courts were also required to consider a spouse's need for career training in determining spousal support.

I was the sole sponsor of a bill that would require the courts to grant joint custody of the children in a divorce if the parties requested it and if the parents devised a workable plan. This was another one that came from my lawyer experience. In Multnomah County it was necessary to go "judge-

Rep. Pat Whiting and Sen. Betty Roberts watch as Gov. Straub signs the joint custody bill. (Photograph by Joseph Tompkins)

shopping," just as it had been in the name-change situation, if the parents had decided joint custody would work best for their family. The bill encountered no significant problems in either the Senate or the House.

Domestic violence issues were also a major part of the Women's Rights Coalition's legislative agenda. These bills, which all passed, would provide shelters for women and children in danger, require police to arrest a person committing an assault during a domestic disturbance, and make provisions for an abused person to obtain a restraining order against an abusive household member.

The women's groups were especially sensitive to the problems faced by rape victims, particularly in a trial. One proposal in the 1977 session built on the rape-shield law passed in the previous session. The new bill, HB 3096, made the shield apply more broadly: "sexual character or reputation for chastity of alleged victim of such crimes [is] not admissible for any purpose." This bill would go a little further toward challenging the prevailing attitude that the victim may have invited the rape.

The bill passed the House and came to the Senate, where it was referred to the Judiciary Committee, of which I was vice chairperson. When the bill was assigned to me to carry on the floor of the Senate, I decided to use a dramatization I'd heard from one of the witnesses at the committee hearings. The scenario was of a robbery. I would play the defense attorney and Senator Wally Carson, a lawyer and Judiciary Committee member, would play the victim.

> *Defense attorney:* "Mr. Carson, you allege you were held up at gunpoint on the corner of First and Main?"
> *Victim:* "Yes."
> *Defense attorney:* "Did you struggle with the robber?"
> Victim: "No."
> *Defense attorney:* "Why not?"
> *Victim:* "He was armed."
> *Defense attorney:* "Then you made a *conscious* decision to comply with his demands *rather* than resist?"
> *Victim:* "Yes."
> *Defense attorney:* "Did you scream? Cry out?
> *Victim:* "No. I was afraid."
> *Defense attorney:* "I see. Have you ever been held up before?"
> *Victim:* "No."
> *Defense attorney:* "Have you ever *given* money away?"

Victim: "Yes, of course—"
Defense attorney: "And you did so willingly?"
Victim: "What are you getting at?"
Defense attorney: "Well let's put it like this, Mr. Carson. You've given money away in the past—in fact you have quite a reputation for philanthropy. How can we be sure that you weren't *contriving* to have your money taken from you by force?"
Victim: "Listen, if I wanted—"
Defense attorney: "Never mind. What time did this hold-up take place, Mr. Carson?"
Victim: "About 11 p.m."
Defense attorney: "You were out on the street at 11 p.m. Doing what?"
Victim: "Just walking."
Defense attorney: "Just walking? You know that it's dangerous being out on the street that late at night. Weren't you aware that you could have been held up?"
Victim: "I hadn't thought about it."
Defense attorney: "What were you *wearing* at the time, Mr. Carson?"
Victim: "Let's see—a suit. Yes, a suit."
Defense attorney: "An *expensive* suit?"
Victim: "Well—yes. I'm a successful businessman, you know."
Defense attorney: "In other words, Mr. Carson, you were walking around the streets late at night, in a suit that practically *advertised* the fact that you might be a good target for some easy money. Isn't that so? I mean, if we didn't know better, Mr. Carson, we might even think that you were *asking* for this to happen, mightn't we? Your Honor, we rest our case."

The bill passed with all senators voting "Aye" with one senator excused.

There were more successes for women, and almost as many bills that failed to pass. "Issues of concern to women fared well in the 1977 Oregon Legislature—as long as there was no price tag on them," said a story in *The Oregonian*. That's an accurate statement, but there were other bills that didn't need funding that also failed to pass. Certainly they would all be back in 1979.

⚭ ⚭

The session dragged on and on, going through June and into July. Part of the problem of winding up the session was the problem Speaker Lang still had with legislators who initially challenged his election as Speaker. Their aggressiveness ended up "demonstrating the need for the authority of a Speaker of the House to maintain order and a sense of purpose," said the *Oregon Statesman,* but given the circumstances that was hard to do.

In addition, we had a big bottleneck in school finance. It started out being a priority, as it had in every session I'd served in, but by the time the end of the session approached there was still serious disagreement on how much funding was needed and how to distribute it. President Boe's proposal for a "safety net" for schools had been defeated by voters in March, so it was back to the drawing board.

On the Fourth of July, a Monday, as late afternoon passed into evening, sandwich-making ingredients were laid out in the Senate lounge to keep us all nearby. We knew it would be a long night. We'd meet and wait, meet and wait, and wait some more. The guys hung around either on the floor or in the lounge. Betty Browne and I retreated to the north-side aisle just off the Senate floor, where we could see and hear everything that was going on, and then step just inside through the small swinging gate to vote when necessary.

Betty had her cigarettes, an ashtray, a tall glass with ice, and a can of Fresca on the wide window ledge. She asked if I'd like a Fresca, and very promptly I had a similar tall glass in my hand. With my first sip, the taste of vodka told me I could see the night through if I could tease that drink for the next couple of hours. Betty and I commiserated. The sessions were getting longer and longer, and we were working harder and harder. I'd seen seven sessions; she'd seen six. We'd both had big responsibilities this session, and here we were, standing in the dim lighting of the side aisle on the evening of the Fourth of July, waiting to do whatever needed to be done to get this session over with. Going through both our minds, although we weren't ready yet to talk about it, was the idea that we ought to move on.

The Legislature adjourned at 2:44 a.m. on Tuesday, July 5, 1977. I called Keith to let him know I was on my way. By 3:30 a.m. I was on I-5, driving north toward Portland, with scenes from the just-concluded session flashing in my brain. I wondered what lay ahead.

As it turned out, the future would take me on a journey more surprising and fulfilling than I ever could have predicted. But I didn't know that then. Then, my most important and immediate destination was—home.

Chapter 18

"Ladies Were Not Expected"

On the day after Labor Day in 1977 I sat at the front of a large legislative hearing room in the State Capitol with nine black-robed men.

Governor Bob Straub read, "Know ye, that reposing special trust and confidence in the capacity, integrity, and fidelity of Betty Roberts, a citizen of Portland, Oregon, I, Robert W. Straub, Governor of the State of Oregon, do, in the name and by the authority of said state by these presents appoint and commission *him*"—the governor paused, said, "We'll have to fix that" to muffled chuckles, and continued, "the said Betty Roberts, Judge of the Oregon Court of Appeals ..."

I too was in black. I wore the robe of Judge Jena Schlegel, my friend and mentor who had coached me for the bar exam ten years before. Jena was now a Circuit Court Judge in Marion County. The effect of the cancer that would soon take her life was painfully obvious in her gaunt frame and dark, piercing eyes. She was a tall woman, and her robe fell to my ankles, wrapping me in warm friendship and inspiring me to be as good a judge as she was.

I thought back to my first day in class at Eastern Oregon College. Then I was a stylish young woman in my dress, high heels, and white gloves. Now I was cloaked in the somber black of a judge, the first woman in Oregon to wear this solemn garb in this court. My decision to go back to school had carried me a long way, further than I'd ever expected.

Three men, George Joseph, John Buttler, and Michael Gillette, were sworn in with me as new judges that day, increasing the court's size from six to ten. In the last legislative session the Senate Judiciary Committee, of which I was vice chair, had approved the bill adding four judges to the Court of Appeals. The Ways and Means Committee approved the funding on the recommendation of a subcommittee that I chaired.

The need for additional appeals judges was great. The Court of Appeals had had only 574 cases in 1970, its first year of operation after the Legislature created it. By 1976 the caseload had grown to 1,847, much of it generated as the result of legislation that had been passed during my tenure in the Legislature.

Soon after the 1977 Legislature adjourned, Governor Straub had publicly announced he intended to name a woman to one of the positions. Newspapers reported his choice to be Lane County Circuit Court Judge Helen Frye. However, Frye took herself out of consideration, not wanting the risk of running a statewide campaign to retain the position on the Court of Appeals in the next election, which is required of all judges who are first appointed to fill a vacancy that is created between elections.

"With Frye out of contention," said an *Oregonian* editorial, "it now appears the strongest candidate for Straub's 'woman appointee' may be Senator Betty Roberts." The writer noted my lack of judicial experience, but called me a highly intelligent lawyer and a quick study. It was true that I'd not been a trial judge. However, I'd had ten years experience working with many kinds of cases, particularly in family law and before administrative agencies, and I'd argued a few of these to the Court of Appeals. My practice had expanded into personal injury, legal and medical practice, and a few criminal defense cases, giving me experience in a wide variety of areas of the law. It was not unusual for me to work up cases, argue preliminary motions. and then have to turn them over to other lawyers in the office when I had to go to the Legislature.

"If appointed, she likely would receive some on-the-job training from [Chief Judge Herb] Schwab, one of the state's best judicial teachers." The press also analyzed the political advantage to Governor Straub in getting me out of another potential head-on campaign against him in the next year's gubernatorial race. He'd beaten me by only eight thousand votes in the Democratic primary three years earlier. The speculation was amusing. I would not have run against the incumbent governor, but it made good political press.

At about that time, I received a handwritten note from the governor that said, "Without making a commitment you should put your name in the bar poll." I assumed other women lawyers and judges had been asked to do the same. The note was a surprise, but I remembered the old etiquette rule that when a man holds a door open for a woman she should always walk through. I'd take that advice. Within days there were twenty-one names on a statewide Oregon State Bar poll (a gauge of the preferences of the association's members). Multnomah County Circuit Court Judge Jean Lewis was the only other woman on the list. I came in ninth in the poll—not outstanding, but not a bad showing either.

The press all over the state began to speculate about possible appointees. Their lists always included Michael Gillette from the Attorney General's office; George Joseph, a Portland lawyer; Wally Carson, my Republican colleague in the Senate and a Marion County lawyer; and me. I had learned that Senator Carson had gone to Chief Judge Schwab to say he was interested in the Court of Appeals and to seek Schwab's advice. Schwab told him he should be a trial judge first. I wondered how much influence the Chief Judge was exercising in the Governor's selection. I didn't feel inclined to seek Judge Schwab's counsel, especially after hearing about Carson's rebuff. There had been too many times in my life when a man had told me, "You can't." I wasn't about to reopen that old chapter and allow another man to tell me I couldn't, or shouldn't, be a judge on the Court of Appeals.

On August 3, while I was at a national legislators' conference in Michigan, I received a call from Governor Straub. He asked if I would prefer to be a trial judge. If so, he would appoint Judge Jean Lewis to the Court of Appeals and I would take her place as a domestic relations judge.

Without hesitation I said, "Bob, I can't be a good domestic relations judge. Hearing divorce cases every day is not for me. I need variety. I know that about myself." I respected Jean Lewis immensely, but I wondered about her chances of winning a statewide election, and there were rumors that she planned to retire soon. There were only five women trial judges in Oregon—Jean Lewis, Mercedes Deiz, Jena Schlegel, and Helen Frye on the Circuit Court, and Shirley Field on the District Court. If any one of them gave up her seat for the Court of Appeals and then lost the election, we'd be down to four. If I took the appointment, we'd have those five plus one more. I knew I was a formidable and experienced campaigner and could hold the seat against any challenger.

The governor did not try to convince me to take the trial position. He said, "Then I am appointing you along with Mick Gillette, George Joseph, and John Buttler."

George Joseph had been one of my law professors and had later supported me in my legislative races. Mick Gillette and I had become instant friends in 1970 when he was in the Attorney General's office and was defending the new 1969 abortion statutes against the federal court challenge. He was young, but a good lawyer. I was not acquainted with John Buttler, but I knew he had served as one of the top leaders in Bob Straub's campaign.

I reflected on my careers as teacher, legislator, and lawyer, all of which would soon be over. Was it scary to give up a secure political and professional life to venture into new territory? Of course. Would I miss politics? Yes, some. How would I hold up on the one-hour drive to and from Salem every day year-round? I'd turn the travel time to an advantage by using it for planning and listening to tapes on the law. Could I do the work well? I knew I could, once I learned the routine and the system.

And finally there would be a woman on the Court of Appeals. Once again I'd be the only woman working with a group of men. But that had been my normal working environment, and it had been productive and enjoyable once the men learned I worked as ably as they did. I had run against some of the most powerful men in Oregon politics—Tom Mahoney, Bob Straub, Jim Redden, Bob Packwood—and loved every minute of it. It would be a new challenge, I decided, to work side by side with men—this time as a judge.

I had no inkling just how much of a challenge it would be.

❧ ❧

The ranking of the four new appointees was determined by the year we were admitted to practice, which made me the "junior" judge. A junior judge has the least seniority in choosing an office, is the last to enter the courtroom when sitting for arguments, and is the last to speak about cases at court conferences. Being last was okay, I thought. At least a woman now has a seat at the table.

As it turned out, I was not only the last to choose an office, I was the last, by several months, even to get an office. Because of renovations to the Court of Appeals quarters in the Justice Building, Chief Judge Schwab suggested that for the time being I use what had been my legislative office in the Capitol Building across the street. That was not good. The other judges and court personnel saw me only when I came to pick up briefs, or at conferences and on argument days. My contacts with judges and staff were so limited that I felt like an outsider.

The four new Oregon Apellate Court judges with Chief Judge Herbert Schwab and Governor Bob Straub, 1977. Left to right: Betty Roberts, Chief Judge Schwab, John Buttler, Gov. Straub, Mick Gillette, George Joseph. (Photograph by Gerry Lewin)

When the office was finally ready some two months later, it was three times larger than my legislative office, but the Chief Judge had ordered me a small desk, much like a home writing desk—symbolizing to me that I was not expected to do as much work as the other judges. Or perhaps I was expected to do the same amount of work with less desk space. Either way, it diminished my presence. I immediately had it exchanged for a big, well-worn desk that I quickly covered with stacks of briefs and other evidence of tasks in progress.

Our offices seemed to be quietly removed from the rest of the world. That was appropriate in view of our sequestered and confidential work, but the quiet often seemed oppressive. It hid more than a desire not to disturb a colleague's work. Each morning I entered the court offices with a "good morning" to anyone I met, but the greeting was rarely returned. Sometimes a secretary would respond, but my male colleagues would usually grunt or sigh. Only the clerks replied with friendly hellos. The judges were always too preoccupied for conversation. All, that is, except Mick Gillette. He and I talked about the oppressive atmosphere.

I knew that relations among some of the judges were burdened with animosities from past political battles. Judge Robert Thornton and Judge Lee Johnson had had a falling-out in 1968 when Johnson unseated Thornton from his long-time post as Attorney General. Thornton sued Johnson, alleging violations of election laws, and lost. Thornton ran successfully for the Court of Appeals two years later, and Johnson was elected in 1976. In all the time I worked with the two men at the court, I never saw them speak to each other directly.

The six judges on the Court of Appeals before the four new judges were named. Top to bottom: Chief Justice Herbert Schwab, Judge Robert Thornton, Judge Jason Lee, Judge Lee Johnson, Judge Jacob Tanzer, Judge William Richardson. (Photographs from *Oregon Blue Book*, 1977-1978)

A similar animosity existed between Judge Jake Tanzer and Judge Jason Lee. Tanzer had been appointed to a newly created position on the court in 1973, but was defeated by Lee in the next election. A lawsuit again ensued, with Tanzer unsuccessfully alleging a violation of election laws. Judge Lee took his seat on the Court of Appeals. Two years later, Tanzer ran for a vacant position and won, but was appointed again before his elective term began. Tanzer's obvious disdain for Lee created unproductive tension. In short, these judges did not display the type of collegiality that I expected on an appellate court.

There was also tension between Chief Judge Herb Schwab and Judge Bill Richardson, a former District Court Judge. The District Court was the lowest of the state's trial courts, with jurisdiction over misdemeanors and traffic violations. In 1976, while serving there, Richardson ran against Court of Appeals Judge Bill Fort (the husband of my Senate colleague Betty Browne) and won. This irritated some of the judges, most particularly the Chief. In Judge Richardson's brief time on the court he had not yet had the opportunity to demonstrate that he was, in fact, a highly capable appellate judge. He later told me of his great relief when we four were appointed. He no longer was the new kid on the block.

The hostilities and conflicts that flowed around us never surfaced openly, but they were profoundly inhibiting on court personnel, especially the secretaries. The unspoken rule, it seemed to me, was that if a judge was not speaking to another judge, their secretaries were not to associate either, or at least to do so in a clandestine manner.

Dorothy Osborne, my secretary, was new, and she encountered her own difficulties. Not only was she the junior secretary, but she was regularly asked, "What's it like working for a woman?" My law clerk, Rich Patton, a young man just out of law school, thought she should say, "It's no different than working for a man," or "I do the same things you do." But Dorothy developed her own reply, which was, "If I'd known what it's like to work for a woman, I never would have worked for a man." In truth, it would have been much easier for her to work for a man and not have to suffer the innuendos and subtle slights that occurred because she worked for a woman judge. But she was a strong, mature woman who supported me in every way she could.

Rich asked me one day how I responded to those who said I was appointed only because I was a woman. I told him that no one said that directly to me, but if they did, my answer would be very simple: "I could be appointed because I am a woman, or I could *not* be appointed because I am a woman. Of the two, I prefer the first."

At our weekly full-court conferences, during which we considered proposed drafts of court opinions, the judges sat around a long rectangular table in order of seniority. The Chief, who presided, sat at one end. To his right was the most senior judge. I, being the most junior judge, sat on the Chief's left. Comments on the proposed opinions were made in order of seniority. The process was quite formal.

It was at these conferences that I encountered "you-are-not-present" discrimination, one of the cruelest forms, for it makes one nonexistent. It is also insidious, for the person practicing it can say, "What did I do? I didn't do a thing." Which is both true and not true, and that is the point: there's been a refusal to interact at all. The Chief Judge never asked me, as the last judge, about draft opinions. He declared discussions done and turned to the next case without looking at me. I wondered if I was invisible, or if he had a blind spot on his left side.

I had not experienced that exclusion before. The signal I was being sent in conference was loud and clear: being a judge was men's work. The Oregon judiciary in 1977 might as well have been a tree house with a sign posted: "No girls allowed." Their fear was that irrational. And it was up to me to modify myself in some way to alleviate their fear. If a woman is doing "men's work," then the woman must change in some inexplicable way to make her work acceptable to the men. The burden was clearly on me to do the impossible. It was an untenable responsibility that placed great stress on me emotionally and intellectually. I'd just come from years in the Oregon Legislature, where I'd worked on every piece of legislation that would give women equal status. I'd worked effectively and skillfully alongside the men, and I was recognized as a confident legislator who used political power constructively. The Court of Appeals seemed oblivious to all that. I couldn't let the indignities continue.

I began to speak up in conference. "Wait a minute," I'd say before the Chief moved on, "we're not done with this opinion yet." And I relished the advantage I had as the last person to speak. By the time discussion got to me I knew the positions of all the other judges. My vote often could be decisive. When an opinion had a majority without me, I could delay it by stating that I intended to write a concurring opinion or a dissent.

It was important not to act out of pique or retaliation, or frivolously or aggressively. None of that was my style, anyway. I patiently waited for the men to learn that I worked the same way they did and often thought the same way, but there were times when I didn't, and at those times—indeed, at all times—I expected to be heard.

The first time I spoke from the bench in the courtroom during oral arguments, I saw a startled look cross the face of the attorney who was presenting his case and a noticeable stiffening of the shoulders of the other judges on the panel. For a moment it appeared the lawyer was wondering if he should answer in view of the reaction of the other judges. My comment was neither brilliant nor silly; it was just something about the facts. Perhaps the lawyer was simply struck dumb by the sound of a female voice. It was a first. No lawyer or judge had heard a woman's voice from that court bench before. I had broken a significant sound barrier.

My relationship with women secretaries was similarly confusing. They, too, seemed uncomfortable in my presence. They may have thought it inappropriate to be friendly with any judge, woman or man. After all the years of working with women in the Legislature, in women's organizations, and in campaigns, I missed being with women immensely. I had not anticipated being separated so completely from familiar faces and conversations, from people who looked like me, thought like me, and talked like me. I felt severed from my gender.

Not surprisingly, given my slow integration into the court that first year, my production in terms of number of opinions was low. Part of the reason was simply the steep learning curve. Part of it also was my reluctance to let go of my interest in seeing the Equal Rights Amendment ratified. I took time to speak to women's groups about the continuing efforts to ratify the ERA. In truth, though, I held out little hope for that, and told my audiences that progress for women would instead depend upon Congress, state legislatures, and the courts.

Overcoming uncomfortable moments, most of them unconscious acts of feigned chivalry, was a priority for me. Whenever my panel of judges went from our office building to the courtroom in the Supreme Court Building, as we entered or exited doors and the elevator, there would be that trained hesitation that said, "You first." The judges' private elevator in the Supreme Court Building was an ancient and tiny cage that barely held three adults. Getting out of it required delicate maneuvering. If the judges insisted I get out first, after having insisted I get in first, there was no way we could keep our dignity intact. It had to be as annoying for the men as it was for me.

There were other embarrassing moments. Once when I was hearing cases on a panel with Chief Judge Herb Schwab and Judge Jake Tanzer, we took a break midway through the morning's arguments. I was last to exit the courtroom. Judge Schwab walked down the hallway talking about the last case we had heard. At the end of the long hallway he entered an unmarked door. Jake started to follow, but quickly turned and said, "Aw, Betty, ..." Jake was obviously torn between following Herb and stopping me. I realized that the door Herb had entered was a men's restroom. When Herb returned he was angry that Jake had not followed him to continue the discussion of the case.

A sign saying "Men" was promptly attached to the door. It was a long time before Herb could see the humor in the situation, but one day he remarked good-naturedly, but with a little sting, that there was only one place the guys could go to talk about cases without me there.

⋙ ⋘

The case work, fascinating and challenging, enabled me to start asserting my place among my colleagues. One case that took my particular interest was a rape case in which the defendant claimed there had been consent to the intercourse.

The man had been convicted at trial on evidence from another woman, not the rape victim. The man, this witness said, had accosted her on the street; she had struggled with him but reached the door of the apartment building that was her destination. She was let in by the person she was to visit, but the man who had accosted her got into the building, too, and went to another apartment. He knocked and a woman came to the door. That was the woman he'd raped. He claimed he'd been invited in. He appealed on grounds that it had been wrong for the trial court to allow the testimony of the first woman, which had been crucial in his conviction.

One of the judges was circulating an opinion that accepted the defendant's argument and found the first woman's testimony inadmissible. If our court accepted that opinion, the man would be tried again without the challenged testimony. Rich Patton, my law clerk, researched the issue and we concluded there was a good argument that the comments were admissible. Rich and I decided before conference that I should dissent. If the court were to adopt my dissent, the defendant's conviction would stand.

We wrote the dissent and distributed it to the other judges for review. Soon thereafter the Chief passed my clerk in the hallway and said, "I see you're working for women's lib." Rich reported to me that at first he "just blew it off," but that the more he thought about the Chief's comment the more he resented it. Finally he decided that if that was the reaction, then the dissent was making its point. I was proud of Rich, for on a man-to-man basis the jibe was a challenge to his status, and on an intellectual basis it said he was not doing his own thinking. Either way, it was an incident that the other clerks quickly learned about, and they rallied around Rich, perhaps influencing their own judges.

For me, that remark by the Chief was the turning point when I realized that these problems between us were harmful to the court and its work, not just to me. No matter the old animosities, the newness of us four judges, and the reluctance to accept a woman, we each had a duty to do good work. That meant we all needed to speak out, whether in conference or by written opinion.

The dissent received a majority vote of the judges in conference and became the majority opinion, written by the Chief Judge himself as he had been on the panel that heard the case. The conviction stood.

> ⊱ ⊰

In April of 1978 I attended my first judicial conference, a three-day meeting of all judges in the state at a beautiful resort on the Oregon coast. The few women judges sought each other out to catch some conversation, but mostly the meeting was a sea of males. On the first night of the conference, after a social gathering, I excused myself from a group of judges I'd been talking with in the cocktail lounge, explaining that I was going to my room. One of the judges said he was leaving, too, and would walk with me. We had a friendly chat as we walked toward our rooms. Upon arriving at my room I leaned over to put the key in the lock and was startled when the judge quickly put his hand over my breast and squeezed. Unbelievably stunned, I couldn't speak. My assailant turned and fled down the nearby stairs.

Fumbling again with the door lock, I let myself into my room. I was shaking with anger and fright. I double-locked the door and pushed a chair against it.

In all my life no man had touched me without my permission. The man's groping, I concluded, was a flagrant attempt to put me in my place. It was an act that said, "Sure, you're an appellate judge, but you're still a woman and I don't respect you as either a woman or a judge."

I called Keith and told him. He was angry and suggested I tell Chief Judge Schwab. I said, "Oh, sure, as though Herb gives a damn about what happens to me. Besides, what will he do? He probably won't even believe me." Nor did I want to be seen as a woman running to a man for help.

As I dressed the next morning I knew what I would do. At the conference that day when I saw the judge, I stared at him until he finally had to catch my eye. I continued to hound him quietly during the rest of the conference, keeping my distance but staring at him steadily. I deliberately placed myself where I could stare at him during meals and programs. Every time he looked up he saw me. Finally, he began to keep his head down—bowed in shame, I like to think. I have never since spoken to him, and on later occasions when I saw him I simply took up the staring again.

❧ ❧

As the summer wound down and all the law clerks began to leave the court for jobs as attorneys, there was a steady stream of goodbyes. I had a fondness for the young clerks assigned to the other judges, as well as for Rich, for they had been my friends at the court during my first year. They seemed fiercely sincere as they wished me well, and they reported incidents they had observed or remarks they had overheard about my presence on the court. Their supportive comments gave me hope. "Getting it off their chests" was a relief for them, too, because they had been troubled by what they had seen and heard.

One male law clerk reported that his judge's secretary had made it known to everyone on the court that she did not believe women should be judges and that she, personally, would do everything she could to make things difficult for me. As a senior secretary she had significant influence on the other secretaries. That told me why I was having trouble establishing rapport with the women. Ironically, her judge was one of my supporters on the court. Two years later, I learned from another clerk for the same judge that the woman had changed her mind about me but was still insisting she would quit if her judge ever hired a woman law clerk. He eventually did, but she didn't quit.

Another clerk told me his judge had asked him when I first came on the court, "How do you think Judge Roberts feels about using the same restroom as the secretaries?" He must have thought it was demeaning for me to share a restroom with the secretaries, but, obviously, I couldn't use the men's restroom. His comment brilliantly reflected his low regard for female secretaries.

For an entire year I had been seeking the meaning behind the events at the court. Now, thanks to the departing law clerks, the puzzle pieces were falling into place. That was liberating. It confirmed that I was not imagining these attitudes and affirmed that I was okay, at least with the clerks. Though other people's beliefs and attitudes were beyond my control, I did not have to remain passive. The situation was not of my making, and I refused to be a victim.

In August, my new law clerk, Marjorie Speirs, came aboard. As an introductory gift she gave me a copy of Virginia Woolf's *A Room of One's Own,* a revealing book about why women had not been able to progress as writers as well as men. I wondered how Marjorie could have been so perceptive without knowing me. It was as though she had been sent to me at just the right time. The importance of Woolf's message pushed me into deeper reflection on where I was in my professional life and the troubling situation at the court. I found in this little book the courage to go forward with my own professional autonomy.

In September I was to give the keynote speech at a luncheon at the state Bar convention for the Women Lawyers Caucus. A few weeks before the convention I had dinner with Judge Kim Frankel, who was running for election to keep her appointed position on the District Court bench in Multnomah County.

It had been a terrible year for women judges. Jena Schlegel had died, Jean Lewis had retired, and Shirley Field had been removed from the bench because of her unacceptable behavior in the courtroom. At least women had been named as replacements for two of the three, but we had a woman running against a woman for the third position, which seemed to me a waste of talent when there were so few of us. Others, however, may have viewed it as progress that two women could run against each other.

Kim had clerked at the Court of Appeals before I arrived. She said one of the judges had told her, "What you need, Kimberly, is to marry and have a baby." I believed her story. As we talked, the subject of my upcoming speech to the women lawyers began to form.

There was a good turnout of women lawyers at the Bar convention, and I saw some men in the audience at the luncheon, too. I began my speech with a quote from Samuel Johnson: "A woman preaching is like a dog standing on its hind legs. It is not done well, but it is surprising to see it done at all." I added, "Today, some believe that to be true of women judges." I followed that with a litany of statistics:

> There is no woman on the United States Supreme Court, and there never has been. Only nine of the 525 active judges in the federal court system are women. Only ten of the 341 state supreme court justices are women. Less than 5 percent of all intermediate court of appeals judges are women. And in Oregon, of 143 active judges, five are women. To see a woman judging is, indeed, surprising.

Then I talked about Virginia Woolf and her statement that a woman needed financial independence and a supportive learning environment—"a room of one's own"—if she were to realize her destiny as a writer or in any other field. Yet not until 1865, when Vassar offered the first college curriculum for women, were women able to venture into the learning environment that men had possessed for so long. There were too many obstacles for women—and all were clearly enunciated and held in place by the United States Supreme Court.

I mentioned cases, beginning with the 1865 case that held that the Constitution's equal-protection clause did not apply to gender discrimination and ending with the 1978 *Bakke* case, which had challenged admissions policies at the University of California. In *Bakke*, the court reiterated its position that, while race discrimination is "inherently suspect," sex discrimination is far more easily justified and is far more readily condoned by the courts.

It was encouraging, I told my audience, that there had been an increase in numbers of women law graduates, from 4 percent in the 1960s to 15 percent in the 1970s. Given the time it takes, however, between graduating from law school and becoming a judge, I could not see a similar increase in the numbers of women in the judiciary in the near future.

I concluded, "Now the time has come for obstacles to give way." The message was clear to the women in my audience. If we work for equal status for women, we will have great women lawyers and great women judges.

This speech was something of an epiphany for me. My mind was clearer about the attitudes at the court, the refusal to see me as a person, and I realized any woman would have had the same experience. It was about deep-seated, unconscious prejudice. How could it be otherwise when the U.S. Supreme Court said discrimination against women was not against the law?

Chapter 19

Transformation on the Court

As 1978 gave way to 1979, my opinion writing was improving considerably in both quantity and quality. I had learned that the court's motto, "Don't get it right, get it written," was said only partly in jest. Statistics on opinion production were on our desks first thing on the first day of each month, and I was becoming well established in the middle tier of those statistics.

I was also becoming bolder in conference. Some of my comments sparked unexpected controversy. Once I asked Judge Lee Johnson to change the use of the words "maiden name" in an opinion to "birth name," "family name," or "surname." We'd never specifically discussed the use of gender-neutral language in opinions, and I hadn't adopted this as a crusade. But here was a specific example about a woman's identity that I felt I shouldn't ignore. Judge Johnson became angry and defensive, saying I knew how he felt about "these things," having served with him in the Legislature, and he certainly would not change now.

Someone asked why it made a difference, since "maiden name" was so commonly used. I explained that many women found the reference offensive because it prolongs the expectation that women must change their names upon marriage, that all women are expected to marry while they are still in their "maiden" years, and that their birth name is only temporary and insignificant until then. There was a moment of contemplation, and then Chief Judge Schwab said, "You mean this is something like 'Christian name?'" Being a Jew, he could recognize the personal significance of a point that others saw as merely semantics. I thought, *Hurrah, at least the Chief is educable.* More importantly, the Chief had supported me, if only indirectly. Nevertheless, "maiden name" stayed in the opinion.

My friends asked me regularly whether a woman on the court made any difference in how the law is interpreted and in the outcome of cases. I had to answer candidly that I didn't think my presence on the court had made much difference yet, but that when more women became judges that would make a difference. It's inevitable, I thought, that when we have judges who are biologically different from men, who have different cultural training and uniquely different life experiences, they will see the law from a different set of values. And, yes, I guessed sooner or later I'd make some difference.

✌ ✌

By the spring of 1979, my working relationship with the Chief and the other judges was becoming warmer. At the beginning I'd been sure the Chief was surprised that I showed up for work every day. One snowy winter day my panel was scheduled for pre-argument conference at 8:30 a.m. Hearing the weather report the night before, I set my alarm for five o'clock to allow two hours for driving from Portland to Salem, twice as long as the trip usually took. My car was equipped with snow tires, and I had chains in the trunk. If court is cancelled, I resolved, it won't be because I'm not there. Conditions were dangerous, but I arrived well before 8:30 a.m. The phones were ringing with lawyers asking if arguments were cancelled. The Chief asked me how the roads were. I told him, "Terrible but improving." He instructed his staff to tell the lawyers that Judge Roberts had driven down from Portland, and that meant there would be arguments.

One afternoon Chief Judge Schwab and I were waiting for two other judges to arrive for panel conference, and he casually asked, "How are things?" I said, "I feel a bit vulnerable right now because I just had a lump removed from a breast this morning. The biopsy was negative, but I have a few stitches."

He said, "You should have told me. I would have postponed the conference." Frankly, I was surprised I'd told him even after the fact, because I feared it would be seen as another female weakness.

The Chief's change in attitude was partly explained by something Mick Gillette told me. He said three judges had gone to the Chief and bluntly stated that it was time he "knocked off" the hazing or whatever he was doing to make life difficult for me. Of course I appreciated that, but I wished it had not been necessary.

Mick had also suggested to me once that I "talk back" to the Chief, or "take him on" in an argumentative sense. I told Mick I would not do that, because I had respect for the position of Chief Judge. And Herb Schwab, as the court's first Chief Judge, had done a fine job of organizing the personnel and work of the court after it was created by the 1969 Legislature. I didn't agree with his administrative style, but I knew his harsh manner was not uncommon among the men who had fought World War II and come back to use their military training techniques in civilian management. I had worked around that in teaching, politics, and law by accommodating the men, but I would not emulate them. "Talking back" would only have created a greater schism between us.

⚓ ⚓

In the first year, when four new judges almost doubled the size of the court, the Chief had arranged us in panels of three, and he himself presided on every panel. Ultimately he decided to make the panel appointments permanent, with one of the three the presiding judge. I ended up on a panel with Bob "Doc" Campbell and Mick Gillette, who was our panel's presiding judge.

I was delighted to be working with those two men. We jokingly called ourselves the eastern Oregon panel. Doc was a Circuit Court judge from eastern Oregon, Mick had grown up in Milton-Freewater, near Pendleton, and I'd spent eleven years in Klamath Falls, Lakeview, and LaGrande. We shared other similarities—we were all decisive, we cut through extraneous matters quickly, and we were not tolerant of long-winded lawyers. Each of us was willing to work on any case we heard and to help our colleagues when asked. We were also highly competitive, and we wanted our panel's opinion-writing statistics to be at the top of the monthly scoresheet. In this we succeeded from time to time, because Mick was a prolific writer.

The court's public profile rose that spring when a series of articles appeared in *The Oregonian*. The first article described the increasing numbers of cases on appeal and the administrative and legislative changes that needed to be made to deal with the workload. The second article categorized the Appeals Court judges as "strong," "middle," and "weak," naming me with Jason Lee in the latter group. There were also two special feature articles, one on me and one on the Chief, and a picture of each of us.

The reporter wrote that I'd been a "fiery" state senator but lacked legal experience compared to the other judges. It quoted one source as saying I "unwittingly" did things that irritated the Chief. Being the first woman was a factor in my low production of opinions, the writer said, but "in recent months her productivity has shot up." Another source said my sex might have been a factor: "'This court tends to be a men's club,' said one female clerk. 'Most of the judges carry their egos around in a wheelbarrow, but Judge Roberts doesn't.'"

The story about Chief Judge Herb Schwab said that "law clerks call him 'old grumble guts.'" It added that some do so "affectionately," but many others didn't have much affection for him. One source said, "He's crude, sexist and crass." The Chief's own clerk said: "I remember him saying to me once… 'You can't be a good administrator unless you're prepared to be a sonofabitch, a gut fighter.'" The Chief's manner was naturally gruff, so when he added disdain to his comments he could wilt the self-confidence of a lawyer and fill the entire courtroom with apprehension if not outright fear. Such was the story about the time the Chief held up his pencil and broke it in half and said to the lawyer, "That's what I think about your argument. You're done."

There were complimentary remarks in the news article, of course, about Schwab as an administrator and judge. One source said, "Beneath some of that blusteriness there is a warm and compassionate person." I was beginning to see that side of Herb. However, on the morning the news articles about the Chief and me appeared, he came into my office with newspaper in hand, obviously angry. He wanted me to know he had not made any comments to the reporter about judges' opinion production. He accused Marjorie Speirs, my clerk, of having talked to the reporter about him. I assured him she had not. I knew Marjorie had refused to talk to the reporter—she didn't trust herself in what she might say, and, more importantly, she didn't think it would be ethical.

Later that same day I encountered Gary Babcock, the state public defender, in the court's parking lot. Chuckling about *The Oregonian* story, he said he hoped it helped me. He knew my opinion production was up, he said, and he knew I was being treated differently from the men on the court. Gary revealed that he had been the source of much of the material.

Support for me was swift and overwhelming. Many people saw the articles as a mixed review of my performance on the court, which, in some respects, demonstrated the schizophrenic attitude that attended the fact of a first woman on the appellate courts. Many, including female legislators who knew me and my work, saw the negatives in the articles as sexist; others saw the positives and wanted to add their words of encouragement. The articles left me feeling bloodied and bruised, but I was emboldened by the support, which gave me courage for the next round.

Instinctively I knew the newspaper publicity was not good for the court. Courts communicate through their opinions, not by talking to reporters about their internal work. The negative comments so publicly displayed might have been as much of a shock to the Chief as they had been to me. Maybe it helped him see that there were changes needed on the court, not only in workload but also in personnel. I believe these changes would have happened without the publicity.

In any event, Herb became less gruff and more friendly toward me. Shortly after *The Oregonian* articles appeared, my panel was sitting with the Chief presiding, which he did from time to time when a judge recused himself from a case or was not present, for some reason or other. An elderly lawyer addressed us as "gentlemen" not once, but three times. This was not unusual. But the third time this lawyer said it, the Chief wrote me a note: "I guess you're not on this case."

I wrote back, "The first time I excuse it as a mistake, the second time I excuse it for age, the third time I vote against him." We still didn't correct any lawyer openly in court, but the fact that Herb noted the error and could communicate with me about it was progress.

⚘ ⚘

With the gradually improving atmosphere at the court, a different but intriguing opportunity presented itself. My two eight-year-old granddaughters enrolled for a month during the summer at a girls' camp, Camp Tamarack, seven miles from Black Butte Ranch, where Dian and I had built a vacation home. I would be able to visit them often. Camp Tamarack's mission was to help girls develop self-confidence, independence, and leadership by learning outdoor skills. My daughters and Keith and I volunteered to help open the camp in the spring and close it in the fall, a commitment requiring two solid weekends of hard work. I loved being there, and I envied my granddaughters their camping experience. I wished I'd had something like it when I was a child.

On one of my trips into camp, I learned the owners were looking for buyers who would continue to operate Camp Tamarack as a girls' camp. Two women were interested, both recreation professors at the University of Oregon. I was offered the opportunity of going in with them as a silent partner.

The idea intrigued me. The two women were highly qualified and capable of actively running the camp. One, Phyllis Ford, was scholarly; she had written books and numerous articles on camping and recreation. The other, Gale Orford, was an outgoing, cheerful Australian with a brand-new doctorate in physical education and recreation that she was eager to put to good use. I drove to Eugene one day after work and met with Phyllis and Gale in their living room to get acquainted and talk about the details of operating a camp. They understood that my role would be limited because of my obligations at the court. They assured me they were prepared for the intense labor required to operate the camp, and they would take that responsibility willingly.

Keith did not interfere with my decision. The only thing he was concerned about was the partnership arrangement. He said, "You know your partners have a lesbian relationship, don't you?" I restrained a "Duh." Instead, I said, "Of course I know, but it doesn't make any difference unless it affects the business of the camp."

In early November, as I was enjoying dinner with my new partners and the former owners, Keith called with the sad news that my mother had died. She'd passed away in the hospital in Kerrville, Texas, at age eighty-four. It was not a shock; we knew Mom's heart was deteriorating, and she'd been ill for some time.

I received abundant condolences from our hostesses and my new partners. Kind as they were, I was glad our business and dinner were over, for I welcomed being alone with my thoughts. As I drove up the freeway to Portland in an autumn rain, I felt grief and hope in equal measures, musing on the fortuitous coincidence that I would be starting a new venture that involved me with young girls' lives just as my mother's life was ending.

Then I vented my sorrow with tears. What a strong woman my mother had been! In two days I would be in Texas to face the fact that I would never hear her supportive, encouraging words again, except in my heart.

❧ ❧

Marjorie Speirs had decided to stay on another year as my law clerk. While that was unusual, I had encouraged it because we were working well together and neither of us was ready for a change. I assured her the conditions at the court looked brighter. Almost half the new clerks were women, which reflected the growing numbers of women graduating from law school. Their presence made the place friendlier, even though the atmosphere was still decidedly masculine. If we could just get another woman judge or two, the Court of Appeals would be an ideal place to work.

Other changes were on the way. The Chief intended to retire at the end of 1980. In the late fall of 1979 Supreme Court Justice Ralph Holman announced that he planned to retire, and Jake Tanzer from our court received the appointment. John Warden, a Circuit Court judge from Coos and Curry counties, was appointed to succeed Tanzer. Ed Warren, a law-school classmate of mine, was appointed to fill the vacancy created by the sudden death of Judge Jason Lee in February of 1980. The court was changing more rapidly than I had expected. I was now seventh in seniority, well into the middle tier, making me a more integrated member of the court. With the arrival of the new judges, the human dynamics changed subtly but decisively.

Judge Warden certainly set himself right with me when he came into my office a couple of months after he had joined the court and told me he wanted to talk about something personal. I was surprised, but said, "Fire away." His observations since coming to the court, he confided, had led him to conclude that I was not being treated the same as the other judges. He wanted my comments on that. I could have jumped from my chair and hugged him. Instead I said, "John, you should have been here two years ago!"

We talked at some length about my experiences. I related some of the incidents, but I assured him that there had been marked improvement. I felt free from discrimination now, I told him, and whatever he was observing was not affecting me. John's sincerity and candor in talking about these things was a good sign that other women would be more readily accepted into the judiciary. While the workload of the court was still a killer, the emotional strain had diminished significantly, making it easier for me to turn all my mental energy to my work.

⊱ ⊰

In the spring of 1980 we new owners of Camp Tamarack began preparing for the outdoor schools that would use the camp until we officially opened it for the summer campers in June. Cleaning the cabins was cold and wet work, but there was always a roaring fire in the lodge and plenty of food and coffee. Jo, Dian, and Keith pitched in again, along with recruits my partners lined up from the university. By early summer the camp was in good shape. Phyllis turned out to be a good plumber and carpenter. Gale repaired the horse corral and hauled in hay for our thirty horses. One weekend Gale donned her wetsuit to help another diver replace barrels under the floating dock that extended into Dark Lake. For relaxation, she split wood. How did women ever get the reputation for being the weaker sex?

When our staff arrived in June, I got in the habit of going to camp after work on Fridays and staying the weekend. On Monday mornings I was in the shower early, then in the kitchen picking up a cup of coffee and one of our cook's freshly baked cinnamon rolls and a sandwich for lunch. I'd turn onto the highway by 7:00 a.m. just in time to see the sun rising in the sky in my rear-view mirror. Returning to work on Mondays was great physical relief. I could sit all day, calmed and relaxed by the weekend's hard work, and I found my mind more ready for the tasks at hand.

⊱ ⊰

Marjorie would be leaving her clerk's position in September; I hired a new clerk, Kathleen Bogan. Kathi told me in her interview that she wanted to work for a woman appellate judge, and since her choices were limited to one, I should hire her.

"Not exactly a compliment," I told her.

She said, "No, it is. Because if I had not liked you I wouldn't work for you." This sprightly, animated, diminutive young woman possessed a captivating self-confidence. She had a journalism background and was highly recommended by her legal writing professor. She wrote poetry. Our initial banter demonstrated her sense of humor and her quick wit. I learned she was just as quick and assertive in her work.

Betty Roberts with her law clerk, Kathleen Bogan, at the Oregon Court of Appeals. (Photograph by Paul Peterson, from *Eugene Register-Guard*, January 3, 1982)

Kathi's cheerful competence soon became apparent to everyone at the court. She established good relations with all the other clerks and began to work her way into the affections of the tight-knit circle of the judicial assistants (formerly "secretaries"). Her interest in politics led to discussions about the Legislature and the personalities there, as well as the politics of the court. She had friends working at the Legislature who kept her informed, and she, in turn, shared that information with me. It had been a long time since I had talked about political events and issues, my life's blood for so many years.

The year also brought more changes to the court. Judge Warden, who had been appointed in February of 1980 to take Jake Tanzer's seat, lost the election to George Van Hoomissen, a Circuit Court judge from Multnomah County. I was sorry to see John go, but I knew and liked Van Hoomissen. He had once written to the editors of *The Oregonian* to complain of their use of "Mrs. Roberts" when referring to me in print, while referring to other judges as "Judge" or using only their last names. He told them rightly it was a sexist practice. I appreciated his efforts, but I had long ago given up on *The Oregonian*'s ever getting it right.

I was delighted when the governor appointed John Warden to rejoin the court in the position to be vacated by the retiring Chief Judge. When Doc Campbell was appointed to the Supreme Court, Tom Young, an eastern Oregon lawyer with whom I had served in the Legislature, was appointed to take his seat. We held a full-court conference to select a new Chief Judge, and George Joseph was elected unanimously. With these changes I had moved up to position six in seniority.

I was comfortable with the new Chief. In the course of a casual conversation I said to George, "You know, I tried for three years to figure out why the Chief acted the way he did toward me. I don't know if it was because I was the junior judge and therefore had to take the hazing for all four of us who came on the court at once, or because he thought I lacked the experience to be a good appellate judge, or because he thought I would bring my partisan politics to the court, or because I had not asked him for permission to be on the court, or if it was because I am a woman." George's reply was simple: "Would you believe all of the above?"

The new Chief assigned Tom Young to our panel. Mick and I were delighted. Some months after Tom joined the court he told me his daughter had passed the bar exam and was interviewing with various law firms. He was proud of her accomplishment but distraught about how she was treated in interviews. He said, "Betty, you can't believe some of the questions they ask and the comments they make." I thought, *Oh yeah? Just try me.* He was outraged that she had been asked if she planned to marry and if she planned to have children. Sometimes she was asked about her men friends and her social or recreational interests. I listened.

We discussed the difficulty women lawyers were having getting jobs, and the attitude that lay behind the kinds of questions asked of women. And then Tom said, "You know, I've always dismissed the complaints of women about a double standard in these things, but I believe my daughter, so I guess it does exist." Mark one up for another breakthrough—but what a tedious task, and at what great cost to women!

≫ ≪

Kathi went with me to Camp Tamarack a few times in the summer of 1981. That fall, she came into my office with something urgent to tell me. She said, "You need to know that I have found a very important friend in one of your women staff members from camp. In fact, we are going to be living together."

"That's very nice," I told her.

"But I want you to understand. This is a very special relationship. I have not had a relationship like this for a long time, and I am very happy about it."

I understood what Kathi was telling me, and, frankly, it made me uncomfortable. I thought to myself, *Why does she feel she needs to explain this to me? Why do I need to know?* I'd had a similar experience when my business partner Gale told me she and her domestic partner Phyllis were splitting up. She'd said, "It's something like a divorce." Why did Gale have to explain her personal relationship with Phyllis? What business was it of mine, anyway?

I was conflicted on why I had those reactions. Homosexuality wasn't exactly a popular topic in those days, and perhaps that was why I felt discomfort when confronted with it. On the other hand, I was sure I had no prejudices about it. Women's organizations had had their own confrontations and conversations, and had universally come out supportive of lesbian and gay people.

I didn't know what I was supposed to say, so I said something like, "Well, Kathi, that's nice. I hope things work out for you." I thought about our conversation on the drive home that evening. Camp Tamarack had introduced me to many aspects of life that I had not confronted before—the most startling being the recognition that many of our staff members were lesbian. Women, as evident in women's magazines and organizations, were becoming more open in their discussions of homosexuality, but in society in general it was a taboo subject. It had dawned on me at some point that I was needed in the camp partnership as a straight woman who loved men—maybe too much, having had three husbands and plenty of boys in the family—and as someone with a good grandmotherly image.

Once I had mentally worked through the issue, I realized that Gale's revelation was intended to help me understand that her breakup with Phyllis was more than just a failed friendship. It was as emotionally devastating as a divorce would have been. And Kathi's compulsion to tell me about her new relationship with Jill was her desire to share her new-found happiness in a blossoming love relationship. While I was not as supportive in both situations as I might have been, I came to appreciate their forthrightness. They had both felt it important to tell me so that I could understand their lives and be prepared for any effect their relationships might have on me. It was healthier than shrouding our differences in mysteries and rumors. And so it was my business, after all.

❧ ❦

Kathi was always cheerful and frequently in a playful mood. Sometimes her impishness made its way into opinions. Once, in a most unusual situation, the court was asked to reconsider an opinion in which the majority of the court had missed the major issue that was the subject of appeal. Fortunately I had not written the first opinion, but it was a blunder for all of us for not catching the error. I was assigned to address the issue that had been missed. Kathi thought it was pretty funny for the court to make such a boneheaded mistake, so she suggested we recognize it good-naturedly.

Here is what went in the opinion—all Kathi's idea, and approved by me: "The author Gertrude Stein is said, on her deathbed, to have beseeched her life-long companion, Alice Toklas: 'What is the answer?' When there was no reply, Stein fell silent, then spoke her final recorded words: 'In that case, what is the question?' We confess to having created a similar dilemma in this case."

All playfulness aside, we never compromised the seriousness of our work, and together we produced good opinions. The Oregon Supreme Court had reviewed a number of my opinions and had upheld about half of them, a good record. They had also taken a few cases in which I had written dissents and had reversed the majority in a couple of those cases.

The work at the court had become exceptionally satisfying to me. The judges, while working very hard to deal with an increasing caseload, were more cooperative and civil with each other. With more women law clerks, the women judicial assistants were more relaxed. Either I had mastered the court or it had mastered me. A little of both, probably.

In July of 1981, President Reagan appointed Sandra Day O'Connor to the United States Supreme Court. What a dramatic breakthrough! O'Connor's appointment was an inspiring event for women in the United States. Asked by a reporter to comment, I said, among other things, "It's terribly important to the morale of women in this country." We knew little about O'Connor at first, but as news items emerged, revealing that she had served in the Arizona State Senate and was at the time serving on the Arizona Court of Appeals, I instantly recognized the similarity of our paths.

As she took her place among the justices in October for the opening of the 1981-1982 term, there was more analysis, especially by women writers, of how Justice O'Connor would fit in at the hitherto all-male court. Ellen Goodman wrote, "If the public expects first women to be either wonderful or terrible ... that woman is inclined to respond by being safe and moderate." I could relate to that and most of the other commentary about how O'Connor would adjust to the court, and it to her. It felt good to have a woman on the highest court in our country. I didn't feel so alone any more.

❧   ❧

Also in the fall of 1981 came a rumor that Supreme Court Justice Tom Tongue would not run for reelection in the following year. I thought about whether I would be interested in moving up to the Supreme Court and what the politics might be in getting there. The status that would come with sitting on the Supreme Court was not important to me, but the challenge of a new job was. I couldn't think of any reason why I shouldn't try. The schedule would be pretty much the same—a killer workload—so that wouldn't require any personal adjustment. The answer ultimately was another, "Just go for it."

Then rumors began to circulate that Justice Tongue would not serve out his term. If he resigned early, Governor Vic Atiyeh, a Republican, would appoint someone to fill the vacancy, and the appointed successor would then have to run in the primary election in the spring of 1982. If opposition developed and there was a runoff, it would mean another six months of campaigning through the general election in November.

At the state bar convention in September I shared my thoughts about the Supreme Court position with my friend Ann Aiken, now a practicing attorney in Eugene. Ann was a good political strategist, and I needed someone to analyze my plan with me. I had not yet told Keith what I had in mind. I told Ann I would run against anyone the governor appointed if, in fact, Justice Tongue resigned. I said I thought I should file for election to the position very soon. That way it didn't matter what Tom Tongue did because I'd be in the race whether he resigned early or served out his term. She said, "Well, filing is an obvious preemptive move. Anyone seeking an appointment will know they will have to run against you." She added, "The press and the governor will see through it right away. You might make the governor mad." She meant he might perceive my actions as an end run around his authority to appoint judges for open seats.

"But Ann," I said, "Vic Atiyeh's not going to appoint me anyway. So what difference does it make?"

She pondered that and then said, "Don't be too sure. At least you have to put your name in for the appointment and give it a try." Then she added, "Go ahead and file. Then if someone else with a good political name and reputation gets the appointment, that just means a good, hard campaign. You've had hard campaigns before. Besides, if you lose the election you'll still be on the Court of Appeals."

Ann had said all the right things. It was important to seek the appointment, if only to let the governor know I felt strongly that I could handle the job. Soon after my talk with Ann, on September 22, 1981, I filed for election to the position. This was news for a few days. *The Oregonian* noted, "Her announcement followed by one day U.S. Senate confirmation of the first woman appointed to the U.S. Supreme Court, Sandra Day O'Connor." An editorial concluded, "[I]t's questionable if a person's sex ever again will be much of a hurdle in most election races in most states. Betty Roberts is one of the people sharing a responsibility for that monumental change in American politics."

Then Justice Tongue announced his intent to retire early owing to poor health. After setting out my political background, an *Oregon Journal* editorial stated:

> [S]he has much going for her in a Supreme Court race and the
> governor would be hard-pressed to find someone who is both a well-

qualified Supreme Court justice and politically capable of overcoming a Roberts campaign. Of course, there is one simple solution to the dilemma. Atiyeh could appoint Roberts to fill the vacancy. She has done well in previous endeavors as legislator and teacher, and has shown impressive growth on the appellate bench. The governor would win some Democratic friends who believe he has been overly partisan in office and draw credit for naming the first woman to the Supreme Court.

I went to see Justice Tongue to ask him if he would consider staying on the court for the last full year of his term so that the vacancy might be filled by election. "I believe I can win the election," I told him. I was sure I still had good political recognition among the voters, and I felt I had a better chance to succeed in a statewide campaign for the seat than I had in getting an appointment from the Republican governor. Justice Tongue had been my evidence teacher in law school, and he was known to have strong feelings that judges should be elected. So I had no hesitancy in asking him the question. But he candidly told me that his health would not allow him to remain on the bench until the end of his term.

Armed with this knowledge, I made an appointment to see the governor. It would be easy to talk with Vic because we had served so many years together in the State Senate. He was cool at first and asked if my filing was intended as a threat. Rather, I said, it was an indication of my interest in serving on the Supreme Court and my desire to see women advance in all levels of the judiciary. There had never been a woman on the Supreme Court. I hoped he shared my concern about that.

The governor had just begun his selection process, so I had no indication of his thinking. Norma Paulus, secretary of state and my Republican friend from legislative days, called to tell me that she and other Republicans were encouraging Atiyeh to appoint me. She said they were telling him it would be a good political move for him, and besides, he would look silly if he ignored my interest and my work on the Court of Appeals and then I beat his appointee in an election. This was backed up by an endorsement from attorney Jack Faust, who had chaired Bob Packwood's campaign for U.S. Senate. In a letter to the governor, he said that, while we had been on opposite sides of "a bitterly fought campaign," I had treated him with "complete impartiality and unfailing courtesy" when he argued cases before the Court of Appeals, proving that I was "completely qualified in the critical areas of judicial temperament and objectivity." Then he pretty much laid it on the line: "My fear is that if you appoint anyone else, the appointment will be viewed as a slap in Betty's face and her election next May will be viewed as a rebuke of you."

Of course, I was grateful for all that unexpected Republican support. Another endorsement came from an even more surprising source. On one of Herb Schwab's periodic visits to the Court of Appeals, he came into my office and said he thought it was "all right" for me to be on the Supreme Court. He said he would speak to the governor about it. He said, "You'll be good for some of those guys over there."

It was not prudent to rely only on political connections. Kathi and I produced a summary of the most significant opinions I had written while on the Court of Appeals and sent the compilation—236 opinions and 33 dissents since September 1977—to Governor Atiyeh, with copies to each member on the State Bar Board of Governors.

In mid-December the Bar forwarded the three names, including mine, to the governor. Late in the afternoon on December 16, 1981, I received a phone call summoning me to the governor's office the next morning. I was told nothing else.

I dressed for a press conference, just in case, in a dark suit and white blouse with a soft bow at the neck. All the way to Salem I wondered what might happen. If not me, who? If not me, why was I being invited to the governor's office? It was a beautiful, sunny winter morning. A good omen. Nothing disappointing could happen on such a lovely day.

Walking in the December sunshine from the Justice Building across the street, past the statues of early circuit-riding missionaries on horseback, I entered the Capitol Building at the east entrance—the exit through which we Democrats had escaped during the turmoil on the eighteen-year-old voting rights bill back in 1971. I thought about how many times in the past sixteen

Gov. Atiyeh's press conference announcing the appointment of Betty Roberts to the Oregon Supreme Court. (Photograph by Mike Williams, from *Statesman Journal*, December 17, 1981)

years I'd gone into and out of the various doors of the Capitol. This time I was entering for what could turn out to be the peak of my long career in politics and government.

I was taken to the governor's assistant, Ede Schmidt, who had been my secretary in the Senate in 1977. As the door closed behind me, Ede came around from behind her desk and with a big smile said, "Congratulations, Betty. The governor is appointing you to the Supreme Court." She added, "It will be announced at a press conference in a few minutes. Perhaps you'd like to be left alone to think about your remarks." Then she was gone. I spent a couple of minutes just absorbing Ede's statement.

A few minutes later the cameras were on me. I said I was pleased that the governor had expressed such confidence in my ability to do the job, and I pledged to the people of Oregon that I would be a hard-working Supreme Court Justice. The reporters began to ask questions, but the governor took over again. This was his press conference and he was making the most of it.

That evening in Portland, Keith and I hosted our annual Christmas cookie exchange party that included family and two long-time women friends and their children. This time we started the celebration with champagne. It was a fitting end to a spectacularly eventful day.

A few days later *The Oregonian* ran the editorial cartoon shown below. What a wonderful Christmas present for me, and, I hoped, for the people of Oregon—especially the women.

Artist: Art Bimrose. Source, *The Oregonian*, December 19, 1981)

Chapter 20

On Being a Justice and Doing Justly

The news of the appointment of the first woman to the Oregon Supreme Court in the 124-year history of the state spread in a hurry. The *Oregon Journal* quoted the governor: "'I wanted to appoint a woman, and I have found one who is eminently qualified." And the Corvallis *Gazette-Times* observed, "Atiyeh's appointment of Roberts is significant for Oregon women, who until recently had little impact on the court system."

I had previously worked with all but one of the men I'd be joining on the court. Chief Justice Arno Denecke was regularly at the Legislature to testify on bills that would affect the judiciary, and he'd been there often in the 1977 session when the bill expanding the Court of Appeals was going through committees on which I served. Berkeley (Bud) Lent had been my long-time legislative colleague. He had been the first to tell me he thought I could beat Senator Tom Mahoney way back in 1968, and he'd been the Democratic caucus candidate for president of the Senate in 1971 when we made our hopeful attempt to end the coalition that had controlled the Senate for so long.

Hans Linde, a former law professor at the University of Oregon, had been my teacher in a course on politics and law when I was working on a master's degree, and I'd known him through Democratic Party activities. Jake Tanzer and J. R. "Doc" Campbell had been my colleagues on the Court of Appeals. The one person I didn't know was Edwin Peterson, but I was told he would be good to work with—a huge understatement, as I would learn early on.

The Friday before the swearing-in on Monday, February 8, 1982, was my fifty-ninth birthday and my last day at the Court of Appeals. On Monday, the family was in my office for pictures before the ceremony. It was a lively scene, with five little grandchildren running around and the office bustling with people. Keith turned to me and said, "This will go well, Queenie. Just relax." As he walked out the door to join the rest of the family he murmured, "Just so you know, I have a little part in the ceremony at the beginning." I looked at him with what he called my "teacher look," and he said, "It's okay—Arno has agreed." And then he was gone.

We judges lined up in the back hallway in order of seniority with the Chief Judge at the head of the line. Then we filed in through the door leading into

Chief Justice Arno Denecke administering the oath of office to the new Supreme Court Justice (Photograph by Bill Murphy, from *The Oregonian*, February 8, 1982)

the courtroom from behind the bench. I was last in line—the junior judge again.

The applause began as soon as Justice Denecke walked through the door and continued until we were all seated and the gavel brought the courtroom to order with a heavy thud. The room was packed with people. They filled all the chairs, stood along the walls, and overflowed out the double doors and covered the staircases as far as I could see. It was a stunning sight. Then Keith stood up and asked the Chief Justice if he might approach the bench. He walked up and handed me a dozen long-stemmed red roses. Again great applause. I managed to discreetly get them between me and Justice Tongue and lay them carefully on the floor.

Governor Atiyeh read the document just as Governor Straub had done at my swearing-in at the Court of Appeals. This time someone had corrected the statement by removing the word "him" and inserting my name. A minuscule change, but hugely significant nevertheless.

As the governor handed me the document, we shook hands across the bench, and I quietly assured him I appreciated the opportunity he had given me and that I would work very hard to make him proud of the appointment.

Then the magic moment came. Justice Denecke asked me to stand to take the oath of office. I raised my right hand and repeated after him, "I, Betty Roberts, do solemnly swear …"

After the final words "… so help me God," the applause was thunderous and sustained. Would it ever stop? I looked at my husband and our combined family of eight children with pride. Gazing at the rows and rows of well-wishers smiling and clapping with all their might, I felt admiration and humility sweep through me for their outpouring of energy and enthusiasm. I vowed I would do good work on the court.

Justice Denecke made no move to intervene with his gavel. I raised my eyes to the beautiful stained-glass dome that dominated the room. It held the Oregon state seal in the center of a large square, framed with mahogany. Four mahogany spokes ran toward each corner of the room, interspersed with a pattern of green and gold stained glass. The dome was still intact after the thunderous applause. Thank goodness. That was a glass ceiling I did not want harmed. The symbolic breaking of a mythical glass ceiling was sufficient for the occasion.

When finally it was my turn to speak, I thanked the governor with heartfelt sincerity. In spite of the politics that went on behind the scenes, the decision was his alone, and I think he finally felt comfortable and proud to name me to the position. My attention then turned to the man I was replacing. Justice Tongue was a good teacher and lawyer who became a good judge. Then I introduced my family. I couldn't have kept the pride out of my voice even if I'd wanted to. Finally, I recognized the women judges who were present.

After the ceremony and the reception, the court was scheduled to hear arguments. As we gathered in the back hallway, Justice Hans Linde took me aside and told me that one judge had wondered aloud about my taking time to introduce my large family, each by name. "I told him, 'But that was important to her; she *is* a mother, you know.'"

"Thanks, Hans," I said, touched at his remarks. "That's nice." He grinned, and we took our respective places in line. Then this mother marched in last behind six men to take her place as an Oregon Supreme Court Justice.

              ✶ ✶

The Oregon Supreme Court sits *En Banc*, that is, as a full court, unlike the Court of Appeals, which sits in panels. Its responsibilities are much broader than most citizens, or many lawyers for that matter, appreciate. All cases that go through the Court of Appeals may be appealed to the Supreme Court by filing a Petition for Review. The judge to whom the petition is assigned analyzes it and writes a memo for the full court to consider. The judge is expected to be thorough, and sometimes this task is as time-consuming as writing an opinion. The court then decides whether to accept review. In general, the Supreme Court is more likely to take review in a case when there is an issue of law involved, and less likely if the only issue is the facts (this is called a review *de novo*), even though, in considering such a case, we might have come to a different decision than the lower court did.

The real power of the Supreme Court lies in its opportunity to rule on constitutional issues and points of law that need clarification, and thus a decision may have a broad effect. In many instances these legal questions stem from new legislation passed in response to changes in public attitudes, or initiated as a result of changing mores and cultural differences. Like society, the law is never static.

The Supreme Court has a wider range of duties than the Court of Appeals. All the judges write opinions covering a broad range of legal issues. The court hears all appeals from the Oregon Tax Court. Surprisingly, I found I liked these cases, because the issues are straightforward with little or no human emotions or conflicted personal relationships involved. The court has responsibility for all appeals from disciplinary actions against attorneys and judges and hears appeals on ballot measure titles. The court also hears *mandamus* petitions, used by lawyers to compel a public official to do his/her duty, and *habeas corpus* petitions, used to seek the release of a person who is unlawfully detained.

We sat for oral arguments three consecutive days a month, and then the Chief assigned the cases we'd heard, taking into consideration the judges' straw vote at conference after oral arguments and the complexity of the cases we were already working on. While the monthly statistics were not as onerous in a competitive sense as they'd been at the Court of Appeals, we all knew how our productivity of opinions stacked up against that of the other judges. Again, once I learned the procedures and how to organize my work, I was always somewhere in the middle.

In contrast to my experience on the Court of Appeals, seniority never seemed particularly important, except that we followed tradition on where the judges sat during oral arguments and around the conference table. This put me to the Chief's left at the far end of the bench; in conference I had the chair near the end of the table on the Chief's left. That happened to be the seat nearest the door. At my first conference the Chief Justice explained in an apologetic tone that, because I was nearest the door, it would be my job to open it when one of the judicial assistants appeared there with coffee around 10:30 a.m. Arno, in his gentlemanly way, made sure I understood that this duty was not assigned to me because I was a woman. In fact, I never did open the door. Instead, I suggested that it might be just as easy if those of us who wanted coffee brought it with us when we came for conference at nine o'clock. If anyone wanted refills, his or her own judicial assistant could bring them. No one objected, and that's how we did it from then on.

※　※

The case I am probably most known for came just two months into my tenure on the court. It was a workers' compensation case centering around a state law that provided workers' compensation benefits to an unmarried woman living with an injured worker, and to their children, as long as the couple had been living together for more than a year.

The claimant in this case, Floyd Hewitt, Jr., had applied for benefits after the woman with whom he had been living for five years, and with whom he had a child, died in an industrial accident. The workers' compensation board denied Hewitt benefits on the grounds that the law provided for compensation only for a woman in such a case. The Court of Appeals reversed that judgment and awarded Hewitt his claim. The Supreme Court took the case to decide the constitutional question. I was delighted when the case was assigned to me to write the opinion.

While I was in the Legislature we had specifically changed the law that benefited only the widow if the couple was married; our revision provided that the husband and children would receive compensation if the wife and mother died as a result of an industrial accident. But the Legislature had not extended the gender-neutral language to unmarried couples in the statute at issue in this case—an obvious oversight, in my mind.

In her research, my clerk, Kathi Bogan, found that many states allowed compensation to men, but some required that the man be dependent on the woman's income. In Oregon, the man was not eligible for compensation under any circumstances. It seemed terribly unfair. Not only had the man lost his lover-companion—who in some states was recognized as being a common-law wife—but he had the child or children to raise on his own.

By August, when my new clerk, Maureen Leonard, began work with me, the case was nearly ready to be submitted into full court conference. Justice Hans Linde had convinced me that we should rely on Article I Section 20 of the Oregon Constitution, which is brief and to the point: "No law shall be passed granting to any citizen or class of citizens privileges, or immunities, which, upon the same terms, shall not equally belong to all citizens." Justice Linde was recognized nationally for his convincing advocacy of basing constitutional questions on state constitutions rather than the U.S. Constitution if equal or greater rights and protections are provided in the state constitution.

After considering legislative intent in the original proposed bill in the 1973 session to make all the language in the workers' compensation statute free of gender discrimination, we found that:

> It is apparent that the gender classification of [the statute] is not
> based on intrinsic differences between the sexes. Rather, it reflects

assumptions about the relative social roles and the probable dependency of men and women. Families of deceased male workers may receive benefits regardless of marital status of the mother while families of deceased female workers may receive benefits only if the parents were married. Accordingly we find the statute unconstitutional.

The next question was whether Floyd Hewitt should be paid benefits. We needed to know what had happened in the Legislature that had changed the intent of the original anti–gender-discrimination bill by leaving this particular provision. Our research revealed that the bill had passed the Senate with the gender-neutral language in 1973, but this challenged provision had been the subject of extensive and heated debate among the members of the House Labor and Industrial Relations Committee. I'd been in the Senate at the time, so I hadn't known what was happening in this House committee during that session.

The entire statute had at first been deleted on a motion from Representative Gary Wilhelms, who argued that "an able-bodied man who was cohabiting with a woman worker who was injured or killed" should not be entitled to benefits. Others emphasized that the benefit was really for the children. After the provision providing gender-neutral language was restored to the bill, a vote was taken that effectively killed the entire bill with all its other important gender-neutral language. Ultimately the old discriminatory language was restored for this one portion of the bill and it went to the floor of the House for a vote. Hence the old language in the statute that was now being challenged in our court.

Maureen and I concluded that the debate in the House committee returned over and over to concern for the family after one or the other parent died. There had to be a child for there to be benefits, and without an entitled parent there could be no benefits for the child. With that in mind, the opinion held that the father and claimant in this case was entitled to benefits.

Justice Betty Roberts with her law clerk, Maureen Leonard. (Source unknown)

When the case went into conference I explained our reasoning in finding the law unconstitutional under Article 1, Section 20 of the Oregon Constitution. Ed Peterson raised the question of whether we should allow benefits to this particular litigant, but my opinion received a majority vote on that point. Ed wrote an opinion concurring that the workers' compensation law was unconstitutional, but dissenting in making the decision applicable to this claimant, because he felt the court was overstepping its bounds. Doc Campbell joined Ed's opinion.

Nevertheless, the whole opinion had been accepted by the majority of the court. That evening as I drove up the ramp onto I-5 to head for home, I had to celebrate somehow. I popped a cassette of "Vangellis," the theme from the movie *Chariots of Fire,* into the tape player. As that energetic music filled the car, I felt I could have run the whole fifty miles home.

I was fortunate that a case with such constitutional significance fell to me early in my years on the court. I was grateful for the lesson on basing an opinion on the Oregon Constitution, and I was delighted that the press picked up on its significance immediately. The headlines said it all. "High court ruling counted victory for ERA." "State court finds ERA." "ERA included in state Constitution." "Equal rights amendment emerges from Oregon court ruling."

An editorial in the *Medford Mail Tribune* headlined, "Equal rights in Oregon?" was important for its explanation of the constitutional provision:

> Compare these two quotations:
>
> *Equality of rights under the law shall not be denied or abridged by the United States or by any state on account of sex.*
>
> And: *No law shall be passed granting to any citizen or class of citizens privileges or immunities, which, upon the same terms, shall not equally belong to all citizens.*
>
> Recognize them?
>
> The first is the operative section of the proposed Equal Rights Amendment to the U.S. Constitution, which failed for lack of ratification by enough states by mid-1982.
>
> The second is Section 20 of Article I of the original Constitution of the State of Oregon, adopted in 1859 and still in effect.
>
> They are phrased differently. But insofar as equal rights between the sexes are concerned, do they not have the same effect? They do seem to, and that is the tenor of a recent Oregon Supreme Court decision.

It's not unusual that one person's case seeking redress for discrimination can have a broad application affecting many citizens. The Equal Rights Amendment to the U.S. Constitution had failed to gain the necessary number of states to make it a part of the Constitution, although the Oregon Legislature had ratified it. I'd predicted the failure in the speeches I'd made to women's groups while on the Court of Appeals, explaining that changes in discriminatory laws would have to come by way of legislation at the state and national levels and through court decisions. Our court had gone one step further by finding the equivalent of an ERA in the Oregon Constitution. Women's groups in Oregon had been divided on whether to work for a state ERA. Now we had one by case law. I was proud and fortunate to have had a hand in making that so.

⋟ ⋞

The court often took cases in which the ruling affected only the party involved, but which would have application for later cases and be instructive to trial judges and lawyers. One such case was *Lyons v. Pearce*, in which an immigrant pleaded guilty to a crime that made him vulnerable to deportation. His court-appointed attorney advised him of that, but then failed to ask the court not to deport him. Our court remanded the case to the trial court for further determination of the deportation issue because of the harsh result of the attorney's failure to make the request.

What was unusual about this ruling was an unconventional footnote. In the drafting stage Maureen wrote a couple of paragraphs citing various law review articles and federal cases decrying the consequences of the routine failure of criminal defense attorneys to seek recommendation against deportation, which amounted to "a life sentence of banishment." Then she added a footnote containing "The New Colossus," the poem by Emma Lazarus that is inscribed on a bronze plaque inside the pedestal of the Statue of Liberty. The poem contains the famous lines, "Give me your tired, your poor/ Your huddled masses yearning to breathe free,/The wretched refuse of your teeming shore./ Send these, the homeless, tempest-tost to me,/I lift my lamp beside the golden door!"

I wasn't so sure about the wisdom of that. I didn't want any opinions going out under my name that might smack of being soft on criminals. She said, "It won't come across that way."

"Okay, Maureen, it stays in," I said, "but two to one it doesn't stay in through full court conference." I lost the bet. The opinion went out with the poem in the footnote. A few weeks later, a letter came from the defense attorney. The poem meant a great deal to his client, he said, and he wanted to thank me.

It was at times like these that I keenly felt my good fortune in having one of the most distinctive jobs in the country. What's more, finally I enjoyed true professional collegiality with my fellow judges. One incident stands out as a stark contrast to my experience on the Court of Appeals. Soon after Bob Jones, a Multnomah County Circuit Court Judge, came to the Supreme Court, we were sitting for argument when a lawyer addressed the court as "Gentlemen." Nothing new for me here, but Justice Jones spoke up. "And Justice Roberts," he prompted.

The lawyer, a young man, was embarrassed. Dutifully he added, "and Justice Roberts." I looked at Bob, seated on my left, and whispered, "Thank you." Word must have gotten around the Bar, because I never heard "gentlemen" used again in that way. It was always "Your Honors."

Another time a few of us were gathered around the conference table waiting for everyone to show up, and someone mentioned *The Brethren,* the book about the U.S. Supreme Court that was written before Sandra Day O'Connor was appointed. The talk turned to what our court could be called. Someone suggested, "The Brethren and Sistern." That got a laugh. Then it was, "Snow White and the Six Dwarfs." What a nice change from the early hostile atmosphere on the Court of Appeals! Our repartee showed that we could break with formality and have a sense of humor about it.

ↄ ↄ

Early in 1983 Chief Justice Arno Denecke announced that he planned to retire on June 30. I'd had so little time to work with this fine man that I hated to see him leave the court, but I was pleased that he would be succeeded on the court by my friend and colleague from the Senate, Wally Carson. Bud Lent succeeded Arno as Chief Justice, but when he decided he'd rather work on opinions than be in the administrative position, Ed Peterson became our Chief Justice.

Soon thereafter Ed began planning a day-long conference on racism and sexism in the courts for all metropolitan area trial judges. Ed's sensitivity to discriminatory language was regularly demonstrated in court conferences—he often asked me if the wording used in an opinion was sexist.

Bob Jones took much of the responsibility for planning the conference. For the keynote speaker on gender discrimination I suggested Lynn Hecht Schafran, Director of the National Judicial Education Program to Promote Equality for Women and Men in the Courts. Her impressive background included a federal clerkship and experience as a practicing attorney. I had heard Lynn at a conference of the National Association of Women Judges and

The Oregon Supreme Court after the resignation of Justices Denecke and Tanzer. Left to right: Justice Wallace Carson, Justice J. R. Campbell, Justice Berkeley Lent, Chief Justice Edwin Peterson, Justice Hans Linde, Justice Betty Roberts, and Justice Robert E. Jones. (Photograph by McEwan Photo, Inc., Salem)

knew she would be just right for ours. Bob Jones urged me to speak about my experiences on the Court of Appeals as a lead-in for Lynn's address. I had not talked to anyone about those experiences, and I had certainly not written anything about them. He kept pressuring me. I finally said I would write something and let him read it ahead of time. Frankly, I wanted to put all that behind me, but Bob thought it was important to personalize the subject of the conference for the trial judges. On the day of the seminar, I stepped forward to deliver the hardest speech I'd ever made, on a subject that was still difficult for me to talk about. I opened by saying that I hoped my sharing of experiences would encourage others to speak about theirs, so that we could all learn to deal with sexism when it occurs. After relating a few of the incidents that had happened at the Court of Appeals, I spoke especially of the "you do not exist" attitude of some judges. I said, "Women are not unmindful that it has been the legal profession and the judiciary itself that has perpetuated the stereotype roles of women."

Then I turned to the more pleasant duty of introducing Lynn Schafran. Lynn related incidents of discrimination that women lawyers were experiencing in courtrooms all over the country. Among other stories, she told about a judge calling a woman lawyer "little girl." After the woman lawyer objected and asked to be called "counselor," the judge at first apologized, but later in the trial he became furious and said, "I tell you what, little girl, you lose!"

Some of the Oregon judges in Lynn's audience reacted positively; others were defensive. One judge asserted that this discrimination stuff was a bunch of lies made up by the women. Just as in politics, we made our points with some and not with others.

‹ ›

I'd been on the court for a year and a half when Helen Mershon of *The Oregonian* wrote a full-page article that included a large picture of me standing inside the glass-paneled doors leading into the courtroom. I am wearing my judicial robe and holding a volume of the Oregon Statutes. The beautiful stained-glass ceiling is prominently displayed above my head. The headline read, "When it comes to opinions, Betty Roberts' are taken seriously." The story reminded readers of my past public life and said, "Some have wondered whether she likes the solitude of sitting on the state's highest court, compared to the '60s and '70s, when she was constantly in the news as an accomplished lawmaker and feminist voice of reason." I did, indeed, like being on the Supreme Court. The working relationship with the other judges could not have been better, and I had the best clerk anyone could hope for in Maureen Leonard.

My part-ownership in Camp Tamarack continued to be a challenge and to provide renewal time, especially in the summer months when I went there on weekends, and the Black Butte house continued to be a welcome respite. Keith had begun to take a greater liking to Black Butte Ranch, and he was often disappointed when he, or we, couldn't stay in Dian's and my house because it was rented. One day, without telling me beforehand—which was typical of both of us at times—he stopped by Black Butte after a hearing in nearby Bend and bought a building lot. He called me from the real estate office, excited to tell me what he'd done, and could I make the two-hour drive to come look at it *right now?* Before it got dark?

As I drove over the pass, I pondered our life together over the past few years. Keith had been working very hard as a workers' compensation defense lawyer, primarily on lung disease cases that were coming to him from insurance companies that covered aluminum companies. His work took him all over the country, seeing the operations of businesses and conferring with lawyers and doctors who were experts on the topic. And he had an extensive schedule of other cases all around Oregon. He'd told me he wanted another home base where he could stay from time to time while working in eastern and southern Oregon. As we walked over the property together, I took the opportunity to ask him how, with all his traveling, he thought he could manage to build a house and then spend time in it. "Well," he said, "my asbestos cases won't require much more travel and maybe I can start winding down." At the time, I didn't place much importance on the "winding down" part.

Keith often talked about the things he could have done when he was younger but hadn't—everything from running for higher elective office to staying in the Air Force Reserve, to keeping his pilot's license active, to being a better dad. I felt it wasn't good for him to have those kinds of regrets, disappointments, or guilt feelings, and I told him so. He had a lot to be proud of: his World War II experience as a bomber pilot, his four children who loved and admired him, his career as a successful lawyer, his political activism including his long tenure in the Legislature, his joy of teaching and our almost twenty years of sharing our lives together. Maybe building the new house would be good for him.

In addition to taking on the Black Butte project, we bought another house in Portland—our old house needed repairs, and Keith, who'd always loved remodeling, concluded he wasn't up to working on that house. Another sign of slowing down that I didn't heed at the time.

That summer the Democratic National Convention was in San Francisco. Walter Mondale was nominated as the presidential candidate, and speculation had begun about his running mate. Late in the afternoon of Thursday, July 20, 1984, I was listening to the proceedings on the car radio while driving to Camp Tamarack. There came a momentous announcement: Mondale had chosen Geraldine Ferraro, a congresswoman from New York, as his running mate.

By the time I reached camp the whole place was celebrating. Even the smallest girls were caught up in the excitement. A woman running for vice president for the first time ever! Later in the evening we listened to Ferraro give her acceptance speech. It had to be a huge inspiration for all those young women when she said, "I stand before you to proclaim tonight: America is the land where dreams can come true for all of us." It didn't matter one whit whether Ferraro was a Democrat or a Republican. She was a woman. When I finally went to bed in my little cabin by the lake, I lay awake a long time, still full of excitement, joy and thanksgiving that a woman would finally be on the ballot for the second-highest position in government.

My business partner, Gale, and I had been running Camp Tamarack since Gale's "divorce" from Phyllis. Before camp opened in the spring of 1984 Gale had asked me to consider bringing in a third partner, Sue Sherman. Sue had been a camper and then a counselor, and was now head of our riding program and took care of the horses year-round, and she now wanted to be an owner. I said I'd think about it. That fall, Sue offered to buy me out and invited me to name my price. Her offer was too good to pass up. I would miss the girls and the staff, but not the hard work and the summer weekends away from home.

❧ ❦

Even as I closed the chapter of Camp Tamarack, I felt my life was becoming more complicated. I didn't seem to have the resilience and adaptability that had been so much a part of my personality just a few years back. Was it just that I was getting older? *No way, not me!*

Keith and I had hardly settled into our new homes when his son came back from service in the Navy. Tom was having a hard time adjusting to civilian life. He'd moved to Portland and found sporadic work at service stations, which fit in with his love of cars but paid almost nothing. He had little self-discipline, and his friends in Portland were not the best company for him.

His first citation for driving under the influence worried us. Keith handled it well by telling Tom he had to get a lawyer and take care of it himself. But then there was another citation, and another, until finally he lost his license. He drove anyway. By this time Keith was having sleepless nights and jumping every time the phone rang.

The call that every parent dreads came in the middle of the night. Tom had gone into a ditch on his way home after a long night of partying. It was a single-car accident, and he'd been alone in the car. He was in the hospital. If he recovered, he would face more citations and possible jail time.

Keith came home from the hospital to tell me that, among other injuries, Tom's right hand was mangled and would probably require multiple surgeries. Keith was inconsolably distraught, filled with that indescribable despair that all parents feel when a child of any age gets hurt. That Tom did it to himself driving drunk made it all the more agonizing. Keith alternated between grief and rage, wanting to help the son he loved and wanting to cut him loose to fend for himself.

The first surgery was more successful than expected. Keith gave Tom a choice. He could come live with us, enroll in an auto-mechanics course at a community college, have no access to a car or alcohol or any other drug, take the bus back and forth to school, and make good grades. Or he could be on his own without help from his dad.

To his credit, Tom seemed genuinely eager for a new chance. We became a family of three, with one needing supervision and constant encouragement, an arrangement that would last for two years. Slowly, Keith and Tom began to develop a father-son camaraderie, and as Tom's hand healed the two of them took on remodeling jobs at our house. Once Tom settled into a routine, including taking his turn at planning and cooking dinner and helping clean house—something the Navy had taught him to do very well—Keith felt comfortable leaving him on weekends. That left us free to go to Black Butte to be by ourselves. The Black Butte house turned out to be our escape, our haven and our retreat.

Later that year, Maureen told me she would not be staying on after completing her third year as my clerk. She felt it was time for her to get out into the world and look for other opportunities. I didn't disagree. She applied for the newly created job of staff attorney at the Supreme Court and got it. I was proud of her for the superb work she did, but I was sad too, because she would no longer be my clerk.

At about the same time Keith began to talk about retiring from law practice. I didn't want either of those things to happen—Maureen's leaving or Keith's retiring—but these events were out of my hands. These two decisions, coming so close together, played off each other in my mind, producing more uncertainty than I wanted to deal with.

I wondered what Keith would do when he wasn't chasing around Oregon for workers' comp hearings. He'd told me he wanted to travel, back to Pennsylvania, where he'd grown up, to Georgia, where his daughter lived, to Phoenix to visit his brother. His tone told me he'd find plenty to do. *But I'm not there yet,* I thought to myself. I wanted to stay on the court until I was at least sixty-five years old, maybe longer, and I'd only be sixty-three on my next birthday.

About that time, Tom got a promise of a job from a BMW dealer when he finished his community college work. To qualify, he would go for training in San Francisco as a BMW mechanic. What a relief! In a few weeks Tom would finally be on his own. Keith and I had weathered a very difficult time, but not without a good measure of stress and worry.

As fall progressed, Keith made his intentions more explicit. He would keep on with his current cases, but he would take no new ones. He anticipated closing his practice by the first part of the year. Then he intended to travel— exactly where he didn't know. He would very much welcome my company.

Thus I was presented with the toughest decision I'd ever had to make.

Was I going to stay on the Supreme Court? Or was I going to traipse around the country and the world with Keith? Something like mental paralysis set in when I tried to sort through my alternatives. This was a strange and unpleasant feeling, and not at all like me. I had faced several difficult crossroads in my life, and I'd made my choices confidently and decisively. This time things seemed far more complicated.

I debated staying on the court and just letting Keith go. But I didn't feel I could do that, not with a full heart. I knew I'd envy his freedom and experiences. And I'd miss him when he was gone.

But without my work, who was I? That was the deeper and more disturbing question. My dedication and the pull of my responsibilities urged me to remain on the court. When I began to feel drawn to the option Keith wanted me to take, I resisted. I didn't feel I had completed either my life's work or my obligation to the governor and the citizens of Oregon. And I was afraid I'd miss the work terribly. I knew I'd very much miss the court and the people who worked there. And yet—all those positive reasons for staying on at the court failed to influence my growing uncertainty and lack of direction about the future.

One dark, rainy November evening close to six o'clock, I was driving home in the middle lane on I-5 with a big white triple-trailer truck on my right. The truck was splashing water all over my windshield. Even with the wipers on high I could barely see the lines on the highway. My plan to pass the truck on the next straightaway was foiled by another long white truck that overtook me in the left lane. The wash from its wheels covered my remaining viewing spot with water. I couldn't see even a part of the highway. My immediate reaction was, "Are those drivers crazy? I could die here." If either of those trucks failed to hold a steady course on that long-sweeping curve, or if I panicked at having only a parallel line of left-curving, moving, shimmering running lights to follow, it was curtains for sure. I eased off the gas and carefully steered while my brain and heart worked as hard as those fast-whapping windshield wipers. As we got onto the straightaway I lagged behind the trucks as they both passed. Then I moved behind the truck in the right lane and followed his red taillights the rest of the way into Portland.

All the way home I thought about not being able to see the highway ahead because of those trucks, but then the taillights on the trucks had come to my rescue. *Pretty lame reasoning,* I told myself. On the other hand, as my mother would say, when trouble comes there's a way to see it through. At the end of grit comes grace.

I thought of the long, dangerous, tedious drives I'd had for the past eight years, and for the thirteen years before that when the Legislature was in session. I'd now have another winter of it. I felt tired just thinking about it. Whether that was enough to steer me into a decision to leave the court—well, that was looking better all the time.

Somehow, I again had to call on that idea of faith leading me into a safe and productive future. I wouldn't be idle, I knew that. So why not take a chance? It wouldn't be the first time, and maybe not the last.

I turned into our driveway and pulled into the garage, feeling safe at last. Then I walked into the kitchen where Keith had the television news on and dinner almost ready, and said, "I'm resigning from the court. I'll need a press release."

Chapter 21

Resignation, Rescue, Rediscovery

Resigning from the Supreme Court would certainly make the news, and doing so after only four years as the first woman justice would raise all kinds of questions and speculations. I needed to think carefully about how it should be done. It wouldn't do to say flat-out I had the symptoms of burnout, but I *was* feeling overworked and stressed. Since selling Camp Tamarack and quitting my jogging routine, I'd lost these regular escapes from the intense mental routine of court work. In retrospect, the momentary panic attack when the two trucks overwhelmed me in that rainstorm on I-5 seemed downright silly—ordinarily I'd have sworn and muttered something about stupid truck drivers and let it go at that. The fact that it frightened me was a sign I wasn't handling unexpected situations well.

I had to admit the idea of traveling on other highways, seeing new places, and visiting with family and old friends, held a certain appeal. Taking the open road, free to wander, finding the sunshine and dusting off the old golf clubs. But I couldn't use that as an excuse to resign, for it would appear too selfish and too irresponsible for the first woman on the Supreme Court.

And saying I was hanging it up because my husband was quitting his law practice would sound hollow, too, because I hadn't quit the Legislature when he quit. In fact, just the opposite—I'd become even more politically active. Coloring all this rumination was my awareness of the old stereotypical perception that women don't stick with jobs—they get married and quit, they have babies and they quit, or their husbands get transferred and they quit.

My deliberations were influenced in part by the separation Keith and I had experienced while I was at Camp Tamarack and he was away on business. Having a grown son live with us for two years had been a big strain. Among our eight children there had been a few divorces to worry through with them. Our grandchildren numbered nine, with the oldest ones looking forward to high-school graduation and college. I truly did want to spend more time with family.

What was really going on was a battle inside me, a battle between my life-long commitment to work that could make a difference in the world and a reasonable desire to live the life I wanted and, I believed, had richly earned. I feared my resignation would appear self-indulgent, a rejection of an important obligation I had undertaken.

Yet with every decision to move on, we leave something behind. There are always regrets, and maybe a bit of fear, too. It was a new feeling for me, not knowing what would come next. Most of the changes in my life had been foreseeable, because I'd initiated them. This time the future was invisible and unpredictable.

≫ ≪

Keith prepared my press release as he'd promised. On November 20, 1985, I would announce to the world that I was resigning from the Supreme Court effective February 7, 1986, two days after my sixty-third birthday. That much advance notice would give the governor a chance to appoint my successor in time for him or her to join the court on that same day. It would also give me an opportunity to finish my cases.

I wrote a letter to Governor Atiyeh and planned to deliver it to his office on the same day I told my colleagues. Then I'd take the announcement to the press room in the Capitol Building. I told Chief Justice Ed Peterson just before our nine-o'clock conference, and I announced it to the other judges at the conference. They were surprised, to say the least. The Chief Justice told *The Oregonian*, "I must confess … I felt a real sadness to lose her." The article continued, "Later, during a conference of the full court, Peterson said, 'The initial reaction was five jaws dropping in unison.'"

After conference, when I delivered the envelope to the governor's office, the receptionist told me that the governor was out of the country on state business, but that she would see that he knew about my letter right away. I learned from the next day's news that Atiyeh had been contacted in Korea, where he was on a trade mission. He had told the press, "Justice Roberts' appointment is one of which I have been especially proud."

When I came by the press room I found only a couple of reporters eating their lunches at their desks. I gave them each a copy and dropped one on all the other desks, knowing that most of the reporters would be back after lunch. The two who were there wanted to talk to me, but that wouldn't have been fair for the others, so I said, "The press release has to speak for me right now."

Done! It was done! I more or less floated out the east door of the Capitol Building and walked back across the street to the Supreme Court Building. By that time the clerks and judicial assistants all knew, so there was more explaining to do and more well-wishes. Then I had calls from some of the judges at the Court of Appeals. Word was spreading in a hurry.

That evening the announcement was on television news. The next day it was in newspapers all over the state, with reactions from women with whom I'd served in the Legislature and from some of my colleagues on both the Court of Appeals and the Supreme Court. As I suspected, one article was full of speculation and actually posed the question, "What is she up to?" The political writer Ron Blankenbaker couldn't resist wondering: "This is the virtual first lady of Oregon Democratic politics. Is she just possibly getting ready for one more big run, say against Bob Packwood in 1986?"

My action puzzled some of my friends. Most gave me their best wishes, but one woman said, "Betty, I don't understand how you can resign from the court when we need women judges so badly and you are that role model. It's a big letdown for me." What a way to make a person feel guilty! Thank goodness for another friend who said a few days later, "I want to hand it to you, Betty, for showing us once again that we women really do have choices that we can freely exercise as we see fit."

Of course I wanted to help women! But that had never been as important as fulfilling my obligation to the people of Oregon and doing what was best for me and my family. I'd followed the opportunities that came my way, and then I'd tried to help other women find their own.

❧ ❧

Who would be my successor? Mick Gillette's name surfaced in the press immediately, as did that of Court of Appeals Judge George Van Hoomissen. I knew that Mick was very much interested. I promised him I'd talk to the governor about naming him, which set up a bit of conflict in me, for I would have loved to see another woman appointed to the court.

By early January the Board of Bar Governors recommended eight candidates to Governor Atiyeh, including two women, Susan Graber and Judge Laurie Smith from Lane County. I was delighted that these women had put their names in for consideration, and it would have pleased me tremendously if one of them had been appointed. However, it didn't take long for the governor to select Mick Gillette.

On the Friday evening before my official resignation, the judges and their wives invited Keith and me to dinner at a local restaurant. We had a private room and a convivial dinner together. After the table was cleared, Chief Justice Ed Peterson gave what I assumed was a farewell message from the court, full of heart-warming good wishes. That was wonderful enough. But then each justice spoke in turn, giving his own thoughts and feelings on what I'd contributed to the court. I was overwhelmed with their outpouring of friendship as they spoke of consensus-building, collegiality, and respect for our working relationship. It *almost* made me want to reconsider. But then Monday came, I said my farewell and Mick Gillette was sworn in as the new justice.

❦ ❧

On our weekends at Black Butte Ranch, I'd always make a trip into the little town of Sisters, a few miles east. The quilt store there held an unexplainable fascination, not because I had an interest in sewing—I never had and guessed I never would. But it soothed me to look at all the pieced fabrics hanging on the walls, the big bolts of beautiful colors and the books of intriguing designs and instructions on how to create them.

One day I bought a beginner's book. The geometric patterns interested me the most because they could be sewn together in various ways to make entirely different configurations. "Jacob's Ladder" could become "Drunkard's Path" by changing the way the same pieces were sewn together. Some of the pattern names were oddly nostalgic: "Rocky Road to Kansas," for example—I renamed it "Rocky Road *from* Kansas" in my mind, in tribute to my family's long-ago exodus to Texas. The versatile "Log Cabin" could be turned into many designs, with only one requirement: the smallest piece, the center square, must always be a bright spot, representing the ever-glowing wood stove or fireplace that heated the cabin.

I started taking quilting classes in Portland. Shortly after that I saw Norma Paulus, my Republican friend. She inquired what I was up to, and I told her. I vividly recall her looking at me as though at a total stranger. Recovering, she said, "My Gawd, Betty, you've either regressed into that generation we worked so hard to put behind us, or you've come full circle and can do that stuff and still be a feminist, and, frankly, I don't know which."

I saw no conflict. Quilt-making is a uniquely feminine art that has held special significance for American women. Quilts were at first a necessity in the early colonies, and then they became a cultural expression, a way to celebrate and commemorate births, marriages, friendships, and deaths. Quilting put me in mind of the women who endured the hardships of the westward movement in the wagon trains. Making quilts must have helped them piece their new lives together, using materials from salvaged scraps, shirts, and dresses they remembered from another place and time, turning them into something new, useful and beautiful. I, too, had migrated west, and now I, too, was piecing my new life together.

❦ ❧

One day, about a year after my resignation from the court, friends from the north side of our Mount Tabor neighborhood came to admire the dramatic new entrance to our house, the result of a recent remodel. They arrived about noon bearing a pot of homemade soup. After they went on their way, I set the table so Keith and I could have the soup together. That was unusual for us. We'd agreed early on that we wouldn't make a big deal about eating together at either breakfast or lunch. We adhered to the saying, "I married you for better or for worse, but not for lunch."

As the soup was going into the bowls, Keith said, "I think I need an Alka-Seltzer." I waited for him. Then he abruptly appeared, saying, "Betty, get me to the hospital quick. I'm having a heart attack." He was pale and perspiring.

"Get in the car while I grab my purse." I ordered him. The Kaiser clinic was a dozen blocks away. I raced through the intersections as fast as I dared. As I pulled up to the clinic I could tell he was about to pass out.

Leaving the door open, I dashed in to the front desk, yelling, "My husband's having a heart attack! Do something!" A woman doctor and nurses sprinted out to the car with a gurney, with me close behind. I took Keith's hand. It was clammy, but he was still able to talk. Within seconds he was in a room with three or four nurses hooking him up to various tubes and machines. Then he was in an ambulance, hooked up to tubes and a heart monitor, heading for the Kaiser Sunnyside Hospital with siren blaring. I followed in the car.

Then the wait began. From a pay telephone I called his daughter Ann and my daughter Dian, and asked them to let the other family members know. Ann arrived at the hospital within the hour.

Occasionally a nurse would come out and give us a report. They were working to stabilize his vital signs. He'd had a quick injection of blood thinner, which had done its job by reducing stress on the heart, and it appeared the damage was small. By early evening they were taking him to the intensive care unit, but they wouldn't let me see him yet.

Sometime around ten o'clock a doctor came into the waiting room where I sat alone. He said there were complications. The blood thinner had caused Keith to start vomiting blood. They suspected stomach ulcers and had done tests. Sure enough, they'd found three bleeding ulcers that had been opened by the strong blood thinner. He was receiving blood transfusions, along with medication to coat the stomach so the ulcers would stop bleeding. The biggest risk was another heart attack because he couldn't tolerate any more blood thinner medication. The doctor told me I might as well go home because they wouldn't know anything until morning.

I asked to see him. The doctor told me to make it brief.

Keith was a sad-looking guy with tubes hooked up here and there and patches with wires all over his body for the monitor. I had hardly entered the room when he had to vomit again. That was scary, but the nurse who had just come on for the night shift said the vomiting was tapering off and hopefully would stop soon. I told Keith I was going home but would be back early in the morning. He nodded.

The nurse followed me out. I turned to her and said, "Take good care of him, please." She assured me she would, but added, "Well, you know, it's Friday the thirteenth, and there's a full moon." I looked at her in disbelief that a nurse would even think such a thing. Then taking on all the authority I could muster, I said, "Look, I'm not a superstitious person, and I don't like what you just said. That man had better be okay tomorrow morning." All the way home I looked at that full moon and said to myself, *In an hour it will be Valentine's Day, and nothing bad can happen on a day set aside for love.* And then I cried.

I woke before the 6 a.m. alarm and called the hospital. Keith's stomach bleeding had stopped. He had slept a little. There had been no more heart irregularities, and the doctor would be in later.

When we learned he would need open-heart surgery which would be done at St. Vincent Hospital, I cried again, this time in the presence of the family. My younger daughter, Jo, told me later that it was then that she realized Keith's condition was serious. She'd seen me cry only twice before, once when her brother John went to Vietnam and again when my mother died.

Before he went into surgery, Keith handed me a small piece of paper. As I settled myself for the long wait, I read it, his true-love note, hope running through every line. Maybe that would carry him, and me, through the surgery.

In the lonely retreat of the waiting room I wondered what Keith's recovery would be like. What would he be able to do and not do? How much help would he need? What would his mental state be? What if the news was bad and I became a widow while Keith was on the operating table? I banished that thought quickly, but not before it prompted memories of my resignation from the court only a year ago. What if I hadn't been home to get him to the clinic? What if I'd still been working?

Did this explain why I'd felt driven to resign? Whatever was pushing me then was telling me that there are more important things than fulfilling a work obligation, no matter how public or how important the position. The crisis with Keith was forcing me to reflect on the decision to leave the court, and I was relieved to be alone with my thoughts. It was becoming clearer that I should have no regrets about that decision. Yes, I'd given up something very important to me, but I was needed elsewhere.

For all my talk about hope and faith and grace, I use those terms more in the secular than the religious sense. We hope something will happen, have faith that it will, and when it does we may feel it was grace that intervened. The progression through those phases is unseen but strongly felt. A growing awareness of forces beyond my control—the spiritually seeking part of me, if you will—made it easier to imagine angels, not in the guise of real people, as television programs portray, but as powerful presences that nudge us this way or that and help us find answers. My angels were surely in the operating room with Keith. And they let me know he would come through it.

The recovery room had a small glass-enclosed area where the nurse watched all the monitors. Every few seconds she looked at her patient. I went to the bedside and took Keith's hand. A puzzle of wires and tubes wove in and out of his body. He opened his eyes and stared at the ceiling. I leaned close to his ear and told him the doctor said he had a strong heartbeat after the surgery. He looked in my direction as best he could but with a strange look of disbelief. Then he closed his eyes again. That look rattled me a little, but I preferred to believe he understood what I said and was pleased that his heart was so strong.

In a couple of days he was strong and alert enough to be transferred to a regular hospital room. He would be transferred back to Kaiser Sunnyside as soon as he was able to move around a little. The day before his transfer he said, "Do you remember when Howard Cherry asked me to run for the Portland Community College Board, and I turned him down?"

"Yes, of course," I said.

"Well, I've changed my mind." Howard Cherry was a doctor and our friend from the Legislature. He had been diagnosed with Alzheimer's disease and would not run again for the board. "The college turned Tom's life around," Keith said, "and I need to do something in return. Besides, I'd make a good school board member."

What audacity! "Keith, for crying out loud, you just had a heart attack. You get better and then we'll talk about it."

He was prepared. "The problem is, the filing deadline is today. So I want you to go to the elections office and get the filing form, bring it to me to sign and get it back in by five o'clock."

"Okay, but who will make up the Voter's Pamphlet statement?"

"You will," he said, not understanding that I was bone tired from worry and lack of sleep. But I did it all, and by that evening this recovering heart attack patient was a full-fledged candidate again. How in the world he expected to campaign was not such a big mystery. *He'll tell me to do that, too,* I thought.

At Kaiser Hospital he began to show more signs of his old impatient self. A good sign, I guessed, but couldn't he just not be quite so demanding?

One evening when I went to see him he told me that a Catholic priest had stopped by during the day. The priest had introduced himself and asked, "Do you have any questions?"

Keith said he thought for a minute and then said, "Yes, Father, I do. Tell me, will President Reagan live out his term?"

The priest, momentarily surprised, said, "Well, sir, I don't talk politics."

To which Keith replied, "Well, Father, I don't talk religion." Right then and there I decided he was well enough to go home and give the hospital staff a break.

❧   ❧

During my nearly nine years on the Court of Appeals and the Supreme Court, I'd missed the company of politically active women more than I wanted to admit. When Maureen Leonard, my former law clerk, and Patricia McCaig, chief executive to then Secretary of State Barbara Roberts, asked if I'd help with a political action committee to raise money to elect more pro-choice women to the Legislature, I agreed. I'd join three other women in the new effort: Gretchen Kafoury, by then a Multnomah County commissioner; State Representative Darlene Hooley; and Jewel Lansing, who had been the elected auditor for both Multnomah County and the City of Portland and a candidate for state treasurer. The committee would be patterned after a new national organization called Emily's List, founded by Ellen Malcolm, a Fleischman yeast heir. The name Emily is an acronym for "Early Money Is Like Yeast"— because "it makes the dough rise." That gave Patricia McCaig the inspiration to dub our group "The Dough Girls" until we could pick a permanent name. Thereafter we became the Women's Investment Network—Political Action Committee (WIN-PAC). We had our first meetings in the fall of 1987, with an eye toward identifying and supporting women in the 1988 elections, and raising money for them.

Between 1985 and 1987 the number of women in the Legislature had dropped from eighteen to sixteen. That was not all bad news, because some had gone on to higher office, but a few of those remaining were on the other side of the choice issue. In any event, women who left the Legislature for whatever reason had to be replaced, and more needed to be elected to increase the pool of politically experienced women for higher offices.

Our very first interviews with candidates took place the following January at Gretchen Kafoury's house. What a great bunch of women! Their enthusiasm and energy reminded me of my own campaigns. Watching younger women run for office would be great fun.

Then Bill McClenaghan, a political science professor at Oregon State University, asked me to be a visiting professor in a state and local government class for one spring term. I'd turned him down before, but now that Keith's election to the school board had put travel plans on hold, I accepted. I taught for three spring terms. While I enjoyed the students and being on campus, I don't think I was a very good teacher—too much time away from the classroom plus other intervening experiences had dulled my enthusiasm for teaching.

Another interesting call came from Governor Neil Goldschmidt's office asking me to work on locating a minimum-security prison in the Portland metropolitan area. It turned out that the superintendent of corrections, Michael Franke, was too new to the state to know the various political jurisdictions in the Portland area, and, more importantly, the elected officials who would be needed to help make the decision. My job would be working with an advisory committee to view sites, reduce the number to three, and submit those to the statutorily created siting committee. This was more in keeping with my interests and would only be for a few months. I took on that project, too.

❧ ❧

We were told in law school that "the law is a jealous mistress." Once you fall in love with its form, language, and mental teasers, its demand on your time and attention is both welcome and exciting. My resignation from the court had created a disturbing mental vacancy. The opportunities to work with women candidates for the Legislature, be a temporary professor and do an even more temporary job for the governor were satisfying for the time being, but nothing but legal work gave my brain so much of a workout, and nothing else gave me the same exquisite emotion of accomplishment.

Two almost simultaneous events brought the law back into my life. The first was the growing concern over how women were faring in the legal profession. The Multnomah Bar Association's Committee on the Status of Women organized a day-long seminar that focused on the need for more women in leadership positions in the Bar and the judiciary. The liveliness of the gathering demonstrated the pent-up desire of women to assume more leadership roles in our profession.

A subsequent breakfast meeting at the Oregon State Bar's fall convention, initiated by Katherine O'Neil, whom I knew only from her appearances at the appellate courts, led to the formation of a statewide women's lawyers association.

Judge Mercedes Deiz and I spoke at the meeting. We emphasized the need for an organization where we could share experiences and help each other; an organization that would help women learn leadership skills that would move them into the larger Bar's leadership positions, and that would also address the many employment issues women lawyers faced, such as adequate child care, parental leave, and job sharing.

The new group, Oregon Women Lawyers (OWLS), held its first annual conference on April 1, 1989. The Board of Bar Governors responded positively to our resolution asking the Bar to establish a task force to study issues facing women lawyers who combine family and career responsibilities.

The second event steering me back to working with legal issues was an invitation to meet with other senior judges to learn about an organization called Judicial Arbitration and Mediation Services (JAMS). Arbitration and mediation, relatively new in the legal profession at the time, offered a quicker, cheaper, and often more effective alternative to trial in solving legal disputes. I was interested enough to attend a three-day training seminar in Newport Beach, California. Then Kristena LaMar, a Circuit Court Judge in Multnomah County, agreed to let me sit in on her mediations. Applying what I'd learned formally in the seminar and then watching it done, there was no doubt in my mind that I could be a good mediator.

The role of a mediator is to facilitate a settlement between disputing parties, not to impose a decision on them as a jury or a judge would do. Court trials can only be won or lost, but the less formal process of mediation allows the parties to reach a compromise. Sometimes neither party is completely happy with the settlement, but they nevertheless are able to agree to it.

Word spread quickly that my cases had a good settlement rate. My phone rang regularly with mediation and arbitration requests. This new role in the legal profession was exactly what I wanted and needed. I could plan my own schedule and still work with lawyers and their clients on all kinds of cases. Later I joined the panel of judges and lawyers at United States Arbitration and Mediation (USA&M), and I continue, even as I write these words, to have cases scheduled on my calendar. I am privileged—blessed, as my mother would say—to have extended my legal career into a personally rewarding activity that fulfills an important function of our legal system.

❧ ❧

As I pursued my expanding new legal career, Keith worked happily on the Community College Board, often fulfilling his desire to travel by going to conferences all over the country. He also worked successfully with U.S.

Senator Mark Hatfield in creating a new federal position as Under Secretary of Education for Community Colleges. As he attended his college class reunions and visited some of his old bomber crew members, and as we initiated home remodeling projects, including a swimming pool, Keith's heart attack seemed far away and less important. I turned to a new project as an adjunct to an already energetic schedule.

My former clerk, Kathi Bogan, once told me, after hearing some of my stories, "You should write a book." I'd been pondering that idea as I moved into this more flexible phase of my life. (I do not use the word "retired" to describe my situation, because to me it signifies declining power, waning productivity, uselessness. I am a former Supreme Court Justice, not a retired one.)

In June of 1995 I took a week-long seminar on memoir writing, held at a retreat center near McKenzie Pass. Keith and I talked on the phone every evening. When I returned home on Sunday I was surprised to find a note from him on the kitchen counter saying he was heading to the hospital.

I raced to the hospital and found him propped up in bed with monitors keeping track of his heartbeat. He said he was feeling better than he'd felt that morning. He told me he'd awakened with a terrible headache, dizziness, and blurred vision. Suspecting he was having a stroke, he had called the hospital, which sent an ambulance for him. He would not be coming home that day.

The next morning the headache was back, and the doctor reported that his heart had stopped for a few seconds two or three times during the night. He stayed another night. His heart had a regular beat all through that night, but in the morning the doctor recommended a pacemaker. Keith responded to that suggestion with an adamant "No."

I remembered back to his open-heart surgery. Before the surgery he'd asked the doctor what the risk would be if he didn't go through with it. The doctor's answer was simple: "Maybe you'll live a few more years, maybe you'll die next week." Keith chose the surgery, but afterward he told me repeatedly that no doctor would ever touch his heart again. He, too, must have remembered that as he returned to his regular routine without a pacemaker.

Three months after he had refused the pacemaker, in the fall, he took a trip to Yellowstone Park with Tom. Then he met me in Los Angeles, where he saw his other son and family, and we began a drive to Texas, where we attended my high school reunion and spent a few days with my sister and her husband. It was a happy but strenuous trip, and I could see it was wearing Keith out. On our way back to Portland he stopped a few days with his brother in Phoenix while I flew home. He arrived home on a Saturday after having been away for almost a month.

The next day he caught up on his mail, paid bills, and planned for a Monday morning presentation at the community college for a senior citizens' class on civil liberties. About ten o'clock I headed to bed. I passed his chair where he was watching television, patted him on his almost-bald head and said, "See you in bed."

"I'll be along as soon as this program is over," he replied.

I don't know when he came to bed, but I was awakened near midnight by a jerk and a noise. I thought he was having a bad dream, and reached over to touch him. I knew immediately that something was wrong. I called 911 from the bedside phone, and in a very short time medics, police, and firemen were in the house trying to revive him. They administered repeated electric shocks. Nothing.

Someone said to me, "What are your wishes?"

What a strange question, I thought. *What are my wishes? I wish this wasn't happening! I wish he'd wake up!*

Then I realized I was being asked for instructions. I said, "What are the options?"

They could put him in the ambulance and continue to try to revive him and take him to the hospital. By this time at least half an hour had passed. His daughter Ann and my daughter Dian had arrived.

I said, "He has a living will." The rescue workers packed up their gear and departed. A police officer stayed with us. We three women decided on a funeral home and made the call. Ann and Dian called the other siblings.

Now what? I wandered around the house. I found an empty wine glass on the floor beside Keith's chair, and on the kitchen counter an empty ice cream carton and a box of bicarbonate of soda. It was Keith's habit to treat himself to whatever dessert he could find after I'd gone to bed. The box of soda was not a mystery—he must have been out of Alka-Seltzer.

Everything so like Keith, right up to the last few minutes of his life.

Many people, mostly men, told me later that Keith had done it the right way. I suppose he did—for him. He always wanted total control over his life and never wanted to be dependent on anyone for anything. His decision to reject the pacemaker was completely in character for him. I was not shocked that he had, in effect, chosen to die as he did. But I was sad, I and his children and all his many friends. We had heavy hearts at the loss of a man who had made all our lives more challenging and more fulfilling than they could ever have been without him.

❧ ❧

My life during the years since Keith's death has been rich with the joy of continuing legal work and involvement with women and men in politics and law who strive to make our political and legal systems fair and just. Happiness has come from the expansion of an ever-growing circle of friends, exceeded only by more grandchildren and great-grandchildren.

I realized early on after Keith's death that there was still that uncompleted task that might help piece everything together. Exactly how, I couldn't be sure until I sat down and let the stories out onto the page, the stories that made up a life that led me to politics and law and the opportunity to make a contribution to women's struggle for equality. I wanted to assemble the information gathered over the years and the experiences collected along the way, much like the accumulation of quilting fabrics, into a design that would continue to inform and perhaps inspire.

There is much yet to be done, for like the universe, the need to work with our fellow human beings for a more tolerant and inclusive world is forever expanding.

What the future holds for any of us and for our society is yet a mystery, but we can influence the way it unfolds. With the hope of every new dawn, and with unfailing faith, we must step out of the places that have always held us and walk into the expanding horizons of our lives.

> When we walk to the edge of all the light we have
> And take the step into the darkness of the unknown,
> We must believe one of two things will happen—
> There will be something solid for us to stand on,
> Or we will be taught how to fly!

For All Those Who Helped

The writing of this memoir began twenty years ago with the words, "You should write a book." Kathi Bogan not only made that statement but encouraged me tirelessly and gave me a good start on the project until her untimely and tragic death. Without her suggestions and continuous prodding this book would not be.

While writing about the legislative sessions I occasionally had the assistance of young women graduate students or legislative aides to do research under my direction in the State Library, the State Archives, the Multnomah County Library, and The Oregonian library. A special thanks to every one of them. I am deeply indebted to Carol McMenamin, librarian for The Oregonian, who expertly and willingly helped locate news accounts, especially when I became stuck in the search for a specific bit of information that she was always able to produce.

Finally, four years ago I had eight hundred pages of writing with hundreds of footnotes. I am exceedingly grateful to Helen Barney for volunteering to read that entire manuscript. Although there was much work yet to be done, Helen's comments about the content gave me encouragement to do the cutting and editing required, for she believed the story was worth the work and the worry.

To Gail Wells, a professional writer and published author, a genuine heart-felt thanks for her expert contribution in making this memoir publishable. As important has been her patient guidance and diplomacy in our working relationship as we toiled together making decisions about the content of the book and meeting deadlines.

Another reader, Judge Kristena LaMar, deserves special acknowledgment for reviewing and editing the condensed manuscript.

I owe tremendous gratitude to three people at the Oregon State University Press, Mary Braun, Tom Booth, and Jo Alexander, who were wisely cautious at first but who were willing to submit the manuscript to the rigorous process that is required before a decision is made on publication. They have always been promptly responsive to my inquiries and, as a team, have lent their considerable talents to transforming a very long manuscript into a readable and publishable book.

With all that in mind, I take full responsibility for the content of the book. My greatest concern is that many people who are important to me will feel left out. To those individuals I say, "Your contribution to my life experiences is not diminished in any way if it has not been reported here. I am forever grateful to friends and colleagues who made my life more fulfilling and satisfying than I would have realized without undertaking this journey back in time."

To the members of my family, especially my daughters Dian and Jo, who have read various parts, given me suggestions, and jogged my memory from time to time, as well as given me frequent computer assists, I want them to know I treasure most the message they consistently communicated: that this was one more goal mother/grandmother set about to accomplish and they would give whatever support was needed.

To the many friends and colleagues who have regularly inquired, "How's the book going?" I express my warmest appreciation for their indulgence and for their encouragement to keep working on it.

To the readers for whom I wrote the book, it is my fondest hope that it will strike a chord of understanding across generations and that you will find something of value for your own life among its pages.

Notes to Chapters

Chapter 1
Historical information on the cause of my father's illness from John Kobler, *Ardent Spirits, The Rise and Fall of Prohibition,* (New York: G.P. Putman & Sons, 1973.)

Chapter 6
Description of the Northwestern College of Law from Scott McArthur, "The End of an Era" (Oregon State Bar *Bulletin*, November 1966.)

Chapter 7
Description of the murals in the Capitol Rotunda from Capitol Guide Service, Oregon State Capitol, Salem.
Information on women who served in the Legislature from author's personal files; *Chronological List of Women in the Oregon Legislature:1914-1993,* compiled by Cecil Edwards, Senate Historian and former Chief Clerk of the Senate; and personal interview with Ken Rinke, lobbyist, campaign strategist, and Democratic Party official.
News articles referenced are by reporters Helen Mershon, Eleanor Boxx, and Doug McKean, *Oregon Journal;* Harold Hughes, *The Oregonian.*
Information on legislation and particular bills from Senate and House Journal, 1965 Session; author's personal file; and tapes of House proceedings in the Oregon State Archives.

Chapter 8
Criticism of the Senate coalition from editorial in the *Oregon Journal.*
Information on the Oregon beach bill from news items by Floyd McKay, *Oregon Statesman.*
Critique on women and equality from news articles by Harold Hughes and Jean Henniger, *The Oregonian,* and Eleanor Boxx, *Oregon Journal.*
Jena Schlegel later became the first woman circuit court judge in Marion County.
Information for references to particular House and Senate Bills from Senate and House Journal, 1967 Session; and author's personal file.

Chapter 9
Quotation from *Time* magazine, January 11, 1998.
Survey in anticipation of running for the Senate conducted by Rep. Richard Kennedy, Democrat from Lane County and owner of The Oregon Poll.
Information on the personal tax issue of Tom Mahoney in the campaign for the Senate from press releases in author's personal file and news accounts in *The Oregonian* and *Oregon Journal.*
Description of historical events of 1968 from Mark Kurlansky, *1968: The Year That Rocked the World* (New York: Ballantine Books, 2004) and Evan Thomas, "RFK's Last Campaign" (*Newsweek,* June 8, 1998).

Letter to Board of Governors of the Oregon State Bar from author's personal file.
Descriptions of scenes at the 1968 Democratic National Convention from David Broder
article and articles by Harold Hughes in *The Oregonian.*

Chapter 10
Quotations from Governor Tom McCall's speech at the convening of the 1969 legislative
session from Senate and House Journal, 1969 Session.
Many major organizations supported decriminalization of abortions, including the
Oregon Medical Association, the YWCA, and Concerned Oregon Scientists
for Legalized Abortion. Among influential persons who supported repeal of the
prohibition were Dr. Joseph Trainer, Director of Health Services at the University
of Oregon Medical School, and U.S. Senator Maurine Neuberger, Chair of the
President's Commission on the Status of Women.
References to specific legislation by bill numbers from author's personal file and Senate
and House Journal, 1969 Session.
Quotation on "grace" from a December 21, 2003, sermon delivered by the Rev. Dr.
Marilyn Sewell at the First Unitarian Church, Portland.

Chapter 11
The abortion case challenging the 1969 Oregon statute is Civil Case No. 70-226 in the
U. S. District Court of Oregon.
For a summary of cases challenging abortion laws in other U.S. jurisdictions, see Betty
Roberts and Keith Skelton, *Abortion and the Courts,* Lewis and Clark Environmental
Law Journal (Spring 1971).
Chronology of the election of the Senate President from Senate and House Journal,
1971 Session; and oral history of Sen. John Burns, recorded by the Oregon Historical
Society.
Descriptions of proceedings in the Senate Consumer Affairs Committee from minutes of
various meetings of the Committee, available at the Oregon State Archives.
References to specific bill numbers from the Senate and House Journal, 1971 Session.

Chapter 12
Remarks about Lt. Calley and the spray painting on the front of the Capitol from article
by Doug McKean in the *Oregon Journal.*
Chronology of the walkout by the Senate Democrats over the ratification of the eighteen-
year-old vote proposal from Senate and House Journal, 1971 Session.
Material on City Club votes on allowing women members from personal interviews with
Gretchen Kafoury; Doug Baker column in the *Oregon Journal;* Margie Boulé column
in *The Oregonian* in 1988 (fifteen years after women were admitted as members) and
author's personal file.
The National Democratic Committee's request that states attempt to diversify their
delegation in keeping with each state's population was best demonstrated by the
Oregon delegation, thanks to the hard work of Blaine Whipple, the National
Democratic Committeeman from Oregon. The delegation was profiled in *Life,* June
30, 1972.
Information on the early formation of women's groups to work for ratification of the
ERA from personal interviews with Eleanor Davis and Gretchen Kafoury and from
author's personal file.

Chapter 13

The *Roe v. Wade* decision is 410 U.S. 113, 93 S.Ct. 705, 35 L.Ed 2d 147 (1973).

Specific bills proposing ERA ratification from Senate and House Journal, 1973 Session.

Account of committee testimony on the proposed ERA from the Oregon State Archives, minutes of committee meetings, and written testimony of witnesses.

Summary of the House floor proceedings, including quotations, from transcript of taped proceedings ordered by Speaker of the House Richard Eymann.

Chapter 14

Bill number, sponsor, and the fate of each bill discussed in this chapter from Senate and House Journal, 1973 Session; *Quick Look*, a publication of Oregon Women's Political Caucus; minutes of committee meetings; tapes from Oregon State Archives of selected Senate proceedings; author's personal file; and personal file of Gretchen Kafoury.

Chapter 15

Survey report by Dave Yaden, Campaign Information Counselors, in author's personal file.

Account of Billie Jean King/Bobby Riggs tennis match from *Newsweek* magazine, September 21, 1998 (twenty-five years after the fact) and author's personal file.

Issues discussed in the 1974 governor's race from multiple news accounts and press releases in author's personal file.

Information on women running for governor in other states from a memo by Huntly Collins and an article by Chuck Stone in *Philadelphia Daily News*.

Chapter 16

Material on State Democratic Committee meeting in Baker from writings of political reporters in the heavily covered U.S. Senate campaign, including articles by Doug Yocom and Tom Stimmel in the *Oregon Journal* and Harry Bodine and Phil Cogswell in *The Oregonian*.

Chapter 17

As further explanation on the confusion surrounding the Roberts name, Frank married again in 1974. His wife, Barbara, worked as his personal secretary during my last two Senate sessions (1975 and 1977). While I was on the Court of Appeals and the Supreme Court, Barbara served in the House of Representatives in 1981 and 1983. She was elected Secretary of State in 1984 and was the first woman governor in 1990, when Neil Goldschmidt declined to run for a second term. Mary Roberts ran for Labor Commissioner in 1978 and served until January 1995.

Events concerning the shaping of women's issues into legislation for the 1975 and 1977 sessions from author's personal file; personal file of Anne Kelley Feeney, lobbyist for the Women's Rights Project in 1975; personal file of Mary Souther Wyatt, lobbyist for the Women's Rights Alliance in 1977; Senate and House Journals for 1975 and 1977 sessions; articles and editorials in *The Oregonian* and the *Oregon Journal;* and publications of Oregon Women's Political Caucus.

The Women's Rights Coalition was composed of the ACLU, the Oregon Council for Women's Equality, the Oregon Women's Political Caucus, the Oregon chapter of NOW, Federally Employed Women, the Coalition on Battered Women, and the Women Lawyers' Caucus.

Dramatization of the robbery scenario from "The Legal Bias Against Rape Victims" (61 *American Bar Association Journal,* 1975: Report of the 1975 American Bar Association Mid-Year Conference).

Chapter 18

The title of this chapter is a reference to Dorothy Nafus Morrison, *Ladies Were Not Expected: Abigail Scott Duniway and Women's Rights* (Forge Village, Massachusetts: McClelland & Stewart, Ltd., 1977). Duniway was the leading force in securing the right of Oregon women to vote in 1912, eight years before women could vote nationally.

Information on the political speculation of naming new judges to the Court of Appeals from author's personal file and from an article by Stan Federman in *The Oregonian.*

The rape case is *State v. Johann,* 34 Or.App. 363, 578 P. 2d. 810 (1978).

Chapter 19

News articles on the work of the Court of Appeals and profiles of the judges from *The Oregonian,* May 28, 1979.

The case in which the court corrected its previous misinterpretation is *In the Matter of Shirley B. Johnson, Claimant, Shirley B. Johnson, Petitioner v. State Accident Insurance Fund Corporation, Respondent,* 54 Or. App. 620, 635 P 2d, 1053 (1981).

Recognition of the appointment of Sandra Day O'Connor to the U.S. Supreme Court from a news article by Fred Leeson in the *Oregon Journal.*

Letter to the governor from Jack Faust from author's personal file.

Chapter 20

Title of this chapter refers to a book by Florence Ellinwood Allen, *To Do Justly* (The Press of Western Reserve, Ohio, 1965). Allen was the first woman elected to the Ohio Supreme Court in 1922 and the first woman in the world to sit on a court of last resort. In 1934 President Franklin Roosevelt appointed her to the U.S. Court of Appeals, Sixth Circuit, where she was the first woman on any federal bench of general jurisdiction. She became Chief Judge of the court in her later years.

The women judges who attended my Supreme Court investiture were Judge Jean Lewis, the first woman to serve on the circuit courts of Oregon; Judge Helen Frye, who by then was serving as the first woman on the Federal District Court of Oregon; Judge Mercedes Deiz, the first woman of color to serve on the trial bench; Judge Laurie Smith, serving on the Lane County trial bench; and Judge Kathleen Nachtigal, serving on the Multnomah trial bench. Two who could not be there were Judges Kimberly Frankel and Linda Bergman, both in Multnomah County. Jean Lewis had retired by then, so we numbered seven active women judges—the most ever in Oregon up to that time.

The workers' compensation case that effectively gave Oregon an Equal Rights Amendment is *Hewitt v. SAIF,* 294 Or 33, 653 P2d 970 (1982).

Justice Hans Linde's article setting forth the reasons for relying on state constitutions before turning to the U.S. Constitution is *First Things First: Rediscovering States' Bills of Rights"* (9 U. Balt. L.R. 379, 1980).

The case on the deportation of a foreign citizen is *Lyons v. Pearce,* 298 Or 554, 694 P.2d 969 (1985).

Figures on the number of women on state supreme courts from Susan Carbon, "Women in the Judiciary" (*Judicature* 65:6, December-January 1982). Only a dozen women served on state supreme courts nationwide. When I joined the Court of Appeals in 1977, I'd been one of only eighteen women on the states' intermediate courts of appeal.

After the seminar "Sexism and Racism in the Courts," Chief Justice Ed Peterson continued to educate judges and lawyers about discrimination in the legal profession. His work resulted in "Report of the Oregon Supreme Court Task Force on Racial/Ethnic Discrimination," published in 1994 by the Oregon State Bar, and "Report of the Oregon Supreme Court/Oregon State Bar on Gender Fairness," published in 1998.

Lynn Hecht Schafran's speech from a copy in author's personal file. The incidents she reported and others like them are presented in the *Women's Rights Law Reporter* 9(2), Spring 1986), a special issue on women and the judiciary.

Chapter 21

News items referenced in the text on my resignation from the court from articles by Alan K. Ota in *The Oregonian* and Janet Evenson and Ron Blankenbaker in the Salem *Statesman Journal.*

Information from the personal file of Jewel Lansing shows WIN-PAC spent $17, 450 to support ten candidates in 1987. Two of them were elected that year, and two more later won political offices. WIN-PAC has grown vastly since then and, as of this writing, continues to recruit and support women candidates for the Legislature.

Katherine O'Neil chaired the Multnomah Bar Association's Committee on the Status of Women and later founded the Oregon Women Lawyers (OWLS) and the OWLS Foundation. She currently serves as a member of the American Bar Association's Board of Governors.

The author of the poem "Edges" is unknown. The poem is used here by permission of the author of *Power in the People* by Jeanette Lona Fruen (New Horizon Press, Fairhills, NJ, 1998).

Index